BEING FREDDIE
THE STORY SO FAR

BEING FREDDIE
THE STORY SO FAR

ANDREW FLINTOFF

HODDER &
STOUGHTON

Copyright © 2005 by Andrew Flintoff

First published in Great Britain in 2005 by Hodder & Stoughton
A division of Hodder Headline

A Hodder & Stoughton book

2

A CIP catalogue record for this title is available from the British Library

Hardback ISBN 0 340 89628 0
Trade paperback ISBN 0 340 89973 5

Typeset in Stone Serif and Mercury by
Rowland Phototypesetting Ltd,
Bury St Edmunds, Suffolk

Printed and bound in Great Britain by
Clays Ltd, St Ives plc

Hodder Headline's policy is to use papers that are natural,
renewable and recyclable products and made from wood
grown in sustainable forests. The logging and manufacturing
processes are expected to conform to the environmental
regulations of the country of origin.

Hodder & Stoughton Ltd
A division of Hodder Headline
338 Euston Road
London NW1 3BH

For Rachael and Holly

CONTENTS

ACKNOWLEDGEMENTS

There are so many people to thank for having faith in me throughout my career and for helping me with this book.

First and foremost I want to thank my wife Rachael for supporting me, encouraging me, putting up with my absences and being there for me when I'm in form and out. She and Holly are my inspiration.

Thanks too to Mum and Dad for setting me off in the right direction. And apologies, Dad, for bringing up that dropped catch again.

To Neil Fairbrother I owe more than I can say. He advised me as we played together and then introduced me to Andrew (Chubby) Chandler of International Sports Management. Between them they nursed me through my weight and attitude problems and tuned my mind and body to turn me into a professional cricketer.

My old friend Myles Hodgson has had a testing time chasing round after me this season as we snatched odd hours to set down my recollections and gather them into this book. I thank him for his patience and perseverance and am glad we are still friends.

Last but not least, my publisher, Roddy Bloomfield of Hodder & Stoughton, who has encouraged and cajoled and not let me see him tearing out his hair. He must have sacrificed many hours of viewing cricket to bring my book out so soon after the Ashes Tests.

Andrew Flintoff

PHOTOGRAPHIC ACKNOWLEDGEMENTS

The author and publisher would like to thank the following for permission to reproduce photographs:

Action Images, AFP/Getty Images, AP/Empics, Philip Brown, Winston Bynorth, Russell Cheyne/*Daily Telegraph*, *Daily Mail*, John Dawson, Kieran Doherty/Reuters, Patrick Eagar, Empics, Kieran Galvin/Colorsport, Getty Images, Tom Jenkins/*Guardian*/2005, *Lancashire Evening Post*, *Manchester Evening News*, Mirrorpix, Graham Morris, PA/Empics.

All other photographs are from private collections.

PREFACE

I don't think any of us realised what regaining the Ashes meant to everybody until we got to Trafalgar Square the day after we won the series at the Oval. Straight after the Test match we started celebrating, but I don't believe we really understood what we were celebrating until that next day. When the open-top bus turned the corner into Trafalgar Square and we saw the thousands upon thousands of people who had all come to welcome us, I think that scene, more than anything, let us know the magnitude of what we had achieved. It was such a massive achievement, not just for us as cricketers, but for the country as a whole. None of us appreciated at the start of the summer quite how much the country was behind us as we tried to win the Ashes.

At the beginning of the summer we had told ourselves that if we won the Ashes it would be a life-changing moment, but I don't think any of us had any perception of what the words meant. It was only in those first few days after the Oval it became clear. People who were not that interested in cricket before the summer were coming up to shake my hand. It has been quite extraordinary how much this Ashes summer has affected everyone.

It has been a dream of mine to play for England in the Ashes ever since I was growing up and playing cricket with my brother Chris as a little kid in Preston. My first real memory of seeing Test cricket was watching Terry Alderman bowling to Graham Gooch in 1989 when he kept getting him out lbw. I remember watching it in the St George's shopping centre in Preston, looking through the window of Martin Dawes while out shopping with my mum on a Saturday afternoon and, like all kids, I wished I was out there playing myself. Now to be involved in a side that has won the Ashes back after such a long time is the stuff of dreams come true.

I still have to pinch myself at times to believe I have been involved in a series like that, played against great players like Ricky Ponting, Shane Warne and Brett Lee and beaten them – it's incredible really. Every so often, even days after all the celebrations had died down, I found myself clenching my fist and punching the air. It all seems a long journey from those early days in Preston.

My early Lancashire cap was my pride and joy –
I never wanted to take it off.

1

A TOE IN
OLD TRAFFORD

I was a late replacement for my first ever game of representative cricket, which was why I didn't have the proper kit and fielded in one of those old black and red Man U tracksuits. I don't know where it came from because I supported Liverpool at the time. I was all of six years old. I'd been recruited into my big brother Chris's Under-14s side as an act of sheer desperation and sent to field somewhere out of the way. When I batted I got one not out, which was a solid start to my cricketing career.

Not that cricket was a great mystery to me until then. My earliest memories are of being wheeled in my pushchair to the boundary every weekend to watch my dad play for the local Dutton Forshaw club. Saturday afternoon spelt cricket in the Flintoff household for as long as I can remember. My dad played and, in the time-honoured way, my mum helped make the teas. I suppose such a set up could have put me right off the game for life, but fortunately it did the opposite and I ended up falling in love with cricket, eventually following Dad into his team.

Unlike a lot of current players whose interest in cricket developed by watching the big stars and going to big matches, I never went along to watch Lancashire when I was a schoolboy in Preston. I don't even remember talking much about cricket, but it was always there in the house. If it was on the television I would always watch it, but like most kids the big enjoyment I got from cricket was running around and actually playing the game. Every night of the week from the age of eight or nine I was playing cricket.

I think I was quite a natural player. I certainly got used to playing with boys bigger and older than myself. Cricket was not something that was difficult for me in those early years. Even bowling didn't seem to cause me any difficulties. I didn't have much coaching until I was slightly older. My dad helped me out with the basics and I just got on with it from there. Catching was very similar – I was so used to messing around with a ball that catching came easily to me. Because I always had big hands I used to field at slip and extra cover, an important position at that age. There's a lot more running involved fielding there, though, and you won't see me volunteering for it now!

I was nine when I was given my first proper representative honours and chosen for Lancashire after my dad brought a coach down to the club. The coach looked at me and suggested I was taken down for trials with Lancashire Under-11s. So off we went to St Helens where they held the trial. Afterwards we all had to sit down on the grass and if your name was read out you were out of it and had to walk off. I was waiting for my name to be called out – it was like one of those *I'm A Celebrity* programmes when they read out who has been voted off – and I was amazed when my name wasn't called out. I was younger than the rest of them, but the same size. I was very skinny but tall and quite strong and I could certainly hit the ball a long way and throw it. My dad is quite a big bloke, so I suppose my strength came from him, although I don't think all my shots are just down to that; a lot of it is timing.

If you look at cricket down the years there have been some little guys around like Brian Lara, Sachin Tendulkar or Neil Fairbrother who have hit the ball a long way and most of that is down to timing and getting yourself in the right position. From a young age I think I had good timing. I was, of course, quite uncultured in the way I played. I held the bat wrong, my bottom hand was dominant and turned me around, so most of my shots were on the legside. All that probably didn't get corrected until I was about 12, but all I ever tried to do when I was young was to hit the ball and I was never discouraged from doing that by my dad or whoever else was coaching me.

Most of my early cricket memories revolve around playing club cricket or for various representative sides, although I remember playing for my school one year when we won the local cup in Preston. A lot of school matches can be very one-sided and I can recall we bowled one side out for 69 and I got most of the runs in reply to win the game very quickly. We also played a few rough schools who weren't beyond trying to intimidate you. I can still remember now being on the boundary under a skier and all these lads started threatening me if I caught it. I was under a lot of pressure but I did catch it, and reminded them that all my mates were around the other side of the field.

Cricket was by no means the only sport I was interested in when I was younger, because I was decent at most sports when I was at school. I played mini-rugby and every year our school had a festival with Preston Grasshoppers, when again I would find myself marking much bigger boys because I was quite big and fast in those days – I don't know where the speed went! I didn't progress to playing fifteen-a-side rugby because opponents suddenly started getting much bigger and the tackles started to hurt. I was better at rugby than I was at football, but I still ended up playing centre-half for the Greenlands school team and played a couple of matches for Preston Boys. My heart was never really in it, though. I only went along with football because everybody else played.

As I've already mentioned, I was a big Liverpool fan in those days and I remember getting that kit with the Crown Paints emblem on the front for one of my birthdays. I used to enjoy watching skilful players like John Barnes, so it was a bit of a culture shock when I was about 15 or 16 and went along with my mates to watch Preston North End. They were terrible then. They had a manager called John Beck who loved them to kick long balls forward all the time on their plastic pitch – is it any wonder my interest in football has faded over the years? I've got little or no interest in it now, although my brother is still a big Liverpool fan. The only time I really go and watch football is at Manchester City because Paul Beck, Lancashire's main sponsor, has a box there and I enjoy the social side of going to the match.

My brother Chris is three and a half years older than me and, although there wasn't that much of a rivalry between us when we grew up, it definitely helped me because I was always trying to keep up with him and compete. From the age of seven or so I played in my brother's side quite a bit, although he was obviously a better cricketer then than I was. He was an allrounder as well, so it must run in the family, with the exception of our dad, who is a bit of a nudger and nurdler as a batsman. I developed enough to be playing men's cricket from the age of 10 and so did Chris. Eventually we both played in the same team as Dad at Dutton Forshaw and he was really made up that all three of us were in the same side. The three of us playing together continued until I moved to St Anne's, another local club, when I was about 13 and my brother followed me there.

St Anne's was a much bigger club with far better facilities and even had a bar. The first game I played for them was for the fourth team and they got me and Chris mixed up. They thought he was the bowler and I was the batter, even though I was doing all right with the ball in those days. My brother opened the bowling and got five wickets and I opened the batting and got 70-odd when it was meant to be the other way around. Moving there certainly helped my development because they were more professional in the way they practised. They had coaches who came along to the club on a regular basis and they also had a professional helping out. There were some decent players there too. I got fast-tracked, moving up into the second team and then, at the age of 14, I began playing for the first team.

My dad was a big encouragement to me when I was younger, but not in a pushy way. If I needed to go anywhere or get any equipment he helped me out. I wasn't spoilt, but he always made sure I had what I needed. He even took me to the Dartford festival with the Lancashire Under-11s, which is a long way from Preston. I remember in my first game for Lancashire, when I was 12th man at Derby, he drove me down there in the pouring rain. Some of the other fathers were really pushy with their lads and I think the way Dad was with me helped me to express myself as a player with no fear of failure because there was nobody on the boundary waiting to give me a right roasting. It certainly helped me develop as a person because I was quite shy as a kid and I probably still am in situations I am not comfortable with.

Cricket was something that enabled me to express myself when I was younger. It is something that has given me a lot of confidence, but has taken it away as well. It can make you feel great when you're doing well, but also make you feel terrible if you're struggling and my career has been like that, very up and down. I've always been searching for a constant rather than all the peaks and troughs and this is what has happened for me over the last couple of years. It's not always been like that but I try to make things as simple as I can so when things do go wrong, which inevitably they will, it is easier to find your form again.

The one time my dad did have a bit of a go at me was the first time I ever played at Old Trafford for Lancashire Under-11s against Northants. They had Alec Swann playing for them, who later became a team-mate of mine at Lancashire. I got bowled off a full toss – my eyes must have lit up at the opportunity to hit it and instead I missed it. That was the only time I can ever remember my dad tearing a strip off me, probably because it was at Old Trafford. Playing there was important to me and my dad even then. That first time the ground seemed a lot bigger to me than anywhere else and I remember going up to Graeme Fowler and getting his autograph on the back of my bat because he'd come in to have an indoor net. Playing there was such a massive occasion because we only got to play one game a year at Old Trafford. It always rained and we never played in the centre because Pete Marron, the groundsman, used to cut a wicket on the outfield. He's still doing it and I pulled him up about it once because when you are kids you want to play in the middle where the Lancashire players play. Playing on the outfield meant we had tiny boundaries on one side, but it was still special for everyone involved.

In 1987 I was given what is still my most prized cricketing

possession – my very first Lancashire cap. My light blue Lancashire Under-11s cap is something I'm really proud of. You had to take five wickets or score a 50 to get one and I hadn't done either of those things, though I had got some three-wicket hauls and a few 30s. But at prize night, which they held every year at Old Trafford, I was awarded my cap in front of all the different age groups. I didn't take it off for weeks; I wore it in the house and everything. Mum and Dad have it now, along with all the rest of the stuff you get given as an international cricketer. I'm not one of those people who displays memorabilia around the house. If Lloyd Grossman were to come around he would struggle to guess a cricketer lived there! I don't want anything like that in the house, I'm not into trophy cabinets. My wife, Rachael, has a go at me every now and then because I won't put anything on show. The only thing we've got on display is a decanter which holds whisky, so that's pretty useful. It was given to me by St Anne's Cricket Club, so that meant a lot.

My last year with the Under-11s was the first time I sensed that I was better than most of the other lads around me, but I was quickly brought down to earth when I moved up to the Under-13s and suffered my first dip in form. By then I was playing in the same side as Phil Neville, who was such a natural sportsman he chose to sign for Manchester United rather than Lancashire, and Mark Chilton, who went on to become a teammate of mine at the other Old Trafford. They were so good I didn't get much of an opportunity because Phil would bowl teams out and Mark would knock the runs off and batting at number 5 I never got in. Those two just scored run after run after run and it was very frustrating not to be able to contribute more. I remember getting very uptight about it at the time, but

I still had another year left in that age group and things worked out much better for me the following year.

Watching those two play gave you an idea of what a good player looked like, especially Phil. He opened the batting and the bowling and was a sound left-handed batsman. I didn't get to know him particularly well, but I was knocking around with lads a year older than me and at that age a year can make a big difference. I think he went on to play for Lancashire's second team as well and I know Lancashire wanted to sign him, but he was also a passionate Manchester United supporter, so as soon as they expressed an interest he was always going to be lost to cricket – I don't suppose he looks back now very often and regrets his decision!

It was while I was playing for St Anne's in 1992 that I enjoyed one of my most memorable days of cricket. It was a cup game against Fulwood and Broughton on a small ground and a good wicket, which made it easier to play your shots. I batted with a lad called Dave Fielding, who was a decent player, and we had an amazing partnership to reach 319 without loss at the end of our 20 overs. The club records say I finished unbeaten on 234, having hit 20 fours and 20 sixes, and Dave reached an unbeaten 66. It was a pretty comprehensive win with the opposition restricted to 43 for four in reply. Hitting that sort of score is memorable, no matter what stage of your career you're at and I can recall a few of the shots to this day. I was very proud of that innings.

It was not until I progressed to reach the Under-15s later that year that I really started to improve under a coach called Derek Jay. He'd been doing the job for years by the time I met him and had a bit of a reputation for being hard. He was certainly strong on discipline, but was always there to encourage you if you'd done well and I really responded to that. He was also manager when I went on an England Under-15s tour to South Africa, which was a tour I wasn't supposed to go on. I had already played for the Under-14s but my back went the first time I played for them. I remember myself and another young player called Ben Hollioake being taken to see the physio for our injuries by my grandad and I got onto the tour because Millfield School wouldn't let Ben go, so I got in through the back door. It was a big surprise to be called onto that tour and I got a couple of hundreds while I was out there and came back a far better player. Mind you, my first game for the Under-15s could easily have been my last had events worked out differently. I got a hundred, but I remember standing on my wicket when I was on nought. However, nobody saw, so I tapped the stumps back down and carried on to get my century. If I'd have walked off I might not have played again and God knows what I'd have been doing now if that had happened.

*Practising a forward defensive stroke during my early days
at Old Trafford.*

2

MAKING PROGRESS

I look back on my time with England's Under-15s with mixed feelings because, although it brought me to Lancashire's notice, it was also the start of the back problems which would plague the early part of my career. Because I was quite tall and grew so fast my body needed to catch up and bowling is a totally unnatural action. I also have a slight curvature of the spine, which is not that unusual, but when you combine it with bowling and growing quickly it causes big problems. The coaching I began to receive with England Schools did not help the situation.

Believe it or not, at the age of 13 I had a classical front-on action which I can only dream about now. I was happy bowling, but one of the staff coaches used by England told me I'd never swing the ball away with that type of action. I am sure it would not happen now because kids seem to be given more opportunity to develop naturally, but it certainly didn't help me. I'm not known even now for swinging the ball away at will, but attempting to change my action to a more side-on approach didn't help my development, resulting as it did in a mixture of the two styles, and that was when my back started to trouble me, probably because of the strain it was under. Those back problems were really something that frustrated me because I like being involved in the game and being an allrounder enables you to do that. But after a year or so of being unable to bowl I just started to accept I could only be a batsman.

It was not until I came into contact a couple of years later with a bloke called Jim Kenyon, who was one of the coaches at Lancashire, that I began to make progress. Jim helped me no end with my batting and enabled me to come to terms with playing off the front and back foot. By now I was all right playing off the front foot, but I wasn't very clever off the back, so I used to come forward to everything. He taught me a back-foot game and now it's come to the situation that the more I have played, the more comfortable I am on the back foot; I prefer playing that way to coming forward now.

Despite my problems with my back, I had been selected for Lancashire Under-15s and had been doing well when my career, such that it was, began to gain momentum. I was playing in a match against Yorkshire in the summer of 1993 when I was approached by Jon Savage, a well known scout with Lancashire, who asked if I would like to play for the second team. I was only 15 at the time and I didn't know who Jon was and didn't know if he was asking me to play for Lancashire or Yorkshire and told him to go and speak to my dad. Before I knew what was happening to me, I was at Old Trafford playing against Glamorgan in a second-team game. Our side included players like Peter Martin, Ronnie Irani and Nick Derbyshire, who went on to play a few games for the first team, and a young Robert Croft got me out in the second innings. Dad was as proud as could be for me, but I was bricking it, to be honest. I'd played against some sharp bowlers in the league, but the step up in pace I wasn't really prepared for when I went out to bat against Glamorgan.

Old Trafford was fast and bouncy in those days and unlike any wicket I had played on before. I remember sitting waiting to go out and bat and wondering what I was doing there. The wicket-keeper was standing back so far it looked like he was almost on the boundary and it dawned on me I didn't even have a helmet, so I quickly borrowed one. When I walked out to bat, my England Schools kit attracted quite a few comments, but after a few minutes or so I gained in confidence and that is when I started thinking I could do this. That match was when it really hit home to me that I needed to learn how to play off the back foot.

I was batting with Digger Martin and I had got to 20-odd when I drove one for four. I don't suppose the Glamorgan bowlers took kindly to this teenager hitting them for four so they decided to pepper me with a few short ones. After the first one whistled past my nose, Digger came down the pitch and told me to expect a few more of those and he was right! I was punching them off my nose and getting hit all over my body.

I played one game for the Seconds and then I went on an away trip with them to Middlesex and that was a real eye opener. I turned up in a blazer to find Ian Austin and Ronnie Irani heaving a huge barrel full of ice and beer onto the coach – refreshments for the journey south, courtesy of Bass the brewers who were Lancashire's sponsors in those days. The actual game was rained off for three days, but I had a big reality check about what professional cricket on the road was all about. During the day I was taken down the bookie's and in the evening we all went out to dinner. Ian Austin, or Bully as he was known because of his similarity to the cartoon figure off the TV programme *Bullseye*, gave me glasses of wine. I had hardly drunk at all by this point, apart from a beer with Dad once, which I didn't really like – that was something that would change when I got older! It was also the first time I was properly paid for playing cricket with Lancashire. I got £55 in my hand for that trip, which seemed like a fortune to me then, but by the time I had chipped in my contribution for all that dining out and wine sampling there didn't seem to be much of it left by the time I got home to Preston.

It was during this time I first acquired my nickname, Freddie. It was a name my brother had been called through school but I had avoided until John Stanworth, the second team coach at Lancashire, christened me with it and it has stuck ever since.

It was a great learning curve for me on and off the pitch, talking and playing with seasoned professionals like Martin and Austin who knew what they were doing. That was the positive side of my time with the Seconds, but what I didn't like was a lot of the young lads coming through who thought they were the bee's knees because they had a contract. The dressing-room could be an awkward place. There were cliques and massive insecurity because there were a lot of lads in there trying to get into the first team. We were a team, but we were also competing against one another and that made for a nasty atmosphere. There was one lad who didn't speak to me until I had scored a 100. Things started to look up for me when Paddy McKeown, who also went on to play for Lancashire, came into the side and ever since then we've been as thick as thieves. Neither of us liked the atmosphere and memory of it has definitely influenced the way I behave to youngsters or anybody new who enters the dressing-room. If anybody joins the first team, whether they're a young lad or not, I make an effort to get to know them and try and make them welcome.

It was also during those early days at Lancashire that I was able to show what I could do on a chess board. Chess was a game I'd played since primary school. We had a teacher there who was mad keen. There were some tough kids at our school and it was a pretty hard place. But during their lunch hours these tough kids would go and play chess like baddies seeing the light at the end of a B movie. In fact, we were one of the best chess schools in Lancashire and quite a few lads, including myself and my brother, went on to play for the county. I was on one of the lower boards, so if we played anybody good I would be the sacrificial lamb who got moved up the order to get beaten. I wasn't really one for plotting many moves ahead or anything like that, I played more on my instincts. However, my proudest moment was winning the Preston Schools tournament. To this day I'm not sure how I managed it.

I had enough gumption not to start bragging about my chess-playing prowess in the Lancashire dressing-room, however, and this stood me in good stead on one pre-season tour with Lancashire to the West Indies in 1996 when we were travelling from one venue to another by coach. A chess board appeared from nowhere and Gary Yates challenged me to a game, thinking he could get one over the youngster. He took my Queen early in the game and got quite confident, but I turned him over, much to his amazement. I also made myself popular in the dressing-room by beating Michael Atherton on that trip. I'm sure Athers thought he had the beating of this young lad from Preston but, despite the bus racing around tight bends at speeds which caused me to throw up out of the window, I beat him. Athers was not too pleased and I don't think he's asked me for a return match since.

The competitive atmosphere eased off when I went on a first team end of season trip to Jersey. We played one game against a team which included Cardigan Connor, the former Hampshire fast bowler. I had gone out there playing a few shots, mistimed one and got an inside edge into a very delicate area of my groin. I limped off to the dressing-room, trying to think the agony away. But a more practical David Lloyd gave me a glass of iced water with instructions to stick my afflicted privates into it. He told me it would ease the pain. I thought I was being sent up but the pain was so bad I was willing to try anything. After ten minutes or so Dr Bumble's remedy did ease the discomfort and I got dressed, leaving the glass by my bag. Later Gary Yates walked in after having a lengthy net. Why he was doing that after the end of the season is anybody's guess, but it summed up what a good professional he was. He had been working hard, he eyed my glass of water, asked if it was mine and didn't wait for a reply before necking it. The rest of the dressing-room, who had witnessed my experiment with refrigeration with keen interest, fell apart laughing, at which point I had to explain what had been in the glass before!

I was playing for St Anne's at Leyland in the summer of 1994 when I heard that David 'Bumble' Lloyd, the Lancashire coach, had come to watch me. I was facing the legendary Malcolm Marshall, who was their professional that year, and felt really nervous, knowing that Bumble was at the ground. I remember quite vividly facing Marshall. His first delivery I thought I had covered but it swung away late and beat me. To the next ball I got into what I considered a good position to leave and it swung back in viciously and bowled me. If Bumble had come to the match that day just to see me he had wasted his petrol money. It wasn't long after that, though, that he came around to our house to ask me if I would sign forms for Lancashire.

He brought with him Geoff Ogden, a member of Lancashire's

committee. Originally I was only going to get a two-year contract but luckily I had just scored a 100 for the Seconds against
Somerset at Crosby, so they upped it to three years. Bumble sat
down with my mum and dad and told them what happens
when you're a professional cricketer and what you get paid and
said you could make a nice living out of it. I always thought
you got into cricket by going to college or university and I
think my mum and dad thought the same, but Bumble and
Geoff explained how other people had come through the ranks
at Lancashire without going to college. They told us about Ian
Austin coming through the leagues to play for the first team
and explained what I could earn as a cricketer. I thought, That'll
do for me! They didn't have to persuade either me or my
parents much – it was what I wanted to do. I was already getting
paid on a scholarship by Lancashire, but for some reason they
were paying me the wrong amount. I was supposed to get
around £80 a week but instead I was getting paid for a summer
contract of around £800 a month for three months. I was scared
they might ask for it back at some stage so I just kept my head
down! I think my first wage as a professional was £5,500 and I
thought it was millions.

I had not realised until just a few years before that that you
could actually get paid to play cricket. Once I found out you
could do it for a living my schoolwork started to suffer and
went downhill fast. I still got nine GCSEs with three or four
B's and five C's, which some people may find quite surprising.
I was reasonably bright up until I started playing second-team
cricket, getting A's on all my reports, then I lost all interest and
cricket just took over. But if you asked some of my mates, they
would all say I'm just thick, full stop.

Playing at Old Trafford has been special to me through my career.

3

LEARNING WITH LANCASHIRE

That meeting with David Lloyd at our house in Preston was to be the beginning of a long association with him, spanning Lancashire, England Under-19s and England. He was a massive influence on me during the early part of my career and almost everything I did was an attempt to impress him; I didn't drink when I was younger, for instance, and one of the main reasons for that was Bumble. He was always there to help me out and give me encouragement and, looking back now, you can see that when he left Lancashire to become England coach things started to go wrong for me. Throughout my time at Lancs he supported me, encouraged me and defended me and if you have a coach doing that, you don't want to let him down.

He was also coach when I went on my first tour with England Under-19s to the West Indies before the start of the 1995 season. I was sent out there as a replacement for Owais Shah, who couldn't get a passport in time. I jumped at the chance because I was working on Woolworths' record counter and going to the West Indies seemed a better prospect to me. I had already been working with the Under-19 team, bowling at them down at Lilleshall and batting with them, so I was on stand-by anyway. I was sent out presumably as a front-line batting replacement for Owais, but when I got there I ended up batting at number 8 or 9 and being used mainly as a bowler. I think that trip was the first time I was ever asked to take the new ball, probably because Bumble was coach and knew what I could do. Having him around helped me settle.

He was as fired up on those tours as he would later be as the full England coach and got into all sorts of rows with officials and umpires about dodgy decisions. Anybody who has met Bumble will know he is not the type of person to just sit there and take things like that in his stride, so he got the hump. He got so much stick in one of the matches he went and sat in the crowd to get away from it all.

Bumble wasn't the only one who got frustrated by various things going on during that tour and I'm afraid I let my temperament get the better of me as well. I had a few verbals with a batsman called Adrian Murphy in Trinidad and I think I encouraged him to get back to the dressing-room when he got out. I must have done this a bit too enthusiastically, because he told me he'd meet me down the beach later. Rather stupidly I suggested he bring his mates along as well. I was only full of it because I was standing alongside Dean Conway, our rugby-playing Welsh physio. Dean's quite a big bloke, the sort you could rely on in a crisis, and he managed to dissuade Murphy from taking the issue any further.

It was a very good squad we had out there with quite a few players who went on to forge bright careers. In addition to myself and Marcus Trescothick, we had Anthony McGrath, David Sales and Usman Afzaal. We were also playing against some good opposition. They had Reon King who was already bowling as fast as he does now when he was only 18 or 19, so he was getting them down fairly quickly. We also faced Marlon Black and the reason I ended up batting so low in the order on that tour was because I just wasn't scoring runs.

I was getting beaten for pace out there and I'm not that sure why. I'd played a bit of League cricket against some fairly quick bowlers like Kenny Benjamin and South African fast bowler Steven Jack in the Seconds. Whether I wasn't watching the ball properly or what, I was not playing well by any means on that tour and really struggled against the quick bowlers. Despite the disappointments with the bat, I was beginning to make progress and impressed even myself with the ball by claiming a five-wicket haul in the First Test at Port-of-Spain. Sadly, my development as a bowler halted after that because my back went on my return to England, probably because of the number of overs I had bowled in the Caribbean, close to 100 in one week. We played a match in Guyana and I had just finished my spell and was wandering towards mid-off as Matthew Dimond, who played for Somerset, prepared to start his over. He went back to his mark, then just blacked out, so I had to carry on bowling – I swear I carried on right through to tea in one match. I just kept going and going and going; it's little wonder my back nearly snapped in half after that. I blame Marcus Trescothick, our captain in the West Indies, for bowling me into the ground. He thinks I'm joking because he always laughs!

My struggles with the bat during that tour did not prevent Bumble promoting me to the first team later that summer. I was given my championship debut mid-way through the 1995 season against Hampshire after Michael Atherton and Mike Watkinson had been called up by England to face the West Indies. My only previous experience of playing a first-team match for Lancashire was a Benson & Hedges Cup game against the Minor Counties and that went all right, even though I was disappointed to be batting at number 10. All the same, I was still extremely nervous playing my first championship match, although going out with the first team the night before was an even more nerve-wracking experience. I remember Warren Hegg was great to me because I was just a nervous 17-year-old drinking milk-shakes while the rest of them were on pints of bitter or lager. You can imagine how I became a target for their mickey-taking! I think I drank about six or seven chocolate milk-shakes and the rest of them had a couple of pints and it was a case of speak when you're spoken to. As if that wasn't bad enough, Bumble talked me up to all these big players in the dressing-room and persuaded the captain, Wasim Akram, to let me field at second slip after telling them I was so good I could catch pigeons. It was a great vote of confidence, but it certainly put the pressure on me.

When we went out to field, Graham Lloyd had been moved out of the slips to make way for me and I'd never seen bowling as fast in my life. Wasim was racing in on this lively pitch at Portsmouth and it was flying through and I ended up dropping three catches. The first one I can laugh about now because there was a left-hander batting, who nicked the ball and it just thudded into my chest before I could react and that was the way it continued. When I came off the pitch and took my shirt off there were three ugly marks on my chest, painful evidence of my three misses!

That was a shaky start and unusual for me because through-out my career I've always found catching quite natural, particu-larly high catches. There was a period when I kept dropping catches at slip, which wasn't down to technique or not being able to catch, that was all about concentration. When things aren't happening is often when a lot of slip catches get dropped because fielders aren't tuned in all the time – it's very hard to keep totally focused over the course of a long day. It certainly was a quick pitch at Portsmouth because even I put the ball through at a decent pace, even if I didn't have any idea where it was going. When I batted I was dismissed twice by Zimbabwe's Heath Streak, which at least showed I was getting out to very good players.

I can't have done too badly down there, though, because I was next selected to play in a Sunday League game against Yorkshire in front of a really big crowd at Old Trafford. It was easily the biggest match I had played in at that point of my career. I opened the batting with Jason Gallian and walked out full of nerves, with my eyes as big as saucers. We both got a huge round of applause as we walked to the crease. I'd reached about ten when I got a short ball from Peter Hartley, which brushed my gloves and looped to slip. It was harder to drop than catch but David Byas, who was one of the safest pair of hands around, dropped it. To this day I'm convinced he missed it on purpose because there were some really good players coming in after me like Neil Fairbrother, Mike Watkinson, John Crawley, Graham Lloyd and Wasim Akram. Even I was thinking I was probably better off out of the way because the crowd had come to watch them and not me! Bingo, as he is universally known on the cricket circuit, probably thought the same and was happy to let this young lad continue batting.

Later he made the controversial switch across the Pennines to join us at Old Trafford and was a major influence on everybody at the club. His love of the game is infectious and it was no surprise to anybody that he ended up returning to Yorkshire as coach. I've asked him since about his dropped catch in that Sunday League match and he never answers, he just laughs at me.

It wasn't too costly for Yorkshire that day because I only got 12 and began a run of disappointing debuts. Looking back on my career, I'm terrible on debuts. It's always taken me a while in almost every form of cricket to get going, come to terms with it and get my head around what I am doing. I don't know what that's down to, but it's something that has afflicted me over the years. Luckily now, I don't have another level to go to, so I shouldn't have to worry about making a debut again.

I was very shy when I first went into the first-team dressing-room. I never said anything and spoke only when I was spoken to. I didn't really know what to say to people. There were all these players I had seen on television like Atherton, Wasim Akram and Neil Fairbrother and I was just in awe of them. They did their best to make me feel comfortable but until you have played alongside them regularly I don't think you ever relax in that situation. I remember my first pre-season net session and in those days Old Trafford had very lively nets. Bumble, always looking out for me, marched up and said: 'Right, you've got to get yourself an arm-guard, and get yourself a chest-pad while you're at it because they're going to come after you.' I was absolutely bricking it about facing the likes of Wasim and thinking to myself, I don't need this. Peter Martin bowled first at me and I was all kitted out, expecting the worst, but after a while, when I found I was still in one piece, I began to think I could handle it and just got on with the job. I've hardly worn a chest-pad since. The only other time was on my first senior tour to South Africa when I was due to face legendary fast bowler Allan Donald.

Young players got treated well in the first team, possibly because the rest of the team had no insecurities about someone coming in and taking their place. They would always help you out, whereas the second team was full of insecure cricketers who had not really played at any great standard, so everybody was a threat. Fairbrother, or Harv as he was widely known because of his middle name, was particularly good to me. He took me under his wing from an early stage, helping me get my first bat contract and generally settle into the dressing-room. He worked me really hard on a bowling machine during a pre-season trip one year and I suppose that was really when we struck up a relationship because he realised I was keen to learn, I felt comfortable asking him for his advice. I was eager to improve and that was probably more evident in me at the time than in some of the other lads in the second team who thought it was only a matter of time before they got picked for the first team instead of concentrating on getting better.

I combined my few experiences of playing for the first team with my first home series for the Under-19s against South Africa, when I experienced one of the fastest bowlers I have ever faced even to this day. We were warming up at Taunton ready for the first Under-19 Test when we were approached by Somerset to ask if Andre van Troost, their Dutch fast bowler, could bowl at us in the nets and prove his fitness for their next championship match. I remember watching Anurag Singh face up to him, thinking I didn't want to be the next man in. The first ball I faced he pitched up and I stupidly hit him back over his head. It was an instinctive reaction on my part and it was one I lived to regret. The next ball hit me on my glove in front of my face, then I got a beamer and managed to duck under his next delivery. After that I thanked him for the net and walked out. He was seriously quick and I just didn't know where the ball was going.

I met up with him again later that summer playing for Lancashire Seconds against Somerset at Preston and we bowled them out for a low score on quite a dangerous wicket. When we went out to bat, Paddy McKeown was opening and hitting van Troost back over his head, just trying to make some runs before he got killed or got out, whichever came first, because the wicket was bouncing all over the place. I was batting at five, but I made sure I was dressed in all the protective equipment I could get my hands on. I was wearing a chest-guard, arm-guard, helmet and lots of equipment I wouldn't normally bother with. I kept telling Peter Sleep, Lancashire's second-team coach, that we couldn't possibly bat in those conditions and, fortunately, the match was stopped in the end because people were getting hit, so I didn't get in.

Paddy obviously didn't learn from this experience because not long afterwards we faced Somerset Seconds again, only this time it was at Old Trafford. Paddy clearly thought he was still batting on that Preston wicket and hit van Troost back over his head for six early in the innings, which wound him up again to bowl short and fast at the rest of us. Thanks, Paddy!

My little experience of first-team cricket ensured I was selected for that winter's Under-19s tour to Zimbabwe, which was one of the best tours I've ever been on, despite the fact that for some reason it had been scheduled right in the middle of their rainy season so was destroyed by the weather. It rained virtually every day and we had very little cricket to speak of, just enough to win the Test series comfortably. You can imagine how 15 lads, ranging from age 17 to 19, coped with the almost constant rain – we went out nearly every night. We would see the rain coming down in the evening and we knew that would be it for that night and most of the following day, so we would all be off out. That tour was a bit like a holiday. We'd do some training, have some lunch at the hotel and then have a kip in the afternoon to build up stamina for the next night out – it was a great trip for a young cricketer.

One of the rare times we did get onto the field on that trip, I once again got a bit too involved and into another dispute with a member of the opposition. We were facing a bloke called Craig Evans, a medium-paced bowler who had played Test cricket for Zimbabwe. He obviously had more experience than any of us and made it known that he thought he was too good for us. His performances didn't back up his opinion, however, even though he kept moaning in an exaggerated fashion every time we got a bat on him, as if to emphasise he'd been really unlucky. His attitude got my back up and when they batted he stood close to the boundary talking to his mates waiting to bat and having a cigarette. When he finally came out to the middle, he was dismissed first ball and I gave him a bit of a send off by shouting after him, 'If you hurry, you might catch the end of that fag.'

I returned from that tour hopeful I could kick on again and get into the first team at Lancashire that summer. Things didn't work out as I'd planned, though, because competition for places was fierce at Old Trafford and I didn't feature again in the championship until the 1997 season. So I spent another year playing for the second team, but it was a hard school at Lancashire in those days and I had no complaints about that.

*Playing for England Under-19s at Headingley
against South Africa at 17. Little did I know what was in store for me
at the ground in years to come.*

4

MAKING MY WAY

I may have been frustrated at my failure to make more progress at county level, but other people were fortunately
impressed with me because at the end of the 1996 season I was
asked to become captain of England's Under-19 tour to Pakistan
that winter. It was an honour which almost passed me by,
simply because of my reaction when I was asked and my
attempt to make a joke out of it. Former Lancashire captain
John Abrahams had taken over as the Under-19 coach from
David Lloyd and came to see me in the Old Trafford dressing-
room, calling me into the captain's room. He told me he had
something to ask and enquired whether I would be interested
in becoming captain. My cocky reply was, 'What are you asking
me for? Doesn't anyone else want to do it?' John got the hump
and thought I didn't want it until I hastily told him I'd only
been joking.

We got a lot of praise on that tour from the Pakistan officials
for being an England team who just got on with things and
didn't let conditions affect us or our conduct; little did they
know we were whingeing like anything behind closed doors.
When you go to somewhere like Pakistan, you have to accept
things are not always as they are at home. The organisers had
tried their best to help us out most of the time, but in one

match the lunch didn't turn up from the hotel and there were little things like towels not being available. None were life-threatening and in the end it gets to the stage where it's quite laughable and you all wonder what's going to not happen next. I was helped by having a good set of lads with me. Gareth Batty, Ben Hollioake, Dean Cosker, Chris Read and Alex Tudor were all on that trip. On the previous winter tour in Zimbabwe, there were quite a few distractions when it rained, but in Pakistan there were none. You go there to play cricket and that's it, there's nothing else to do at night.

It was also the first time I came across Steve Harmison, although he only lasted a couple of weeks before going home. I must admit I didn't realise quite how bad Pakistan could be until Harmison came up to me and told me he wanted to go home to Ashington! Quite a few people who had been on several tours found Pakistan difficult, but he was on his first trip, so it must have been even worse for him. He came in the middle of the night to tell me, as captain, that he wasn't enjoying himself and was really struggling. He desperately wanted to go home. I told him to give it another day and think about things. I did a lot of talking with him during this period and I think we became closer as friends because of it. But it was obvious he wasn't going to change his mind.

It was a shame because I'd have liked to have captained Harmison; he had serious pace even then. In one of the few matches he played I remember catching someone at slip off his bowling and we were standing as far back as I'd ever known at that stage of my career. He was very raw, but he obviously had pace and great potential. He had been picked on the tour from out of nowhere and everyone had been talking about him.

I enjoyed being captain on that trip, even the public speaking, thanking the hosts at various official functions. Stringing a few words together wasn't a big thing for me, even if it did cause hilarity among the rest of the lads. It was stressed to us before we left that we were ambassadors as the first England side to visit Pakistan since the major flare-up between Mike Gatting and umpire Shakoor Rana in 1987. Funnily enough, Shakoor umpired one of our matches and I was struggling to understand why Gatt had a row with him because he couldn't have been more charming to us. I had threatened to take the lads off the field because we were getting bottles and all sorts of rubbish thrown at us, so Shakoor calmly walked over to one part of the ground, spoke to the crowd for a few minutes and we carried on the match without any further incidents. I didn't do much bowling on that trip because of my back, but I enjoyed the tactical part of captaining the side and the field placings. Ben Hollioake and Alex Tudor used to open the bowling and once the shine had gone off the new ball, I used to introduce our two spinners, Gareth Batty and Dean Cosker, and their batsmen couldn't play against them.

Captaining at such a young age has helped me think more about the game during my career. I probably don't get that much credit for my cricket brain. I know I stand at slip and mess about a little between balls, punching first slip and having a laugh, but I do think a lot about what is happening. I should like to think I have been a help to Michael Vaughan while he has been England captain. I'm not saying he's going to do everything I suggest, but I'm always willing to offer my opinion, both for England and Lancashire. That experience of captaincy taught me that to be a success, you have to lead naturally and not do things which are alien to your personality. Should I ever be offered the captaincy of England or Lancashire in the future, which are both opportunities I'd be proud to accept if they ever came along, I would have to do things my way. I know some people believe that when you are in charge, it's good to assemble the best parts of others' captaincies, but that's not for me. My strength as a leader is in being one of the lads. If you can be that, players will play for you. Of course the hardest part of being a captain is telling friends they are out of order or even dropping them. That is a tough thing to do and I have been very impressed with the way Michael Vaughan has handled that side of things.

After returning from that tour I had high hopes of breaking into the Lancashire side for the 1997 season. Instead of that summer becoming my breakthrough season, however, everything seemed to stall after I got off to a bad start with new coach Dav Whatmore. He had been brought in to replace David Lloyd, who had left to become England coach the previous summer, after guiding Sri Lanka to a shock World Cup win. We were taken out to Cape Town for a pre-season trip with everyone, myself included, keen to make a good impression on our new coach. Things didn't go as planned, though, and after meeting the coach for the first time, we had a bit of a night out as a team and a few of us came in a little bit later than the rest. Richard Green, Neil Fairbrother, Glen Chapple and I all got in very late, even though we knew we would have to get up early for practice.

The morning after the night before we were all feeling a little the worse for wear, but Glen Chapple and I made it to the nets at 9.30. Fairbrother turned up, almost falling out of the van, and told everyone he couldn't do anything because he was too ill. Richard Green never turned up at all. Funnily enough I wasn't too bad at the practice session, had a bat and a bowl and got through it. But it still got me off on the wrong foot with Dav. In fact, he barely spoke to me for the rest of the trip and for a long time after we got back. So I didn't really get a look in with the first team and kicked my heels in the Seconds for a long time the following summer. I know Fairbrother and some other players tried to plead with him on my behalf, but nothing changed.

Some of the fault for the situation lay with me. By then I was developing as a person and starting to come out of my shell with people around the dressing-room. I must admit I was quite difficult at that age and the way I prepared for games must have driven the more experienced players and the coach mad. Cricket wasn't the be-all and end-all for me then and it should have been. But there were so many other things going on in my life; I'd just moved into digs on my own and I simply got sidetracked from what I should have been doing. It was a very frustrating period for me, but even then I never thought about leaving Lancashire. For as long as I can remember I had wanted to play for my home county and I don't agree with players moving around all the time. There were a few rumours I was going to leave a couple of years later. There was talk about Sussex being interested in me, but I don't think it came to any more than newspaper talk. Almost all Lancashire players over the years have had other counties interested in them and I was no different. There was nothing concrete in it and I have only ever wanted to play for one club and I want to see my career out with Lancashire.

For all the frustration of that summer of 1997, the gloom was lifted when I scored my first championship century against Hampshire at Southampton, but even that didn't earn me an extended run in the side. It was a great wicket and the outfield was rock hard and like lightning. I was also fortunate that John Stephenson was bowling when I went out to bat, because he kept bowling bouncers at me with a man out for a catch. But he wasn't really big enough or quick enough for the bouncers to be effective, so I took him on and that got me in and settled. I played well and it was nice that Mum and Dad were there to watch me reach such a milestone. When I'd got to 99, the Hampshire captain brought the field in to try and stop me stealing a single and increase the pressure. I was thinking differently because I was planning to hit it back down the ground if I received anything that was pitched up to me. I was batting with Mike Watkinson, who asked me what I was thinking of doing, so I told him. I ended up trying to hit over the top and spooning the ball to mid-on for one and scampering through to the single.

Mike told me later that now I'd got my first century I wouldn't be thinking of hitting sixes the next time I got into the 90s. How wrong he was. I think I've been out three or four times trying to hit a six when I've been close to my century.

I also had a bit of a do with Australian batsman Matthew Hayden, who was Hampshire's overseas player that season. He had got to 90-odd overnight and at the end of play we all sat around in the middle talking about our plans for the following day. Hayden had a reputation for having a lot to say for himself on the field and Neil Fairbrother suggested that the best way to get Hayden out was to upset him, rattle him and generally have a go. They looked around for volunteers and, as I was the youngest, I was chosen. I was put at silly mid-off the following morning with Gary Yates bowling and Hayden trying to murder everything to get to his century. All the time I was chirping up, calling him things like 'kid', 'lad', 'young 'un' and generally being obnoxious. After just a little of this he started to have a go back at me – you could see he was fuming. Just a few minutes later, Yates dropped one short and Hayden tried to cut it, but hit it as hard as he could. I don't know if he was trying to hit me or not, but he nicked it behind and walked off for 94. We all enjoyed that.

It soon became clear that Hayden wasn't very happy with his dismissal. In those days the dressing-rooms at Southampton were on stilts and you could hear the banging going on in the home dressing-room – it looked like it was shaking too. When it came to lunch-time he just stood outside with a glower on his face looking straight ahead. As I walked off, tall and skinny, I was dreading going past him, but none of the other Lancashire lads were queueing up to support me. I avoided the confrontation by not going to the dressing-room at all and headed straight to the lunch room.

When I went out to bat in the second innings, he was chirping like mad at me, saying that cricket has a way of coming back to bite you on the backside and he was right. I got a pair just a week or so later at Derby and was banished to the Seconds in shame. I heard later that Hayden had said some complimentary things about my batting and particularly how hard I hit the ball. I'm taking that as a sign he may have forgiven me by now.

After scoring a century I was feeling good when we played Derbyshire, but I got out to Devon Malcolm for a duck in the first innings. He seemed to be bowling at the speed of light and firing down 100 mph outswingers. The second innings was the start of my rivalry with Dominic Cork. He was bowling a lively spell at some pace and swinging the ball and he hit me on the helmet with a bouncer. Being the type of player he is, Corky came down the wicket and gave me a few verbals and I gave him plenty back. There's no doubt who won that duel, though, because I nicked the very next ball behind and trudged off after a pair of ducks. He's an aggressive cricketer and I was pleased he joined Lancashire years later – he's the sort of cricketer you'd rather be playing with than against.

The strange thing about getting a pair is everyone else finds it funny. I went into the dressing-room and there was Ian Austin hiding behind his newspaper. You could hear him chuckling and see the paper going up and down, and there is always some joker who puts a pear by your kit.

When I got dropped after that I ended up playing for the Seconds against Yorkshire, who had Matthew Hoggard and Gareth Batty playing for them, at Bradford Park Avenue. I remember facing Batty and trying to hit him over the top for six and getting caught at long-off, which was a familiar form of dismissal for me at the time. The dressing-rooms are downstairs at Bradford and I had a bit of a temper on me in those days. I booted my helmet across the dressing-room and threw my gloves and bat after it. By now I had got my head down in my coffin, probabably looking for something else to throw, and for some reason as I came up I just punched out at the brick wall. I didn't think anything of it at the time, but a bit later I was sitting on the toilet with my head in my hands and and something didn't feel quite right about one hand. I looked at it and saw a massive egg had swelled up on it. I told Paul Ridgeway, one of the lads in the dressing-room, that I thought I'd broken my hand hitting the wall. He immediately told me not to say anything to our coach Peter Sleep.

I stewed for a while and after about an hour I went to see

Sleepy and told him I'd broken my hand while I was batting. He didn't seem very convinced, but sent me off to have it X-rayed anyway and it was confirmed I had broken it. When I told him the bad news I admitted I hadn't done it while I was batting and explained how it had really happened. His first reaction was, 'What are you going to tell Dav?' I missed the last six weeks of the season because of that. A few weeks later I was in Old Trafford with my fingers plastered together and I knew David Lloyd was on the ground. Normally I would have sought him out because he was such a big influence on me, but I was avoiding him like the plague this time. Dav Whatmore had said nothing to me, but I remember coming out of the shower that day and Bumble walked past saying, 'Stupid thing to do that, wasn't it?' That was all he said to me on the subject. He could have rollicked me for 20 minutes and I still wouldn't have felt as bad as hearing him say those few words. It taught me not to punch walls in future.

Since then, when I get out, I don't react. Generally I try to keep my temper in check. There are times when people wish I would show more emotion, but just because I'm not making a big show of it doesn't mean I'm not absolutely gutted to get out. I can't see that shouting and screaming is any good for the dressing-room, either. If I come in disappointed to get out and smash my bat and throw things around the room, what's it going to be like for the poor bloke sitting there trying to focus in on batting next? More often than not it's my fault I've got out and I don't want to affect whoever is in next. I'd rather help them by telling them what the opposition are bowling like. I want the next man coming in to be able to approach me, no matter how I've got out, and not worry about my reaction, and ask me for the lowdown on the wicket or the bowling. No matter who I'm playing for I will always stop when I'm walking off and tell the next man in what's going on in the middle. Once you are out you are not in the game, so you have to try and help your mate and the team in any way you can before you depart.

Because I wasn't playing regularly with Lancashire, it came as something of a surprise to me when I was picked for the A tour that winter of 1997 to Kenya and Sri Lanka. I was really looking forward to going on my first A tour with a group of young players, many of whom had graduated with me from the Under-19s. There was Dean Cosker from Glamorgan, David Nash of Middlesex, Ben Hollioake and a number of other people I'd played alongside, but that tour turned out to be a big disappointment and I didn't enjoy it whatsoever. It started badly when we went for the fitness test before the start of the tour, because I'd put weight on.

I was a young lad living in digs and doing the wrong things and didn't think how it might affect my cricket. Everything was a bit out of synch. I was eating and drinking more than I should have done as a young professional cricketer. When I was younger I didn't put weight on at all. I didn't drink, but I ate pretty much what I wanted, then when I started drinking, I was still eating what I wanted and I began to put weight on. I didn't really notice this at the time. I don't remember looking in the mirror and thinking I was getting fat, but when I turned up for the fitness test prior to the A tour there were several harsh words said to me along the lines of 'Look at the state of you . . .'

Nowadays, all the young players that come up through the England system have strict diet and exercise regimes to follow, which we didn't have then but it would be too easy to blame my condition on their absence. I was a young lad going out and having a good time. I was enjoying my cricket and it was important to me, but there were other things in my life at that stage as well, which pushed cricket to one side. I was exploring life to the detriment of my cricket and after the A tour that side of things probably got even worse. I had more money in my pocket than I'd had before and not a great deal to do with it, so I went out and enjoyed life. I bought a house in Preston and lived with Paddy McKeown and kept open house to all my mates. I wasn't doing anything they weren't doing, but as a professional cricketer it didn't help me much. Looking back, I still don't think I would swap that time for anything. I learnt a lot of lessons from what I was doing and now, if I have the odd drink, I know when to stop and I know when I need to get my head down and start training.

It was at that A tour fitness test that I saw Glamorgan physio Dean Conway for the first time since he had been physio on the Under-19 tours. Dean barely recognised me when I got on the scales because I was so out of shape. After that uncertain start, I began well in Kenya and got runs in the matches there, but I never felt comfortable. After several games we moved on to Sri Lanka, where they had political troubles and there was a constant bomb threat. We were told that if anything like that happened we would go home. We were told it wouldn't be left to individuals to decide, we would go home as a group. Instead, when a bomb did go off, we stayed on out there with a changed itinerary to take us away from the trouble spots. I really wanted to go home and I was probably one of the last to be persuaded to stay, mainly because I wasn't enjoying my time out there.

The main reason for that was Mike Gatting, the tour coach, who seemed to enjoy having a go at me. It was the first time I'd ever come across Gatt and there was a group of us, David

Sales, David Nash and Owais Shah, who used to hang around together that he would pick on. Before games I would be training on a tennis court and then be expected to stand all day in the field and I wasn't enjoying it at all. To this day I don't know why Gatt decided to pick on me and the others; all I can think of is that we were easy targets. We were three or four young lads who couldn't really defend themselves and his little remarks made him look better. After eight weeks of that I was really glad to get home.

Having said all that, the cricket in Sri Lanka was perhaps what I needed at the time. I was only just 20, had very little experience in first-class cricket and it was about time I was stretched to see what I was capable of doing. I batted well out there against some very good players like Marvan Atapattu, who captained the Sri Lanka A side, and others like Mahela Jayawardene, Russel Arnold and Hashan Tillekeratne – all of whom I would come up against later in Test cricket. I crammed a lot of learning into that short tour and I'm sure I came back a better player from it.

*Celebrating beating South Africa at Headingley
to win the series in only my second Test.*

5

ENGLAND DEBUT

My winter may not have finished in particularly high spirits, but I got off to a flier at the start of the 1998 season by scoring a then career best 124 at Northants in a big partnership with John Crawley. I always liked batting with John because he's such an intelligent player and incredibly versatile, no matter what type of wicket he is confronted with. He was also very good at spotting the times when I was getting het up and playing daft shots through not concentrating enough. All John had to do was give me a quiet word and that would make me take notice. He had the same effect on me as Neil Fairbrother and, later in my career, Graham Thorpe. They all seemed to know what I was thinking and, if it was a bad idea, talk me out of it. I have always responded well to batting alongside an experienced player at the other end, helping me along with advice and encouragement, and John was one of those people I listened to.

That innings gave me a lot of pleasure, but the performance which really made people start taking notice and earned me a bit of media attention was against Surrey a few weeks later in the championship match at Old Trafford against my old mate Alex Tudor. We have known each other for years, either playing with or against each other, and we've had some good tussles in that time. He either gets me out pronto or I smash him all over the place. On this particular occasion we were in a run chase, I was batting with Nathan Wood, and Alex was bowling pretty quickly with the wind behind him. In the previous over I had played a lofted drive which went straight over his head for six, which was a shot I didn't play that often then. As the bowling got quicker, the adrenalin got flowing and my bat got a lot quicker. I hit a couple of sixes, Alex dropped one short and I hit another six, and the rest of the over seemed to take care of itself. It wasn't a conscious decision to try and smash him everywhere. I remember one of the Surrey players going to sit down in the stand as a joke because I kept clearing the boundary.

I didn't know I had hit 34 off the over and it wasn't until after the game that one of the lads told me it was a world record score for a first-class over and I'd be in the *Guinness Book of Records* – I pointed out it was Alex who had the record and not me! But I got out shortly after that over – I couldn't start blocking after an over like that, it just wouldn't have been me. Fortunately, by then we didn't need many to win the game.

Unfortunately, my good start tailed off in the second half of the season and I failed to score another century for the rest of the summer. Whether that was because my fitness wasn't up to the required standard or I wasn't working hard enough at my game I don't know. Ironically, by the time I was called up for England later that summer my form had definitely tailed off and I'd gone off the boil. I knew I was being talked about for a possible England call-up because of what was being said in the papers and television. The call finally came when I was on the Lancashire team bus on the way to an away game. I'm not really one for mobile phones – in fact, I hate them; I like the feeling of being out of contact – but Mike Watkinson had his phone on the bus and handed it to me, telling me that David Graveney, England's chairman of selectors, had been trying to track me down and was on the phone. As you can imagine, I thought it was a wind-up and at first I was reluctant to take the phone. But once I heard Graveney's voice I knew it was for real. He was asking me to present myself the following week for the Fourth Test against South Africa at Trent Bridge. I immediately told the rest of the lads on the coach and then I rang my mum and dad. Once the excitement had worn off, it dawned on me what I had in store. Turning up the following week in Nottingham was a terrifying experience.

Going into a dressing-room full of established players was not easy. It was like Lancashire all over again only more so. I didn't know where to put myself and it was extremely unnerving. The only people I knew in there were Mike Atherton and David Lloyd. So I kept extremely quiet and only spoke when I was spoken to. I changed in a room at the back with the washing machine in it and a lad called Theo, who was baggage man for the team. I remember Graeme Hick being good to me during those early stages and Ian Salisbury was also nice, but he was in a similar situation to me because he had just been called up again and I suppose he was finding his feet. The best thing about that whole nerve-wracking experience was going out to dinner on the Monday night in Nottingham with Athers, Angus Fraser and a journalist called Michael Henderson. I knew Athers from Lancashire, but not that well, but he invited me out for dinner that night and I immediately clicked with all three of them. Gus was great to me and we've got on ever since. I still consult him about my bowling.

I was made to feel welcome to some degree by the other

players, but that was a totally different dressing-room in 1998 to the one we have now. Today newcomers like Andrew Strauss or Ian Bell will find plenty of familiar faces from the Academy or Under-19s or A tours and they are people who are actually pleased to see you and with whom you get on. When I made my Test debut, members of the squad were so wrapped up in their own games that the mood in the dressing-room was significantly different. I don't know if selfish is the right word for it because people say you need to be selfish to play cricket in the first place, but there wasn't much emphasis on helping each other out. In today's England dressing-room, everyone is concerned with how we are all doing. But back then it was a very strange environment for a 20-year-old from Preston to walk into. I think part of the trouble was that players were unsure of their places in the team and, just like the Seconds at Lancashire a few years earlier, it possibly made them nervous when someone new came in. England had not won a major series for 12 years, which tends to concentrate the focus. And there was an Ashes tour on the horizon. The change in the dressing-room between then and now that Michael Vaughan has taken over as captain with a new crop of players has been enormous. I have played in sides when there has been a disgraceful attitude, when even some of your team-mates were half-hoping you failed, but that's definitely not the case with the present-day England team. Now we all enjoy each other's success.

My first net session with the senior England team was an experience in itself. Graham Gooch, who had been manager of the previous winter's A tour, was trying to change my backlift, suggesting different grips and all sorts of things which was not what I needed just a couple of days before my Test debut. Then my back went in the nets when I was bowling, but nobody wants to miss out on making their Test debut, so I took a couple of anti-inflammatory tablets and got on with it.

The actual game started well for me and I got Jacques Kallis out in my sixth over in international cricket. It's a dismissal I can still remember now, an inside edge onto his pad and through to Alec Stewart behind the wicket – not a bad first scalp by any means. When it was my turn to bat I felt as good as I had done all season. I was feeling really comfortable while I was out there. The first ball I faced from Allan Donald coming around the wicket hit me right on the backside and in those days it was a big backside. He was bowling quite quick on a slow wicket, but I felt fine and the confidence grew enough for me to play a nice cover-drive off Jacques Kallis early on in my innings. I was going all right and then I got over-confident and tried to hit a wide one over extra cover and snicked it behind instead. I was out for 17 in a manner that was to become distressingly familiar. It was an early lesson for me that you can never completely relax in Test cricket. I was annoyed with myself for throwing away the chance to make a more significant score, but at the same time I was pleased that I hadn't felt totally out of my depth once I had got out there.

My debut was something of a sideshow to the main event, however, and nobody who was either at Trent Bridge that day or has watched it on television since will ever forget the great second-innings duel between Donald and Atherton. I'd never seen anything like that before. People talk to you about the massive difference between Test cricket and first-class cricket and this was certainly the case here. It was one of those occasions when you could do nothing but look on in admiration. The intensity of it was incredible and it has since gone down as one of the all-time classic passages of play. We were chasing 247 to win and Donald came in bowling like the wind against stubborn Athers, with neither of them giving an inch. I was on the balcony, the next man in but one, hoping and praying I wouldn't be needed to bat in this situation in my first Test match. Nasser Hussain got caught behind but was dropped by Mark Boucher and Atherton was caught behind but not given – it was dramatic stuff!

How Athers stood it out there I'll never know, but this was the sort of situation he took in his stride and his ability to withstand it helped win us the game and level the series. Donald was absolutely furious when Athers didn't walk and came snarling down the wicket at him. Athers, as usual, looked totally unmoved by it all. I remember him telling me when I was a bit younger at Lancashire that if bowlers came down the wicket trying to stare you out or giving you verbals you should just stare back at them because they've got to back off and return to their mark at some point – so a batsman can't lose. It's easier said than done at times, but that duel with Donald was a great example of a batsman refusing to buckle when a bowler is fired up and shouting at him. Captain Alec Stewart went in and got a quick 45 to finish the game off and I was more than happy that he had saved me an anxious few overs out there.

The scenes after we had won the Test were unbelievable. We stood on the balcony at Trent Bridge with 5,000–10,000 supporters in front of us singing and shouting and waving banners. That experience had really opened my eyes to what was required at Test match level. I now knew just how fast guys like Donald could bowl and how intense a passage of play could get. I had never seen it like that before. Quite often these

Above: The Flintoff grin was evident even as a toddler.

Right: I always enjoyed playing chess when I was younger. Here I am, aged nine, considering my next move.

Below: Keeping wicket to Chris in the back garden, aged just six.

Below right: In smart attire to pose in front of the Old Trafford pavilion for my first visit there with Lancashire Under-11s.

Preparing for an away game with Lancashire Under-11s with me on the right and future England footballer Phil Neville third from left.

Splashing about with my parents. We are a close family and they still travel to watch nearly every match I play.

In my Lancashire sweater at Old Trafford. Most of my cricket memories are tied up in the place.

Bowling for England's Under-19s against Zimbabwe in Harare.

I really started to develop during my time at St Anne's. I'm the one standing in the centre of the back row.

The catch I took as slip to dismiss Chris Adams in a match against Sussex was one of my best.

Celebrating lifting the NatWest trophy at Lord's in 1998. We captured the Sunday League title the following day.

Talking to David Lloyd before I made my Test debut against South Africa at Trent Bridge in 1998. If I look a little nervous, it's because I was.

Claiming my first Test wicket by getting Jacques Kallis, one of my heroes, caught behind.

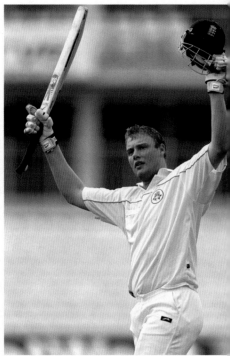

Hitting out during an innings of 142 off 66 balls against Essex in the build-up to the 1999 World Cup.

Reaching my century against Surrey in the 2000 NatWest Trophy quarter-final at The Oval.

Enjoying life with my mates Darren Gough and Graham Thorpe during the 1999 World Cup.

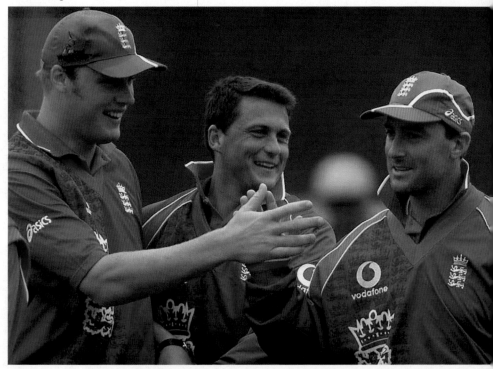

Right: My unlucky return to Pakistan in 2000. I'd barely stepped off the plane when I got hit in the face trying to pull shots in the nets.

Below: Bowling Sachin Tendulkar at Eden Gardens. The whole ground went quiet.

Below right: It took a dramatic victory against India in Bombay to level the one-day series.

Above: Muttiah Muralitharan – what a bowler and what a great friend.

Above left: I can't believe I've just scored my Test century against New Zealand at Christchurch. Graham Thorpe is offering his congratulations.

Left: Steve Harmison took his first Test wicket during the Second Test against India at Trent Bridge in 2002.

days you see big bold statements from players claiming they would have loved to have tested themselves against the best in the world, but on that occasion I can tell you that, hand on heart, I was happy not to have been called to the crease a second time.

From there we went straight to Headingley, where I suffered the first of many disappointments there by recording my first pair in a Test. I got a bad decision in the first innings when I was caught bat-pad. I thought I'd got too far across to interest the umpire in an lbw appeal only to find out I'd been given out caught when I returned to the dressing-room. Like any player on a pair I was keen to make amends in the second innings, but I got caught behind off a Donald slower ball. I came off and had my head down in the dressing-room, the tears welling in my eyes. I went and sat in the sauna for God knows how long and I remember Mark Butcher being the first person to come over to me and bring me out of my mood. My failure at Headingley hit me hard, but I was also pleased with the team's success because we won the match and the series, even if I hadn't contributed much. I have played with some players who struggle to enjoy victories if they haven't done well personally, but I was proud I had been part of that success.

The game finished early on the Monday and there were cele-brations all over the pitch, but I was left in no doubt as to the insignificance of my contribution when Sky Television inter-viewed the whole England team except me, Hick and Salisbury, who had all done nothing in the game. We just looked at each other and felt very sorry for ourselves. I may not have featured in the papers or on the television for my efforts on the pitch that Test, but I still managed to get into the *Daily Star* for other reasons. The cameras were allowed into the dressing-room and there, pinned onto my locker, was a picture of topless model Jordan with her boobs out of course, and someone had written across them: 'Dear Fred, nice pair, love Jordan'. I think I may have been set up by one of the lads; Darren Gough would be my chief suspect.

In those days there was no thought given to the side staying together to celebrate and anyway Atherton and I had to fly down to Southampton for a NatWest Trophy quarter-final match the following day. The enjoyment of winning the Test and the series soon wore off when we needed runs and I didn't get any. So I felt I had let everyone down again – myself, the team, the coach, my family, it was a horrible feeling. That game made me realise how much more you are in the public eye playing for England. I got abused by these two blokes in the crowd for two hours or more. They had a go at my pair at Headingley, my weight, my family and everything. I know it was wrong when Eric Cantona went into the crowd to sort out that fan, but I was sorely tempted to follow his example that day. I have got used to being abused by the Western Terrace at Headingley because I am a Lancashire player and I've been given some real stick there over the years, but this was the worst yet. It was the first time I realised that, as an England player, you are a target as well as a hero.

Perhaps the perfect answer to the abuse was helping Lancashire to a double success that summer, my first domestic honours at county level. We beat Derbyshire at Lord's to win the NatWest Trophy and also lifted the Sunday League title. The only thing that spoilt the final slightly was that it was rain-affected, so it spilt over into a second day, but the first day in front of a packed crowd was great. Playing for England at

Lord's is fantastic, but playing for Lancashire there in a major final was just as good, if not better. That doesn't mean I don't enjoy or am not proud to play for England, but playing for Lancashire with all my mates in the team is very special. I was really nervous the night before the final so Ian Austin took a few of us for a curry and about five pints in Hampstead – it certainly cured the nerves. I didn't get to bat in the final, but I took a wicket and a catch. My abiding memory was of myself and Neil Fairbrother getting stuck into Australia's Michael Slater, who was Derbyshire's overseas player. We were fielding either side of the wicket to him and talking to him all the time. He got some runs but we bowled Derbyshire out pretty cheaply and it was a great experience lifting the cup with Lancashire. Sadly, we couldn't go too mad with our celebrations because we had a game the next day against Hampshire at Old Trafford which would decide who won the Sunday League. Victory the following day marked a memorable weekend for everyone involved with Lancashire and to cap the celebrations I won the man-of-the-match award. The celebration after that more than made up for having to be restrained the previous night – we were celebrating two days in one!

That domestic success almost made amends for being dropped by England for the Final Test against Sri Lanka at the Oval, which was a sure sign I was not going on that winter's Ashes tour. I don't think my start with England was helped by being labelled 'the next Ian Botham' virtually from the moment I was first picked. It has happened to nearly everyone who has been selected since Beefy, from Derek Pringle to Darren Gough, and will happen to others in the future, I'm sure. It was a tag I was given, but never something I've believed in at any stage. It could have been a lot worse for me; Michael Vaughan was called the new Chris Tavare when he first broke into the side. Everyone wants somebody of Botham's calibre to come along again and do the sort of things he did. I do my best but I've got a long way to go to match his efforts.

Some people believe we play in a similar manner and if that's the case, then great. I just play to enjoy my cricket. But I'm a lot more calculating than I used to be and I've got a better gameplan. There have been times in the past when I've doubted my ability and I've doubted myself. It's taken a long time to get where I am now. I've chatted about this to Dave Roberts, who has worked with Ian Botham as a physio in the past. He told me that Beefy never doubted himself and perhaps that's something I still have to add to my game. Getting to know Botham as a person has also helped because I'm no longer in awe of him as much as I was when I started. We meet up every now and then and I have talked to him about parts of my game. People with his sort of knowledge need to be used and getting the advice of people like Ian Botham or Geoff Boycott can only help. I'm sure Beefy would like to be playing out there with us now and, although he has strong opinions at times on Sky, he basically just wants England to do well. Mike Atherton is another person whose advice I ask at times. He's not the sort of person who would put on their kit and get in the nets to help you out, but he's good to speak to. I know some players are reluctant to speak to commentators who might have been critical about them in the media. My attitude is that they have all had good careers, that's why they are there, and I'd be a fool not to listen to their advice.

I wasn't that disappointed at missing out on the Ashes tour at the time because it gave me a chance to go on another A tour, this time to Zimbabwe and South Africa. I was quite pleased to get on that tour, not least because it brought me back together with Steve Harmison and Robert Key. I'd played Under-19s cricket with Key and played against him at county level, but it was the first time the three of us had spent a decent amount of time together. We had a great trip and my form was good as well, which was a major bonus for me. I came home averaging more than 80 and I got picked for the 1999 World Cup on the back of that. It was during that tour that the three of us became really close, and sometimes Graeme Swann would join us. We were accused of being a clique by both the other players and the management who did try to separate us at one stage, but they had no chance. We get on well and enjoy each other's company. I'm sure at times we can be annoying. I know I can be and even Robert Key annoys me when he takes the mickey but I don't think our friendship has been detrimental to any team we have been involved with. We are all good team men as well.

That tour was also useful in getting to know Michael Vaughan, who captained the side well and has since developed into a good captain of England. Vaughan gained my trust on that tour. You could speak to him and I enjoyed playing under him. He had the same mentality then as he has now, although he is probably a bit more polished as a captain now he is doing it full-time. He was very relaxed on and off the pitch even then, and encouraged people to enjoy their cricket. I always rated him as a player anyway and the way he handled himself on that trip as captain made you think he had the potential to go on and achieve exactly what he has done.

I was really pleased for him when he got the England captaincy, and I think that has helped my performances as well, being under a captain whom I like and trust. From the word go he has encouraged everyone in the side to express themselves and have no fear of failure. That's the type of environment that I want to play in. I don't want to turn around and see my captain throwing his cap on the floor or kicking sods out of the ground or rollicking people right, left and centre. That doesn't make anyone feel better. I want his support and that's what Michael Vaughan has done since he has taken over.

We did a fair amount of fitness training on that tour as well, especially in Zimbabwe because it rained a lot. As a result, I became much fitter, but once again I had problems with my back. It was preventing me from bowling and I went for an injection at a place just around the corner from the ground in Harare. Big mistake. He was a specialist who trained in Scotland but the treatment I was given was barbaric. I braced both hands against the wall and he just stuck the needle into my back, without an anaesthetic, and not even hitting the right spot, so he had another couple of goes to make sure as he filled me up with cortisone. After six injections I was able to bowl for the remainder of that tour at least. And then there would be the World Cup.

Playing with Murali in 1999 made up for the letdown of that summer's World Cup.

6

WORLD CUP
DISAPPOINTMENT

Preparations for the 1999 World Cup, which was to be based in England in May, began with the squad being sent off to Pakistan and Sharjah to warm up for a tournament being played in English conditions. It was my first overseas trip with the senior England side and I was understandably nervous, but before I could begin to think about the cricket ahead of me there was the small matter of a cash row to sort out with the England and Wales Cricket Board. As I came late into the saga, I wasn't that aware of the players' unhappiness until we flew out on this trip. The contract on offer for the World Cup amounted to a basic fee of around £12,000, and bonuses if we should win the competition on home soil. It was a strange situation for me because here I was, aged only 21, and delighted to be called up for the World Cup, but there were all these underlying things knocking the shine off it. I kept my head down during all the meetings about the contracts because I didn't really know what to think and left all that to the older players.

The basic fee of £12,000 we were being offered wasn't much, but the management argument was that we were playing for our country in a World Cup and it should be a great honour.

It wasn't ideal being stuck in a room until 2.30 in the morning before the opening match of our mini-tournament in Sharjah discussing the contracts with the ECB's chief executive. Tim Lamb had flown out to talk to us about it all and it was during that period I started taking most of my advice from Neil Fairbrother, who had begun to help me with my affairs. He would eventually take them over completely after going to work with the International Sports Management group owned by Andrew 'Chubby' Chandler. The contract dispute wasn't settled until we arrived back home in England, but I tried not to let it affect my preparations for my first World Cup.

We began in Pakistan with a few warm-up matches in Lahore, playing on quite a small ground at the Gymkhana Club. The England team chosen looked as if it was going to be the one that played in the one-day Internationals in Sharjah and I wasn't in it. Instead, I was included with the spare parts for the opposition, so I went out to make a point and try and get in the side. I played pretty well on the day and got a century, which included hitting Angus Fraser for a few boundaries – much to his irritation. I hit Gus back over his head for six, so Alec Stewart was gesturing to him from behind the stumps to try a bouncer at me with the next ball. He tried that, but I managed to get hold of it and hooked him for six. He just stood there in the middle of the wicket with his hands on his hips and turned around and swore repeatedly at Stewart. I didn't really know what to do that day and I think my team-mates were starting to get fed up with me staying in. I'd got to 110 so I asked Stewart whether he wanted me to carry on or get out. He told me it was up to me, but the game was going nowhere so I just tried to hit every ball and eventually I spooned one up in the air, but by then I'd made my point.

From Lahore we moved on to Sharjah for a triangular tournament against India and Pakistan and I was given my one-day International debut in the opening match against Pakistan. It was a very mixed experience for me because my bowling cost around eight an over and I also bowled at the death. I wasn't used to doing that in those days, but I did manage to get Wasim out. I remember turning to Neil Fairbrother and saying that now I'd got Wasim out I needed to try and work on my economy rate – only for Moin Khan to come in and start hitting me for six. They posted a monster score, 323/5, and when we batted it was the first time I had seen Shoaib Akhtar. He was seriously rapid and Graeme Hick was murdering him. If he dropped short, he pulled him and if bowled full he was driven. Fairbrother and I were sitting together in the dressing-room area, getting ready to bat and counting down the number of overs Shoaib had left. Harv did get in to face his last over and just dropped his bat on one which flew for four. I was lucky because I got in when the spinners were on and could have been stumped off my third ball, but I recovered to hit a half-century. I was helped because there wasn't really any pressure on me when I batted. Hick and I needed something like eight an over. We played a few shots and I nearly ran him out. I was very nervous and called for one. There was a terrible mix-up and Hick would have been stranded had Wasim hit the stumps. The minute I realised what I had done I was praying the ball would miss so my debut wouldn't be remembered for me running out Graeme Hick.

It was the first time I'd played against Wasim. I had played a lot with him for Lancashire, but when you play against county team-mates you don't really know what to expect. Do you have a chat with them when you're playing or what? Wasim answered that one by looking straight through me for the entire game. That was my first taste of playing against someone from a different country who I knew really well and being ignored. After the game, which we lost by 90 runs, it was back to normal again: we were the best of mates. England struggled throughout that tournament, mainly because it was a squad selected for English conditions and we quickly got eliminated. We managed to beat Pakistan quite comfortably by 62 runs in our last game, although there have been rumours since that it was not all it should have been.

We were leaving at 4 a.m. for our flight back to England so a few of us went for a drink, coming back to the hotel just in good time to get the plane. I was sharing with Ian Austin and woke him up when I came in. It was the first time I'd woken him up during the entire trip after he'd had me up until two in the morning most nights watching the Masters Golf on television. I hate golf! Anyway, on the last night I woke him up coming in, then nodded off for a few minutes. By the time I came to, ready to get dressed in regulation trousers, blazer and shirt for the journey home, I didn't have a shirt! The management were not amused I had to board the airport bus bare-chested in a blazer and tie, looking a total prat. When we got to the airport my shirt mysteriously turned up. Ian Austin was the man responsible and he's definitely on my list for future retribution!

When we got home we all went back to our counties for a couple of weeks before reassembling for the World Cup. The summer started really well for me. At a one-day game against Essex at Chelmsford I played some outrageous shots to score 143 off only 66 balls. It was one of those days when everything I tried came off. I came down the wicket early on to hit Paul

Grayson over the top for six and then went down the wicket and played a slog-sweep for six and after that I just started playing shot after shot after shot and every one seemed to hit the middle of the bat. It was a great game of cricket because we only won by a few runs. I was in good form, but that was to be my last major innings for a few weeks and I hardly ever got to the crease during the World Cup.

Our final build-up for the World Cup took place in a really good spot just outside Canterbury. It was a country mansion and the outbuildings had been turned into terraced houses. I was put in with Gus Fraser and Neil Fairbrother, two of the more experienced members of the squad, and we had a really good time during our stay there. We would train and practise and then return to the house. Gus had a deal with a wine company so a case arrived early on and we sat around talking and drinking. I learnt a lot at that house just talking to Gus and Harv. Here were two professionals who I respected enormously. I listened to and learnt from everything they had to say about the game – it was an invaluable experience for a young player.

The tournament itself was a big disappointment to us all. I didn't bat much in the warm-up matches, so I was desperately out of touch by the time the tournament started and I ended up only batting twice. The first was against South Africa at the Oval when they blew us away by 122 runs and I got a duck. I missed out against Zimbabwe and then we went to Edgbaston to face India in the crunch game. Because of Zimbabwe's surprise victory over South Africa, we had to beat India to go through to the next stage.

I thought I got a bad decision at the time, leg-before to Anil Kumble for 15, but the one thing that stands out from that game was the dismissal of Graham Thorpe because once he was out it was one of the final nails in our coffin. It was a rain-affected match, going into a second day and it proved too much for us on the second morning. It was also one of the most intimidating atmospheres I've ever played in at home. Edgbaston was packed with Indian fans screaming and shouting. I remember going out to meet Neil Fairbrother in the middle and he told me to soak it up and enjoy it because I was unlikely to come across many atmospheres like that again. Unfortunately, that defeat ended our involvement in our own tournament, which took me some time to recover from. We were out of the tournament even before the official World Cup song was released and it was hard to accept that we hadn't made a proper challenge on home soil. I was a young lad in his first tournament, but I felt even more sorry for the older more experienced players who were unlikely to play in another big tournament.

Everyone in the squad was so dejected and I know some players have stuffed their kit and memorabilia into their shed or attic and have not looked at it since. I didn't go that far, but I know exactly where all my stuff ended up! I had too much baggage and I couldn't get it all into the car to travel home so I collected all my World Cup kit and a few casual clothes in a coffin and put it on the team bus that we'd travelled around on during the tournament. The coach company we used was based in Manchester and told me to pick up the stuff when I was ready. I didn't bother. Maybe it's hanging around a bus depot somewhere still. Maybe a bus driver has it and, if so, he's welcome to it because it means nothing to me except massive disappointment.

I had the option of playing in the next game for Lancashire against Gloucestershire or sitting it out and, to be honest, I had nothing else to do so I thought I might as well play. I'd had a few drinks the night before and I wasn't really tuned into the game at all. I went out to bat just feeling empty. I didn't feel anything, I was totally carefree. I remember Jon Lewis bowling me a rank half-volley on my legs which I clipped for four to get off the mark and he responded by calling me a fat so-and-so and that sparked something. After that it was a bit like that innings at Chelmsford. I played shot after shot, smashing 158 off 105 balls. They weren't reckless shots, though, they were all proper shots. I think Gloucestershire got the full brunt of my frustration over the World Cup that day.

That game was also the first time I met Muttiah Muralitharan. It was his first game as our overseas player and right from the word go he was absolutely brilliant. From the very minute he walked into the dressing-room you just couldn't shut him up. It didn't seem to matter that his English wasn't great, he chatted and chatted. He knew everything about everyone and could tell every player about their career. He was telling players like Ian Austin about what they'd done and when, which he must either have looked up or else he follows cricket very closely. He knows everything about everyone and he's just a lovely bloke.

He did well for us and actually enjoyed doing well for Lancashire. We, for our part, went out of our way to make him welcome. It couldn't have been easy for him in a foreign country with not very good English, but we helped him all we could and it was a pleasure doing it for Murali. He would invite us round to his house and cook dinner and soon became a very popular member of the dressing-room. He endeared himself straight away to the lads simply because he agreed to dress up in a German costume, complete with Lederhosen, for a picture to celebrate the fact Lancashire were being sponsored by a German beer company. We all looked ridiculous, but the fact that Murali was prepared to do it earned a lot of Brownie points for him – I can think of other overseas players who wouldn't have done it. (I think the sponsors also asked Athers, but not surprisingly he refused!)

Murali was always one for coming to talk to you almost as soon as you'd got out. I've lost count of the number of times I walked into the dressing-room that summer after getting out and went to sit by my locker and think. He would come up to me with a big beaming smile and say: 'Freddie, how out?' I would usually answer that I'd been caught somewhere and he would immediately reply: 'Ah, crap shot,' before walking off with an even bigger grin on his face. The two of us became very close and he even flew all the way to London in 2005 to attend my wedding to Rachael.

That first day we met, Murali was very complimentary about my innings. I think he thought I did that every time I went out to bat. A few other people made encouraging comments about my potential, but the big problem then was fulfilling it. After the World Cup I was overlooked by England, who had replaced Alec Stewart as captain and appointed Nasser Hussain in his place. I liked being back on the county circuit and enjoyed a decent season when I averaged nearly 40. But, as in the previous summer, once again I tailed off towards the end. I was also troubled by my back that year and had another injection prior to the World Cup to ease the pain. At that stage I just went along with it if they told me I needed an injection. But I was beginning to notice that the period of relief the injections gave was getting shorter and shorter. At first I was getting three months' relief out of a jab but gradually the period got shorter, to such an extent that by the time I had my last injection I only had a week and a half before my back packed up again.

It was towards the end of the 1999 season that I first got an inkling that I might be picked for the England tour to South Africa that winter. We had played a day-night match against Yorkshire at Old Trafford and after the game players from both teams went to a place called the Conti Club, a famous venue in Manchester. There was plenty of talk that night and Neil Fairbrother told me he thought there was a chance I could get on the tour, but I needed a knock. I went out in the next championship match and hit 160 against Yorkshire at Old Trafford. I think that innings sealed my call-up because a few weeks later I was confirmed as one of a number of new players in the England squad for that winter's tour to South Africa, a trip which would begin the partnership between Nasser Hussain and new coach, Duncan Fletcher.

Gary Kirsten frustrates me during his 275 against England in the Fourth Test in Durban.

7

TENTATIVE STEPS WITH ENGLAND

Playing for England was still a new experience for me and to be chosen for a Test tour squad was a big step up. It was a new look squad that winter, including several other players on their first tour like Michael Vaughan, Chris Adams, Gavin Hamilton and Chris Read. We also had a new coach in Duncan Fletcher and a new captain in Nasser Hussain. For most of my brief England career I had played under a coach I knew well from Lancashire, David Lloyd. Bumble is definitely someone who wears his heart on his sleeve. Duncan Fletcher is totally different to him: he is much quieter and tends to keep his thoughts to himself. He prefers to have a quiet word rather than relying on big speeches. I met Duncan for the first time at a training session before the tour when he outlined what he expected of everyone and how he wanted us all to improve.

The one thing he has done with England is raise the standards that he expects in players, even in something like slip-catching practice. I've been involved in sessions when maybe ten catches have been dropped and nobody is really bothered about it, but there's a lot of pride involved in practice sessions now and nobody wants to drop a catch. I would say that when we practise slip-catching these days I will probably drop one a month, if that. It's the same when you go into the nets for a bat. Duncan is very keen on players working on specific things at practice, so hopefully you'll come out having worked at a plan; I used to go into nets and finish on something like 80/5, playing all my shots and get out a few times. Everything that's done is done for a purpose. It's not just aimless practice, everything has a meaning to it.

Technology has also changed so much since David Lloyd was in charge. Bumble was animated and passionate and I thought he was great to play for and I thoroughly enjoyed that time in my career. Duncan is a lot more technical in his approach. He loves computers and every ball gets documented so you can slow it down, speed it up and do what you want with it. He likes that side of things, but I'm not that interested in all that. I don't mind watching an innings, but I don't like breaking things down and analysing them. Even simple things like the movement of my feet is a bit too involved for me. I don't really want to be aware of what my feet are doing. I know what my feet do, but I don't want to be too aware of it because then you are thinking about that rather than letting it happen naturally. If you start thinking too much about these things, the movement may become false and you may get your timing all wrong.

Mind you, my approach probably doesn't benefit you too much if you're playing badly because if you're not aware of everything you do you can't work out what you are doing wrong. Someone like Marcus Trescothick will get out and, after he's said a few words to himself, he'll go straight to the computer to check where his bat's coming down from and see where his feet are. That works for him, but may not work for me. Fortunately, Duncan is aware that not everybody likes to work the same way. But he is a big perfectionist and expects a lot of his players. No disrespect to the way county teams prepare for games, but you do notice the difference in what's expected each England session from players who are, after all, probably at the pinnacle of their careers.

Duncan was keen for people to get to know each other quickly on that tour and organised an early team outing to a restaurant near our Johannesburg hotel. It was a good night for all of us and I remember one of the highlights being Chris Read standing on his chair singing a couple of songs after being egged on by everyone in the team and the management. People can criticise us for being out enjoying ourselves when we were preparing for a Test series, but I thought it was a really good idea. I've found through playing over the years that one of the best ways to get to know people is by having a beer with them. That's been especially true at Lancashire. There isn't a drinking culture at the club by any means, but there is a core of blokes in that dressing room that have always got on socially and if you get to know people I'm sure that helps when you are on the field together. You can go on team-building exercises and spend fortunes climbing trees or go-karting, but what I've found is that people who are interested in things like that are not necessarily people you would turn to in a cricket situation.

Unlike my first experience with England, this time I knew a few people, and had already encountered a lot of the newer players, like Michael Vaughan, Gavin Hamilton and Graeme Swann. I had been a bit intimidated going into a dressing-room with the likes of Alec Stewart and Atherton the previous summer, but on tour it wasn't so bad because we spent a lot of time together and I began to feel more comfortable in their company. I got to know Chris Adams quite well on that trip.

The new guys tended to stick together quite a bit simply because we didn't know the others that well, but as the tour progressed we all got to know a few of the more senior guys and started spending time with them.

I started the tour quite nervously, although I did pretty well with bat and ball in the warm-up matches before we arrived in Johannesburg for my first overseas Test, and what a strange experience that turned out to be. I very nearly got caught out by the speed of our collapse on that first morning after we were put in to bat in dark and damp conditions. I was in the shower as the wickets began to fall and we slipped to 2/4, but quickly got my kit on and by the time I joined Michael Vaughan in the middle we had recovered to reach an almost respectable 34/5. It was bad enough for me, but Vaughan on his Test debut was on a hat-trick ball in the dark. When I walked out to greet him he just gave me a wry smile, but that's the way he is: he doesn't get flustered, no matter what the situation is. I don't think either of us could believe the mess we were in. I think it helped that we knew each other and our inexperience probably also helped because we didn't take much notice of what was happening. It was more of a case of simply trying to hit the ball than worry about the situation. We tried to play and every time one of us played and missed the other one would just grin. Between us we got more used to the conditions and the bowling and ended up putting together a partnership of over 50.

I was expecting Donald to be bowling seriously fast when I got out there, but he was just coming back from an injury so maybe that limited his pace. Instead of bowling flat out he tried to bowl in good areas. The previous summer he had been bowling into you all the time, but this series he was bowling away from the bat, which was slightly more comfortable, if you can ever be comfortable in that situation. I got off the mark by clipping him off my legs and as I ran down the pitch he snarled: 'That's the last of your freebies.' I just thought, Great! I got peppered a bit by their other main bowlers and Shaun Pollock bowled extremely well. I was quite fortunate because he bowled short at me and he was probably easier to play at that length because he pitched the ball up and bowled some absolute beauties to Vaughan.

After Vaughan was out I was left with the lower order and I got it quite wrong. I got out caught behind trying to run it down to third man in order to get down the other end and it turned into a horrible shot. Knowing what I know now about batting with the tail, when you are seven wickets down you shouldn't really manufacture the strike. I should have waited to do that with the last two. It was a disappointing way to get out because I'd done all the hard work and the wicket had calmed down a bit and wasn't doing as much by then.

South Africa went on to claim a big first-innings lead and by the time I went out to bat in the second innings, Donald was bowling at what seemed like the speed of sound. His spell that day is still one of the fastest I've ever faced. When I arrived at the crease it was reassuring to see Alec Stewart at the other end, who was one of the best players of quick bowling the world has seen. Quite early in my innings, Donald tried to bounce him. Stewart went to hook it and his bat didn't get anywhere near. The ball flicked his collar on the way through to the keeper and he mouthed to me, 'That was quick!' I hadn't faced a ball at this stage and I just thought: 'Thanks, Al – that's just what I needed to know.' When I got to the other end Donald bowled me a few bouncers and I played them all right and I decided that if he bowled another I was going to have a go at it. Sure enough another bouncer came along and I pulled it over mid-off for two because it was too quick to get my bat around it. I tried again with the next bouncer which just flew past me before I could even react.

I ended up batting with Andy Caddick and we managed to get through to the next morning when they brought Paul Adams on to bowl, their unorthodox spinner. Having done all the hard work of seeing Donald off, I was annoyed with myself when the inevitable happened and I gave Adams a return catch for 36, two less than my first-innings score. I was attempting to turn the ball to the legside for one and got a leading edge. When you've been hit all over the body from Allan Donald, on hands, head, in the ribs, the last thing you want is to be caught and bowled to Paul Adams – I was kicking myself when I came off. It was all part of the learning curve for me. But who knows how I would approach it now in the same situation – I may even get out for nought. If I was playing that innings now I probably wouldn't change my gameplan and my mindset when Adams came on. I still believe the way I approached Adams was right, it was just the execution of the shot that went wrong.

We moved on to Port Elizabeth after our heavy innings defeat in Johannesburg and again I scored runs by being positive. I got off the mark by hitting Donald off my legs for four, but this time it was a slow wicket. I wouldn't say it took bouncers out of the game, but they certainly weren't as effective as they were at the Wanderers. After what he'd said about the freebies in the previous Test, I couldn't resist grinning at him when I got off the mark in an identical fashion. Once he was taken out of the attack I had to face Pollock and hit him for four boundaries in an over. He was bowling in the areas I like, so I could hit straight back down the ground, but I was bowled for 42 with the next delivery after I got into a horrible position. It was a disappointing way to get out to say the least. I spoke to Atherton about it and he described situations like that as 'when the beans are going', in other words the adrenalin is pumping and you just can't stop yourself doing what you are doing. Understanding, but not a remedy!

I was coping with the pressures of Test cricket without doing really well, even if my performances were an improvement on my first Test summer. I was facing Allan Donald, the best fast bowler in the world, and he was getting me into trouble every so often, as he would do, but I was handling myself all right. Once again I needed to have three injections to get my back through that tour, which enabled me to bowl 30 overs in the second innings of the next Test at Durban. It was a really flat wicket and we did well to bowl them out cheaply in the first innings and put ourselves in a position to win the Test. Unfortunately, we came across Gary Kirsten in the second innings. I've faced players in my career who can really take you apart on their day, but I don't think I have ever been as frustrated as I was bowling at him during this Test. Kirsten just ground you down hour after hour and went on to score 275 after over 14 hours at the crease. At least when you are bowling to someone who is playing shots you believe you have a chance, but he was just not getting out. He set his stall out second innings to bat for a couple of days. Towards the end of my 30 overs I began to feel a slight niggle in my foot. I thought nothing of it at the time because you do get niggles when you bowl and I had odd boots on as well. I had chosen to wear different boots from different pairs because my left toe was hurting in the original pair.

When we moved on to Cape Town I was hit on the head

twice – again – this time by Kallis, after Pollock and Donald had done it earlier in the series. Kallis totally set me up during the first innings at Newlands; he bowled within himself and gave me a couple of short balls and then I went to hook him and he hit me flush on the badge on the helmet with a quicker delivery. I was playing all right, but we lost a few wickets and I was left batting with the tail where my inexperience was exposed again and got out to another soft dismissal. Lance Klusener was brought on to bowl and I went down the wicket to his first ball. He dropped it short, but I still went through with the shot and got caught at third man.

When it came to bowling I delivered a couple at a decent pace, but my foot felt quite weak. I thought I'd get through this and there was nothing to worry about, but I bowled another ball and it got worse. I tried once more, my foot gave way and I had to go off. I was in plaster for the next few weeks. I felt I had improved during my time in South Africa, even if my statistics were not great. I was beginning to feel more comfortable playing at Test level and it was a real kick in the teeth when I had to hobble home early.

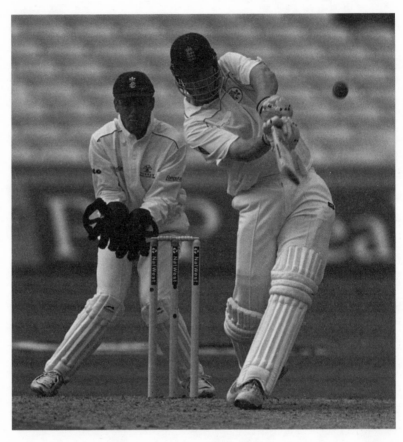

Hitting out during my 135 against Surrey in the NatWest quarter-final at The Oval.

8

NOT BAD FOR A
FAT LAD

The summer of 2000 once against started well for me and gave me little indication of what was to lie ahead. I travelled around with John Crawley, Lancashire's captain, quite a bit at the start of the season and had managed to persuade him to bat me at number 3. He had been forced into an unfamiliar role as an opener because we expected Indian batsman Sourav Ganguly, who had joined us that summer as our overseas player, to play at number 3. But within a couple of weeks of his arrival, it was pretty evident that was not where he wanted to bat and he preferred to bat down the order. I was batting at number 5 or 6 so I told John that if he wanted me to move up I would. John was unsure about that at first, but finally let me do it and I scored a century against Leicestershire, the first time I batted at number 3. Sadly, it didn't go too well for me after that.

England had kept faith in me by including me for the Test series against Zimbabwe, but I failed to build on my South African progress and struggled against them. I didn't make much of an impression at Lord's, even if England won comfortably, but I was confident of scoring runs in the Second Test at

Trent Bridge. Unfortunately, it did not work out that way. They had Heath Streak bowling from one end, a fine bowler, and Pommie Mbangwa from the other, who didn't look that threatening even if he did get me out in the first innings. When you looked at him from the side there didn't seem to be much to him and I thought that if I got in to bat I was going to go after Mbangwa because he didn't seem to have any pace. The problem was that when I did get to face him the ball never seemed to arrive. Heath Streak was tying things up at one end and I was blocking away, but then it clouded over and he got the ball to start swinging and zipping around. Streak was bowling in areas that I didn't want him to bowl and I played and missed several times before edging behind.

People interpreted that as me being too aggressive for the situation, but Heath Streak had already bowled two good overs at me and I wasn't playing too well at the time. Perhaps my mistake was thinking I could do well against Zimbabwe after performing reasonably well against a much stronger side in South Africa. I think a few members of our side thought that, because Mark Ramprakash also had a torrid time after moving up the order to open. Zimbabwe had a good batting line-up but not much in their bowling attack. Mbangwa had got into the top ten in the world and you couldn't understand it as you faced him and tried to time your shots when he was bowling at 75 mph.

I carried my struggles into the opening Test against West Indies at Edgbaston, which was the first time I had come across Courtney Walsh and Curtly Ambrose. They had both lost their pace by that stage, but they were still very fine bowlers. I'm probably not best placed to make a judgment on them, however, as I only faced two balls from Walsh and a couple of overs from Ambrose in the first innings. The first ball I faced from Walsh I pushed through mid-on for four and I thought to myself: This is all right. The next one was just back of a length, which straightened and I nicked it to slip – thanks for coming! Just to complete my miserable start to the summer, I had hurt my back again so I missed the great victory at Lord's and didn't feature again until later in the season for what turned out to be an eventful time for me in the one-day series.

By now I was having to face up to the fact that the jabs were no longer doing the job they were supposed to be doing, and I was now having them every couple of weeks. I have spoken to Mike Atherton about his back trouble over the years because he has always been very open about the problems he has had and how he was helped by doing pilates regularly. After the injections began to stop working I even resigned myself to not being able to bowl again at one stage. I've also done pilates exercises, which helped to a degree, but I found all that a bit finicky and a bit pedantic. In the end it was the old-fashioned stuff that worked for me, strengthening my stomach area to take the strain off my back. I've not got a six pack by any means these days, but underneath it all I've got what they call a good strong core.

Not for the first time, my back problems gave Craig White an opportunity to get back into the England side and he did so well against West Indies that I didn't get back in again that summer. We have agreed that it has worked both ways. We have each won a few Test places at the expense of the other's injuries.

The next time I was involved for England was in the triangular one-day series against Zimbabwe and the West Indies, when there was an experiment to bat me at number 3. There had been a lot of talk at the time about pushing me up the order and dropping Nasser farther down and it was decided that if we lost a wicket in the first 12 overs then I went in, otherwise I resorted to my usual position. It was batting at number 3 that I claimed my first man-of-the-match award with an unbeaten 42 against Zimbabwe at Old Trafford. It was not the innings I remember most from that time, though, because this was when it all kicked off about my weight.

When I look back now and see the pictures it's obvious I was out of shape. The press got stuck into me for it and that fuelled the crowd to get on my back as well. It was a really difficult time for me and embarrassing to have people always going on about it. Possibly the most disappointing part was that my weight – 19 stone – was actually disclosed to the press by the England management. The newspapers called me all sorts of things – I was a porker, a fat slogger, you name it. It was a very low period in my life and there were times when I questioned whether it was all worth it. But realistically what else was I going to do other than play cricket? It is my career, after all. I was supposed to be wearing a girdle around this time to help with my back, but that made me look even bigger so I stopped wearing it because I was so paranoid about my size. I was also desperate to get rid of it so I could bowl properly.

The root of my problem was down to my lifestyle. I was behaving like a 22-year-old with cash, not a professional sports-man. When I got back from South Africa I bought myself a three-bedroom loft apartment in the centre of Manchester. Paddy McKeown moved in with me, my cousin Neil stayed for a bit and both Glen Chapple and Mark Harvey were in a flat in the next development. Cooking isn't a lot of fun for me and it was so easy to go out and get a takeaway. Everything was on your doorstep. You could walk out of the flat and within minutes there were bars and chip-shops and kebab houses. In those days diet and nutrition were not such a big part of the England set-up as they are now, but we were spoken to about it and there was no real excuse for the way I was living. Diet is common sense really and going for a late night curry is probably not the best thing to do. My timing of my social life wasn't great either. Because a lot of my mates worked in the week, their days off were Friday and Saturday and I would go out with them then, even though I would probably be playing over the weekend. When I look back now, it's clear I lost sight of what I was doing and what I should have been doing. Success possibly came a little too quickly for me. Maybe I played for England before I was ready, who knows? What is for sure is that I didn't handle it very well and put weight on. My cricket wasn't great and I wasn't practising. But throughout this period, I never got told England were unhappy with my fitness, although their informing the press I was 19 stones might have been a hint that they were a bit fed up with me. We had fitness tests and got weighed and were given targets but it was never a case of you should do this and you should do that. I've grown up since then. There is no way I could live like that now, even if I do still enjoy a pint every so often.

I had a heart to heart with Chubby Chandler, my business manager, and he informed me the *Sun* had been on to him, asking if they could do a positive interview with me. I didn't really want to do it, but Chubby suggested it might be a good idea so I spent 20 minutes on the phone talking to their cricket correspondent. The result was not the positive piece I was hoping for. Instead they printed what they called a tale-of-the-tape comparison between me and Lennox Lewis, the world heavyweight boxing champion. They compared our weights, reach and all sorts of things. I was less than impressed. I was also embarrassed for my family. My dad didn't say much to me about it. He worked at British Aerospace and God knows how many of the blokes there would have seen the papers and had a good snigger. My mum was working as a reception teacher at the time and I'm sure she must have had some comeback too. I was in a situation that would be hard enough to deal with now, let alone as a 22-year-old who had only been playing professional cricket for two and a half years.

It got so bad that I didn't really want to step out of the house for anything other than cricket. It's periods like this when you get to know who your friends are, though, and I spent time with people who were close to me. I was given a lot of support by Darren Gough. Darren was really good to me, but then again he always is. He's a very positive person and good to be around at the best of times and during that period he was great. I've always had a good relationship with Darren and he sat me down during the net session at Old Trafford prior to that Zimbabwe game when the flak had just started to fly. During that session I'd played really badly and smashed the stumps out of the ground in frustration. It was not something I would normally do, but of course television and all the photographers were there to see it. After watching me do that Darren went out of his way to pick me up.

At least I showed I could still play by winning the man-of-the-match award the following day, which meant I had to do an after-match interview with Paul Allott for Sky Television. Paul, a former Lancashire player himself, had been pretty horrible about me on the television for a while. When he congratulated me on my performance, I replied, 'Not bad for a fat lad,' which was aimed at him and all the other people who had been having a go at me. But I don't bear grudges and there's no animosity between Paul and myself now – we go fishing together every so often these days. I have a better understanding of how things work with the press now and I conduct myself much better now than I did then. Then I was quite fragile as a player and as a person, but I'm much more confident now in everything I'm doing and I'm happier with the people I spend time with as well.

That one-day series was pretty average for me on and off the pitch, with my only innings of note being that 42 I scored at Old Trafford. There was a lot of flak flying around about my weight and my next game for Lancashire plunged me into a big NatWest Trophy quarter-final match against Surrey at the Oval. We were chasing 210 for victory and the way things happened you could say it was a turning point in my season. Everything I tried seemed to come off that day. I went on to score 135 with four sixes and 19 fours. I played very well that game and David Gower said on TV that it was one of the most awesome innings he had seen which did my confidence no end of good at the time.

We were due to drive back on the bus after the game, but it broke down which was perfect because all the lads went to a pub around the corner for two hours to celebrate our win against one of the best teams in the country. I remember sitting there with a huge grin and a bottle of wine – it was a big relief after what had happened over the previous few weeks and months. At that stage I wasn't thinking about it being a turning point, I was just enjoying the moment after the bad run I'd had.

If I was thinking that my bad run was over, however, I was

wrong. I thought all the stick I had been getting would end once I returned to county cricket with Lancashire, but I got into the papers again just a few weeks later and, once again, not for my cricket. There was a big headline in the *Daily Express* which I still remember – 'Flintoff Punch Drunk' – and which I think was harsh to this day. Lancashire had a game on the Friday and I had had a back injection on the Wednesday which would keep me out for four or five days so I went out for a drink with a friend of mine called Iain Fletcher, a journalist I had got to know on the A tour to South Africa and Zimbabwe a few years earlier. We met up in Manchester and went to a couple of pubs where I got involved in an incident which just about summed up the sort of time I was having at that point when a bloke in one of the bars threatened to shoot me. We finished up at the Press Club, a well known late night drinking bar in Manchester, which is somewhere I've been before without too much trouble. Unfortunately for me there was an *Express* leaving party going on and someone must have recognised me and told the paper I was out on the town the night before a game. I had not been out for two or three weeks and that happened! The *Express* did ring the club, asking for their reaction to my behaviour, and Jim Cumbes, Lancashire's chief executive, backed me up and told them I had five days off. But they ran the story just the same. It just showed what a stinker I was having off the pitch at that time.

The rut I was in only ended and my fitness to improve once I started training with Steve Hampson, a former Wigan rugby league player and a mate of Neil Fairbrother. He was coaching Lancashire Lynx at the time and by training with him I started to turn things around a little. He was very good with me and helped me lose quite a bit of weight that year through regular visits to the gym. He also helped me realise how my lifestyle was affecting me. After I had been training with him for about three weeks my weight had not changed at all, despite all the training. Steve asked me about my diet and suggested I gave up drinking in the remaining time before I flew out. I also started eating properly with more salads and things like that and I lost about 20 pounds as a result and got down to under 16 stones – unfortunately I put it all back on while I was away in Sri Lanka. It is easy to put weight on when you are on tour, eating out every night and I still was not being as professional as I could have been with my diet.

After that one-day series I returned to Lancashire where it was clear Ganguly was not settling in at Old Trafford. I suppose we have been a bit spoilt with our overseas players because in my time there we have had Wasim Akram, who was a terrific player and a great bloke. We had a South African bowler called Steve Elworthy who was an all-out trier and we've also had Muralithran who has been fantastic for us. Ganguly just didn't work out at all. You can accept a player not playing well, because we all have our ups and downs in our career, but he just didn't want to get involved. He wasn't interested in the other players and it became a situation where it was ten players and Ganguly in the team. He turned up as if he was royalty – it was like having Prince Charles on your side. There were rumours he was asking people to carry his coffin for him, although he never asked me. He turned up for his first net session with Lancashire, when you would have thought he would have wanted to make a good impression, and got hit on the back of the knee by Mike Smethurst. Those sort of blows do hurt, but you normally rub it a bit and make sure you grin because everybody else is laughing. Ganguly didn't see it that way and got the hump and we didn't see him again for two days. He also ignored simple things about life at Lancashire. On the first day of every championship match you turn up in your blazer and tie and after that we are expected to dress smart-casual. He wore his tracksuit on the first day and sometimes he would turn up in his whites and go home in them, just to get out of the place as quickly as possible. Even when we did try and make him feel at home by going out for dinner, he left early.

His first game was at Kent and he got out first ball lbw to Mark Ealham. He came in not looking that bothered and we heard that Paul Nixon, the Kent wicket-keeper, had said something to him along the lines of 'hard luck, first ball and all that'. Ganguly turned around and told him, 'I'm not going to waste my runs on these games. I'll save them for when it matters.' That's fine if he wants to be like that, but then why bother coming to Lancashire – he doesn't need the money. I've been out for dinner with him since that season a couple of times on England duty, the most notable time being that winter in Kenya for the ICC Trophy. We went out to a little curry house he had found and saw the umpire Venkat sitting over the other side of the room. Straight away he got up and went over to talk to him for 20 minutes while I sat like a spare part eating my curry on my own. We say hello to each other now and we are pleasant to each other, but it doesn't go any further than that. I don't dislike the bloke, but it's a struggle with him.

You could not help but learn from a coach like
Bobby Simpson.

9

HOME TRUTHS

Despite the worries about my fitness and the miserable summer I had just experienced, England showed I was still in their thoughts by selecting me for the first tour to Pakistan in decades, but for the second successive winter my trip was interrupted by injury. We began that tour in autumn 2000 with the one-day series and I started well in Karachi when England chased down a score of more than 300 for the first time ever in a one-day international.

I had faced Wasim briefly the previous year in Sharjah, but if you ever wanted to face him in Pakistan it would probably be in Karachi under the lights. By the time I went out to bat there was so much dew the ground was wet through and it was impossible for him to reverse swing it. He was even having trouble holding onto the ball and because of that he bowled me a beamer, which I pulled for six. It was one of those deliveries where self-preservation kicks in and it was either my head or the ball. Once again he preferred not to have a chat at all while we were playing against each other. I had played with him for a few years by now and it was really strange to be treated like he had never met me before in his life. But off the pitch was totally different and I spent most of my time with him. I was always around at his house and he took me to meet all his mates and family.

With Wasim hampered by the dew, Graham Thorpe and I were able to take advantage and put on 138. That match was also notable for another man-of-the-match award after I hit 84 off 60 balls and, unlike in England, where you are normally presented with a bottle of something, I was given a car. The only problem was that when I went to sit in it after the prize ceremony, it was clear it had not been made for someone my size. I could barely squeeze in, it was so small – I'm not sure what happened to it after that.

I was unable to have the same impact in the second match in that series at Lahore, which we would all remember for a swarm of large flies which descended on the ground while we were fielding. Gough had to run in to bowl with his mouth shut because otherwise he'd have had a mouthful of these horrible things and Mark Ealham bowled in sunglasses to stop them getting into his eyes. I hate creepy crawlies at the best of times, I'm scared of them, and these bugs were enormous. I'm sure some of them were the size of a hand, and there were so many of them. When you looked across the ground from the boundary you couldn't see the middle properly because these flies just swarmed all over the place. They were not the reason we lost that match by any means, but they certainly made our job that much harder. Shortly after the final one-day match in Rawalpindi, which was eventful in itself with tear gas disrupting play after floating into the stadium from a disturbance outside, it was clear my back had flared up again and this ended any hopes I might have had of playing in the Test series that followed. I was sent home after the last one-day international for more injections.

At this stage both England and I were wondering how much longer I would be able to continue bowling. It is still a slight worry for me, even now, because I am never quite sure what is going to happen with my back. I had problems with it for about eight years and, while I have not had any trouble for the best part of four years now, the fear of those old problems returning is always at the back of my mind. Every day I bowl I do wonder how much longer it is going to last. I was so worried about my bowling I did even think about becoming a spinner to lessen the impact on my back. The trouble with that idea was that when I tried bowling offspin in the nets I wasn't very good. I just couldn't do it, I wasn't landing the ball anywhere near where I wanted it to be. I wondered about legspin because I had bowled a little of that in junior cricket, but it is not the type of thing you can just pick up and start doing. Legspin is one of the most difficult arts possible in cricket and takes years of practice to become competent. Duncan Fletcher told me he thought I could develop into a player capable of playing Test cricket just as a batsman, even if my figures didn't suggest that at the time. That provided a big boost for me because at least it showed Duncan rated me enough to consider me again for England, even if I couldn't bowl. I was prepared to go back to England and work just on my batting if necessary, but I've always been the sort of person that likes being involved in the whole game. It's just not the same if you're only batting. I like knowing I'm involved all the time and I'm sure I wouldn't have enjoyed it as much just as a batsman.

I had only been home for a short while when I was summoned to go back out again as a replacement for Dominic Cork, who himself was flying back with an injury. I flew back out there with David Graveney, who gave me his congratulations for my recall but then took the edge off things by informing me I was flying out because I already had a visa and it meant the ECB wouldn't have to organise one for someone else! To make matters worse, when I arrived there was no room for me at the hotel and I had to spend my first night on a camp bed. Despite these minor setbacks I was keen to make a good impression and that probably contributed to the dramatic end to my first net session the following morning. I was trying to do the right thing and stayed on at the end of the practice session to try and do a bit more batting but I was bowled a bouncer. I went to try and hook it and got through with the shot but the ball flew through the gap between the grill and my helmet and hit me just below the eye – welcome back to Pakistan!

I woke up with a major black eye and that was my last real involvement in the tour. I knew I was going out there as a back-up batsman and that's how it proved because I carried the drinks for the rest of the trip. My only real contribution was in the dramatic final few overs of the last Test in Karachi as we closed in on victory in virtual darkness. The local ground staff weren't pushing the sightscreens very quickly because of the state of the game and no doubt hoped the umpires would call a halt to the match because of the light. Duncan wasn't happy with what was happening so he sent me and Matthew Hoggard out to start pushing the sightscreens and that was my contribution to a fantastic victory and the series win.

I am fortunate that the trip to Pakistan that winter is one of the few tours I have been on where I haven't been a member of the side. Some players go on several tours without really playing, but this was my only experience of that and ever since then I have felt for 12th men. It is even harder for them now with the compressed itineraries we have today. It's a horrible job just carrying the drinks because you want to get involved and you want to feel part of it. You do as much as you can for the lads who are playing, but you do feel on the outside. It's a strange one. I enjoyed being out there and I was really pleased we had won the Test and the series, particularly after the hard work the lads had put in, but it is totally different when you are not part of the side and you don't play.

We managed to sneak a couple of beers into the dressing-room to celebrate a great victory, but the real celebrations were reserved for the way home. As chance would have it, we had to stop in Dubai on the way back to London, so most of the lads charged into the Irish Bar there to toast our victory in Guinness before continuing our journey home.

I was overlooked for the Test series in Sri Lanka after Christmas 2000, but I wasn't greatly surprised. We had used two spinners for most of the tour to Pakistan, and Sri Lanka was going to be more of the same so I was always up against it, trying to force my way into the side. My back was still troubling me as well, but England showed they had not forgotten about me entirely by calling me up for the one-day series in Sri Lanka at the end of that tour. Having not played for some time, I should have gone out there keen to make a good impression but didn't do my cause much good by turning up with a dodgy ankle. I had done it playing football with Lancashire. I went to trap the ball and stood on it instead – perhaps that shows the extent of my football skills. England were annoyed because I had not told anyone about it and even Lancashire weren't aware I had a sore ankle. It meant I was unable to do the bleep tests at the start of the tour because I couldn't turn properly and ended up playing with my ankle heavily strapped up. It made little difference to that series because we were well beaten. Nasser Hussain had gone home with an injury and Alec Stewart had turned down the chance to captain the side, so Graham Thorpe ended up leading us. Sri Lanka were the better side in the first two games before beating us convincingly in the final match in Colombo. It was the first time England had ever suffered a ten-wickets defeat in a one-day international, but the conditions were as tough as I can ever remember. The temperatures were something like 35°C in the middle and it was very difficult to breathe. Even Graeme Hick, who was always very fit, had to have a runner because he was so knackered. I made 24, but as soon as I walked out from the dressing-room to go out to bat I was wet through with sweat. I had to change my gloves after four or five overs it was that bad – I've never experienced anything like it before or since.

When I returned from Sri Lanka we had a new coach at Lancashire with the appointment in 2001 of former Australian captain Bobby Simpson. He was great for the club and a great influence on a lot of players during his stint at Old Trafford. I feel a bit guilty about what little we achieved while he was there. His cv speaks for itself and then right at the end of an illustrious career he came to Lancashire and we just didn't play very well through no fault of his. This is a bloke who had played Test cricket for Australia and turned them into the best side in the world as coach, but we let him down. Working with Bob definitely improved me as a player and even players like Neil Fairbrother, who were coming to the end of their careers, said he had done wonders for them as well. I think you would have to be pretty stupid not to learn something off Bob Simpson.

He was particularly good with me on catching and I would say he is the best coach I have ever worked with on that area. He improved that part of my game no end. I've always had good hands in the outfield, but you do drop catches from time to time in the slips and since working with Bob I think the number I drop now has been reduced by at least 20 per cent. He taught me an awful lot about the technique of catching. It sounds very basic but he taught me about really watching the ball into your hands and also using the ball's momentum instead of grabbing it. Instead of taking a catch in front of you, Bob taught me to cushion the ball and allow the momentum of the ball to take it behind me.

He was also very keen on each player contributing their own wisdom, taking ownership of the side, he called it. We had a pre-season trip to Cape Town and he made Neil Fairbrother get up and talk about playing and building a one-day innings, which was obviously something he excelled in. Bob wanted every player to become involved and have input. After the way I got off to a bad start with Dav Whatmore, I was keen to get off to a good start with Bob and I hit it off with him straight away. He used to call me the fruit bat, which is what he used to call Merv Hughes when he was in charge of Australia. I took this as a compliment until he explained the fruit bat is regarded as the great Australian pest. He also changed my stance at the crease. I went from being really crouched to a more upright stance and since then I have probably gone to somewhere in between with my bat between my legs when I'm ready to face. I am sure the time I spent with Bob Simpson gave me the launch pad for going on to play as well as I have over the last couple of years. It would have been really nice to work with him now I am playing better because I think he could have helped me improve even more. I got a lot out of working with Bob and he still writes to me. Last year he sent me a three-page letter giving me encouragement and telling me what he thinks. I'm really bad at keeping up correspondence, but I made sure to seek him out when I was in Australia a couple of winters ago.

Although I was enjoying working with Bob, the 2001 season was very frustrating for me and I never really got going. In 13 matches that season my highest first-class score was only 68 and my only century was against the might of Durham University. It was very hard to put my finger on what was going wrong for me. It wasn't as if I was getting out to the same shot all the time or I was making the same mistake. I was getting to 30 or 40 and then I would get out in all sorts of different ways. Looking back now I probably wasn't professional enough at what I was doing.

If I go and have a net now I make sure I work on something in particular, a particular shot maybe which I haven't been playing very well. I go in there now to try and build an innings just as if I am out in the middle. Whereas back then I would bat for 15 minutes, play every shot in the book, get out four or five times and think that was OK. I tend to practise getting in these days, which is something I've always struggled with, or perhaps to get to know where my off stump is so I'm better at that. Bob had a big influence on making my practice that much better and more focused, but for a while I wasn't even playing well enough to get into the Lancashire side, never mind think about being called up for England. While they were playing a home Ashes series I was struggling and my only form came in the C&G Trophy, where I got man-of-the-match awards for my performances in successive rounds against Sussex and Durham.

Bob even tried shock tactics with me by giving me what I can only describe as an Australian pep talk. He called me into his office and said, 'Fred, you're a cunt.' That was it. That was all he said before walking out and leaving me in his office. Those few words were enough to make me sit down and think about it. There was no big sermon from him and it worked to a degree. I tried harder, but I still wasn't getting the results and that season remained a real struggle, finishing with a pivotal meeting in my career taking place at the end of that season.

By now my business relationship with Neil Fairbrother and Chubby Chandler had developed to such an extent they were managing just about everything in my life. It makes things much easier to have someone you trust looking after you and I trust them both implicitly. Chubby and Harv look after everything from contracts to my day-to-day diary and even help organise my finances. A lot of my post goes to their office and they pay a lot of my bills for me. For me that help is absolutely invaluable because it means I don't have to worry about anything other than my cricket.

They could see, though, that during that season things were not right and they decided to give me a few home truths. They arranged to see me at Old Trafford where in those days they had a first-team and a second-team room. I was up there chatting to Jamie Haynes, who was then Lancashire's second-team wicket-keeper, and went through to the other room when Chubby and Harv arrived, while Jamie continued sorting his locker next door. He might as well have been in the room with us, because the conversation got so loud and heated he must have heard everything through the wall. Both Chubby and Harv gave me a roasting for my attitude and commitment, but once that was over the conversation became a bit more constructive. We talked about how I was going to get out of this rut and how I was going to get back into the England team and we devised a cunning plan. They got me to talk about what I was doing wrong and what I intended to do about it. But talk is one thing, and they made it clear I had to go out and do it, which I actually did. Because the third degree had come from Harv and Chubby, whom I respect, I think the penny finally dropped on what I had to do to have a successful career.

Keeping fit and training hard has now become a major part of my life. The trick is to have a routine and that is what I have now. I still don't look forward to doing it, and sometimes I still dig my heels in, but once I come out I feel really good about myself – energise through exercise as Lancashire physio Dave Roberts keeps telling me. When I look back now I am very proud about how I turned my career around, although I am not too proud about having to turn it around in the first place. I'm sure I wasn't the first young player to learn that lesson and I won't be the last, but I'm very proud of what I am doing now and what I have achieved. I had already taken some steps towards improving myself by moving out of my Manchester flat and away from the temptation of bars and takeaway places on my doorstep, but the training part of the Flintoff plan was when I first started to benefit properly by reaching a better level of fitness.

The lifeline for me around that time was being selected on a one-day tour of Zimbabwe because I knew if I did well on that I would be right back in the frame for England. The selectors had overlooked me even for the one-day matches that previous summer while they had a look at a number of new players, including Paul Collingwood. I probably didn't deserve to be selected for Zimbabwe on form but I wanted to take the chance they gave me. That tour could have gone a lot better for me but I did all right, and the team did well to win the series 5–0. I got 46 in successive matches but I couldn't seem to get beyond that. I felt I batted and bowled reasonably well and I think my performances on that trip did just enough to remind England I was still around and ultimately got me on the tour to India in November 2001.

Another key part of the Fairbrother–Chandler plan was to ring Duncan Fletcher and ask if I could go with the Academy squad to Adelaide that winter. It was a way of me showing willing and I also thought it would be a good opportunity to improve on my game away from everything. It didn't really work out as well as I had hoped over there, but it was important for me to go as a statement of intent to England to say I've not been that good so far, but I'm trying to get better. The accommodation in Adelaide was basic, but it was fine and I shared a room with Steve Harmison. I thought, however, the practice and training facilities were not a patch on what we had in England. That was a massive shock because I always thought of Australia as having some of the best facilities in the world. While I was there, there was not an awful lot of cricket going on either or time to work at your game. There was a lot of sitting around talking about different things and we learnt to do a bit of cooking, which didn't really suit the lads who were on the course that year because we weren't a young intake. I was 24, Andrew Strauss was 26 and Mark Wagh from Warwick-shire was 27. If I had gone there as a 17- or 18-year-old it would have been great, but I think we were a bit old for it. There was also a lot of fitness work, getting up early in the morning and that sort of thing, but no more than I was doing back at home anyway. By then it was probably more of a shock to the others than it was to me because I had already got into my new train-ing regime.

But it achieved one result. I must have impressed Rod Marsh, England's Academy director, because when Craig White informed Duncan Fletcher and Nasser Hussain on England's tour in India that he could no longer bowl as fast as he used to be able to, I was the one they sent for. It was a bit of a shock to say the least. Robert Key came to my room and told me and, just as on the occasion of my first England call-up, I thought he was taking the mickey at first. But after it dawned on me that he was telling the truth, off I set on a tour I had never expected even to get near just a few months earlier.

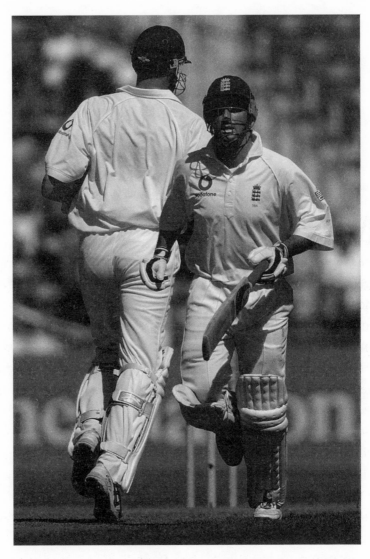

Graham Thorpe was a big influence, helping me to my first Test century in Christchurch.

10

FINDING MY
WAY BACK

My tour of India didn't get off to the best of starts because
I left my bowling boots at the Academy and had to
borrow some. These were clearly OK, because in my first game
against India A I did quite well, opening the bowling with
Richard Johnson. I was pleased with my efforts because I had
done very little bowling ever with the new ball. The previous
time was years ago when I played for the under-19s, so I was
pretty much a novice at it. I must have taken to it reasonably
well, though, because I got a wicket in my second over,
although the wicket was fairly green and had quite a bit in it
for the seam bowlers. Sadly I got a duck in our first innings,
which was pretty much how the rest of the tour went for me
with the bat.

It was really hard work bowling in India, not just because of
the conditions, but also because of the standard of the players
we were bowling at. Coming up against Rahul Dravid, V. V. S.
Laxman, not to mention Sachin Tendulkar, was as difficult a
batting line-up as I had faced at that stage. The wickets were
very flat and once the shine went off the ball there was nothing
there, so we tried either to bang it in short or throw it out a bit

wider and let them try and come at us. They never really clob-
bered me during that series. Endurance was also a key factor
because I bowled a lot of overs. Whenever I have been involved
in the sub-continent I have always bowled my share of overs
because I have got decent control and the extra bounce I get
enables me to put it in areas which allow me to get away with
things without getting slapped.

The amount of bowling I was doing was always going to
make batting much harder, though I would not make that an
excuse for my form with the bat on that trip after scoring only
26 in five innings. But I have found that whenever I've bowled
a lot of overs, as on the previous winter's tour to South Africa,
it is very hard after putting in all that effort to buckle your pads
on to bat at number 5 or 6. If you look at South Africa's Jacques
Kallis, who bats at number 4, he hardly bowled in the 2004/05
series but the times when he does bowl a lot, he doesn't get as
many runs. It wasn't as if I hadn't been playing well because I
think my form with the bat had turned around. I had scored
40-odd twice during the one-day trip to Zimbabwe prior to
going to India and was feeling quite good going into the first
Test at Mohali. I had got to 18 when I was facing Harbhajan
Singh and tried to hit him for six. He delivered the other one,
the one that goes the other way, which I had been waiting on
but tried to hit too hard and spooned it to backward point.
After that it all went wrong and my contribution during the
three-Test series read a dismal 18–4–0–4–0.

At least I was contributing with the ball and I was pleased
with the way I bowled in the First Test, even though I failed to
take a wicket. Gus Fraser, who was now working as a journalist,
sent me a nice note which he pushed under the door of my
hotel room to tell me it was one of the best nought-fors he

had ever seen, which lifted my spirits just at a time when I needed it.

Maybe the management thought the same because after that Test, I was given the new ball after previously coming on first change while Hoggard and Jimmy Ormond opened the bowling. But I was becoming very frustrated with my efforts with the bat, particularly after all the hard work I had put in. I didn't think I was getting any justice. I had volunteered for the Academy, I had lost weight, I was bowling and I was working hard, but I still couldn't score runs. No matter how hard I seemed to practise, it didn't improve my performance out in the middle and I struggled throughout that tour. I practised and practised with the local spinners in the nets, but it failed to change my fortunes. I particularly had trouble with Anil Kumble. Every time he came on I would struggle to get a run. Naturally all the fielders closed in and there didn't seem to be any gaps whatsoever, while the close-in fielders seemed to be right on top of me. I didn't have a clue what to do about it. And that is when people started saying I couldn't play spin. They seemed to have forgotten that I had got runs at county level against international spinners. When I got a duck in the last Test in Bangalore I was ashamed and embarrassed. Getting out to Sarandeep Singh, a part-time spinner, in my final innings was the last straw. Because I had been shot at after my previous performances I daren't hit the ball properly and just chipped it to mid-wicket and toddled off. I was in tears and went to sit away from the dressing-room. But Graham Dilley, our bowling coach at the time, came to find me. Dill was great with me, sitting down and talking to me for a couple of hours. He has been through a lot in his own life and that talk lifted me and enabled me to go out and feel better about myself when

I bowled again. This talk obviously helped because I got four for 50 and man-of-the match.

At the time I thought my batting form was a disaster but experience since has taught me that it is important not to look at these things as though they are the end of the world. Nowadays I have learnt not to dwell on things or have a tantrum. I just sit there now, have a think about what I've done wrong and how I've played and then I crack on. I have acquired a perspective because there are more important things in my life now, like my wife Rachael and our daughter Holly. As disappointed as I am, if I get out it is not going to be the end of me.

We returned to India after Christmas for a one-day series, which began in January 2002 in the huge stadium that is Eden Gardens in Calcutta. It's one of the few grounds I've been to where you can hear the roar from inside the dressing-room and, when we went out, we were hit with a wall of noise. It wasn't even like the noise you get from your average football match. Those erupt when one of the star players gets the ball or the home side scores a goal, but here it was continuous. I don't know what the crowd figure was that day, but people said afterwards that it was getting close to 100,000. Not surprising, because there were two or sometimes three people to a seat virtually right around the stadium. It typified the passion they have for the game in India.

We thought the noise level was loud when we walked out, but when Tendulkar and Virender Sehwag, their opening batsmen, started walking to the crease it went higher by several decibels. The place just erupted with thousands and thousands of people screaming and shouting. They got off to a decent start and every boundary got the crowd going even more. The noise came to an abrupt halt, though, once Tendulkar was out in the thirteenth over. I don't know quite what happened, but I bowled a full-length ball and he just seemed to miss it and the ball carried on to hit his stumps. I think he was trying to hit me into the stands and perhaps he tried to hit it too hard. I simply went mad when I realised what had happened, running around shouting and screaming. The only trouble was that you could hear everything. The ground had gone deadly silent in shock that he was out. We all looked around and there were a lot of people walking out, even though the game had only just started; they had come to see Tendulkar bat and we had spoilt the party. We lost that first game by 22 runs, but it was a good series to play in because we were two evenly matched teams.

There was a bit of nastiness when I got hit by a pellet gun fielding on the boundary during the fifth match in Delhi in which I was pleased to score 52. I felt something hit me and, looking down, saw pellets on the ground. You expect to have plastic bottles thrown at you when you are playing on the sub-continent, but you don't expect to be shot. Nasser got very heated about it in the middle and Phil Neale, the tour manager, came to find out what was going on. We carried on, but the whole thing seemed to get swept under the carpet. There was a big story back home to do with crowd disturbances but Andrew Walpole, the ECB's Media Relations Manager, told me to play the incident down when I was interviewed the following day. Looking back now, I think I should have made more of a stand because I wasn't there to be shot at. I realise on the sub-continent that the crowds are extremely excitable and enthusiastic, but I thought a line was crossed that day. We explained it away as the crowd just being over-excited at the time, but I wasn't sure about that at all.

It built up to a finale in Bombay, which we needed to win to draw the series. It was a close match throughout and we got to a decent total after Darren Gough and I put on a few at the end of our innings. Tendulkar, who had never scored a one-day international century in his home city, absolutely tore into Andy Caddick early on and then Ganguly also started having a go at him. They lost their way a bit and we got back in it with a few wickets. It came down to the final over with them needing just six runs to win the series with two wickets remaining. I was tense and nervous, the whole series was resting on that last over. I managed to run out Kumble by side-footing the ball onto the stumps after they went for a quick single.

I returned to my mark with two balls of the over remaining and six runs needed and Javagal Srinath on strike. I just checked with Darren Gough, who was standing at mid-off, about what he thought I should bowl. I knew myself, but needed to hear it from him. 'What are you talking about?' he said. 'It's got to be a leg-stump yorker.' I ran up and bowled just that, knocking Srinath's leg stump out. It was a massive release after what I had been through to win the game like that. I started running off and, almost as a reflex action took my shirt off, whirling it around my head. Thankfully I ran away from most of the photographers. All the lads were laughing when they caught up with me and I suddenly realised what I was doing. There I was in front of 70,000 people with the palest, whitest body possible. You would never have known I had spent so long in India that winter; Gough said I looked like a farmer. Everyone was taking the mickey out of me for it. I put my shirt back on, inside out, I realised later. Murali was in the crowd. He had flown in from Sri Lanka a few days earlier and we had had dinner a couple of times. I don't think he could quite understand what I was doing. We got a late flight to New Zealand a few days later and people there were still talking about my stripping off. It was only then that I realised what a fuss I had caused. Anyone would think I had done the full monty! But people still seem to remember it, even now; they talk about the night I ran around without my shirt and the time I broke my bat a couple of years later.

Duncan Fletcher made a point of praising my dedication in the media after that performance, which was timely encouragement after the amount of hard work I had put in since that meeting with Chubby and Harv at the end of the previous season. Even though I hadn't been scoring runs in India during the Test series, I was working really hard and had got rewarded for my efforts during that one-day series.

After that first game at Eden Gardens, Duncan Fletcher bought the whole team a tequila in the bar. We followed that with a few pints and it turned out being a great night. There was a band on, who were terrible, and once they had finished I got hold of the microphone and that was the start of our regular karaoke nights. We started calling it Karaoke Night at the Nag's Head and it was good fun. Everybody would get together and almost everyone sang. Graham Dilley always used to sing 'Sultans of Swing' by Dire Straits, Martyn Ball would try a David Gray song and I would belt out a few Elvis numbers; even the press got involved one night with Mike Dixon of the *Daily Mail* standing up to give us a song, but he got pelted with nuts because he was so awful.

New Zealand was always going to be a different challenge to the one we had just faced in India. My confidence was good after the way the one-day series finished and I began to spend a bit more time with Graham Thorpe during the early part of this tour. I had always got on well with Thorpe and on that trip we were the only two single lads around when the wives and girlfriends came out to visit. We'd have a few beers and the odd game of pool and we'd talk about cricket and life in general. We had both been through rough times off the pitch so I suppose we had that in common. He was still going through a bad time after the break-up of his marriage, but I was coming through the other side of my problems and I was feeling quite happy. We seemed to spend a fair amount of time together out in the middle too. Getting to know each other better I think helped us when we got to bat together. Thorpe is very good, and similar to Fairbrother, in that he senses when you're going to do something, and he's right more often than not; I don't know what it is about little left-handers.

This rapport came in particularly useful during our big stand during the second innings of the opening Test at Christchurch. We had talked about my batting problems in Test cricket and he thought I should be more positive so when I went out to bat with him I was determined to play that way. I got to 26 off my first 13 deliveries. Having Graham at the other end was a big bonus for me because every time I got too excited he would come down the pitch and get me focused again. As I approached my century Craig McMillan kept trying to tempt me with bouncers and I kept resisting until he bowled me one too many and I edged it over the slips to the third man boundary to go from 98 to 102 and claim my first Test century.

When we got back into the dressing-room at the tea interval everyone was buzzing. I went up to Warren Hegg, who knew better than anyone what I'd been through by sharing a dressing-room with me at Lancashire, and I just grinned. 'I've done it,' I told him. 'I've got a Test match century.' I'm not sure I could quite believe it. After getting a duck in the first innings, I had only been thinking about avoiding another pair. I ended up being quite disappointed when I holed out to deep mid-wicket for 137. I had got carried away and should have gone on and got a double hundred like Thorpe, but we had shared a huge stand of 221 which put England in charge of the match with a 551-run lead.

During that series we used drop-in pitches, which were slotted in almost ready to play on. In that Test it was difficult to bat on early on but flattened out into a really good batting surface. So by the time New Zealand batted again Nathan Astle was able to play one of the best innings I have ever seen. He hammered the ball everywhere to score one of the quickest double hundreds ever and New Zealand fell only 98 runs short. It was an amazing innings and should have won him the man-of-the-match award, which was given to Thorpe. It's often the way, though, that these awards never go to the losing side and, by winning with a day to spare, it enabled us to celebrate St Patrick's Day properly at an Irish Bar we found near the hotel. Looking back now, that celebration with Butcher and Thorpe was only a week before we received the shocking news of the death of Ben Hollioake in a car crash in Perth.

We found out about Ben's death on the third morning of the Second Test in Wellington. I was sitting waiting to bat, the next man in, when I noticed a few of the lads looked quite upset, particularly Thorpe and Butcher, who both played with Ben at Surrey. Not knowing what was going on, I turned to Warren Hegg and said, 'What's wrong with everyone? Has someone died?' Warren told me to keep quiet and get ready to bat, but I kept on at him to tell me what was wrong until he finally told me about the fatal car accident. I was absolutely devastated by the news. I first got to know Ben when I was about eight or nine and we had played together in all the different England age-groups. I had been his captain for the Under-19s and I had toured with him for England A. I regarded him as a good friend and one of those characters that everyone seems to think is invincible. He was so highly talented at everything he did, but laid back with it and almost always had a smile on his face. It was horrible to think someone like that could die in such a way. It hit a lot of us hard because it was also, for most of us, the first death of someone of our own age.

One of my favourite memories of Ben is his fantastic perform-ance for England in that one-day International at Lord's against Australia back in the summer of 1997. I'd been really chuffed for him getting a call-up by England in the first place as I had always thought he could play, but his performance that day surprised even me. I'd been playing with him for the Under-19s the previous summer and I remember sitting in the dressing-room with a few of the Lancashire lads and telling them to watch carefully because this boy walking out could really bat. From memory, I think he nailed his third ball straight back down the ground off Glenn McGrath, which is quite an achievement in itself, but then did it again for good measure. It was an amazing innings to watch. For a lad to walk out at Lord's at 19 years of age and do that defied belief.

Playing cricket was very difficult after what had happened. We did think about asking them to cancel the remainder of the series, but there were a lot of English fans who had paid a lot of money to come and watch and we thought we owed it to them to continue playing. We had a memorial ceremony for Ben and Mark Butcher sang a song he had written. Phil Neale spoke very well too and then we went to the Irish Bar and had

Running down the beach in East London during the 2003 World Cup in South Africa.

Batting against Makhaya Ntini while scoring 95 against South Africa at The Oval in 2003.

The nine-wicket victory over South Africa at The Oval levelled the series in 2003. Mark Butcher is the one spraying champagne.

reaking my bat during my 142 in the
)03 Second Test against South Africa at
)rd's.

Muralitharan slogs out against me in the
opening Test at Galle in 2003. I wouldn't
mind but he'd borrowed my bat!

etting bowling tips from Angus Fraser shortly before the opening Test against Sri Lanka
Galle.

I can't tell you how hard it is to play cricket in Sri Lanka with the heat and humidity. It shows in my face as I bowl during the Second Test in Kandy.

My dad Colin pictured after his infamous dropped catch in the stand at Edgbaston against West Indies, 2004.

I've just realised my dad has dropped me. He prides himself on being a good pair of hands.

My 'home' Test at Old Trafford against West Indies turned out to be a good one for me when I dismissed Brian Lara twice.

A special moment. Walking off with my good mate Rob Key after we'd won the Old Trafford Test and the series against West Indies and I'd hit the winning runs.

Sparring with Jamie Moore, the British light-middleweight champion, at Oliver's Gym in Salford. I enjoyed learning the different disciplines involved with another sport.

Taking a break from a gym workout with Steve Harmison. Fitness has been a key factor in England's success in the last few years.

Above: With new born Holly. A wonderful moment.

Right: Getting married to Rachael was the happiest day of my life.

With the ICC one-day player of the year award in 2004. I was still celebrating the birth of Holly just days earlier.

Acknowledging an important century that helped us beat Sri Lanka and set up a semi-final meeting with Australia in the ICC Champions Trophy 2004.

Michael Vaughan encourages us all to go out and enjoy our cricket.

a few in Ben's memory. Quite a few of us wanted to go to the funeral in Perth, but logistically it would have been a nightmare so in the end it was decided that Nasser should go as captain.

We lost the Final Test in Auckland after a few decisions went against us, but I returned home in good shape. I was pleased with the way I had performed in New Zealand and was pretty hopeful I could put pressure on to keep my place for the following summer. I felt I was getting somewhere.

The 2003–04 Ashes tour was an unhappy time for me.

11

FEELING THE PAIN

I returned home from New Zealand to disappointing news from Lancashire. John Crawley had left to join Hampshire after a long-standing dispute with the committee. I had enjoyed playing under his captaincy. He was a straight talker, which not everybody liked, and I think he was disappointed when Bob Simpson left because he got on well with him. Of course, he carried the can for our C&G semi-final defeat at Leicester the previous season. Paul Allott, who was also on the Lancashire committee, had slagged him off on Sky and I felt for Crawley because the game went over two days and it was a difficult decision whether to bat or bowl. The batsmen didn't want to bat because the ball was doing a lot and the bowlers didn't want to bowl because it was too wet to run in properly. He chose to bat. I don't think it made much difference in the end anyway because Shahid Afridi played one of those innings that if we'd have got 300 he would probably have knocked them off. John Crawley was one of a number of players who came up through the ranks at Lancashire and had been a Lancashire player through and through, so it was very sad to see him go. I hope he doesn't look back on his time with Lancashire with bitterness, because that's really disappointing after spending so long at a club.

We started that season with a new captain in Warren Hegg, but I was soon coming into contact with an old friend in Murali, who was touring with Sri Lanka. The start of that 2002 summer was the first time I had faced Murali in a Test series, although I'd played against him before in a one-day International in Colombo. The First Test was washed out at Lord's, but we beat them convincingly at Edgbaston when Murali got me out caught at bat-pad for 29. To this day I'm convinced I didn't hit it and I still rib him about it when I see him! By this time I knew him really well, having played two seasons with him at Lancashire. There was none of Wasim's on-the-pitch vow of silence with Murali. He can't help talking, and if he does speak to you, you can't help but talk back to him because he's such an infectiously nice bloke.

That Test was also significant because it was where I first met my wife, Rachael. She was working in the hospitality area provided after the game for sponsor's guests, which the players sometimes go along to and have a quick drink after a day's play. The way I remember it is that I went up there, saw her and began to woo her on the spot – she says she doesn't remember even meeting me! I managed to get her number off a guy from the Professional Cricketers' Association so I sent her a little text message the following day and we met in the bar for a drink. That was on the Saturday night and we had a nice time, but I feared the worst the following day when I was told my ex-girlfriend had slagged me off in one of the Sunday papers. I remember going into the dressing-room that morning to see most of the lads hidden behind the papers avoiding my gaze. I thought there was something wrong so I asked what was going on and they showed me what they were reading. On the same day there was a piece in one of the other papers which was quite flattering about my batting so I asked Rachael if she had seen that. Sadly, she had seen the other piece. Rachael had her own company, Strawberry Promotions, which supplies promotional staff nationwide and kept her very busy. My life changed after we met and we spent most of that summer together. Rachael's been very good for me. She keeps me in line because I have got the capability to push my luck a little bit. Having a stable life at home also helps my cricket. When I was single I would be out until all hours because I always used to find it difficult being on my own. I needed to keep myself occupied and have other people around. I would go and sit in the Old Trafford dressing-room after training until four in the afternoon. Now I get home as quickly as I can to spend time with Rachael and our daughter Holly.

After beating Sri Lanka by an innings at Edgbaston, the series moved on to Old Trafford for my first Test on my home ground. We forced Sri Lanka to follow on, but Andrew Caddick broke down to leave most of the bowling with myself, Matthew Hoggard and Alex Tudor, who also began to fall apart by the end of the match. I bowled all right without much reward, but I had a lot of work to do and, looking back now, it probably didn't help the pain I was beginning to feel in my groin area. I had felt it first at the start of June when we were beaten by Warwickshire in the Benson and Hedges Cup semi-final at Old Trafford. As I was a centrally-contracted player, all medical treatment was England's responsibility, but it would be several months before I finally had an operation.

Despite the major discomfort I was feeling, I was playing all right going into the Test series against India at Lord's. In the first innings I got out fishing at one for 59, a horrible shot. That Test was also notable for me getting out my old team-mate

Ganguly in the first innings quite cheaply after I hung one out a bit wider and he guided it straight to Vaughan at gully. As I recall I got quite a few texts on my mobile phone from the Lancashire lads congratulating me on that one.

Throughout that Test, though, I was really feeling the pain in my groin after once again bowling my fair share of overs and the feeling continued right through to the next Test at Trent Bridge. But now the pain just got worse and worse and went from being merely uncomfortable to absolute agony by the time I got to Trent Bridge. By then I could barely walk. It got to the point where I was even struggling with day-to-day things. Getting going in a morning was just awful. I couldn't even put my socks on. I needed Rachael to help me fasten my laces. But I had more injections in my backside before the Test and they seemed to ease my condition enough to be able to play. Even so, Trent Bridge was not a happy experience for me. I bowled a lot of overs, despite being in bits, and I was starting to get concerned with the damage I might be doing to myself. I let England know of my concern, and I thought Trent Bridge would be my last game of the summer. When I hobbled off at the end of that Test I couldn't even walk properly.

It was at Trent Bridge that I was reunited with Steve Harmison, whose call-up for his Test debut marked his emergence as a high-quality fast bowler. He started off quite nervously, but bowled four successive maidens, even if you couldn't reach all of the deliveries. After that start, he ended up getting three wickets in the first innings, including bowling Ganguly on 99. (More glee at Old Trafford.) He bowled really well and really fast. I remember him being very nervous but whatever you say to people in that situation, the occasion is there, they have to overcome it, and he certainly did.

After my experiences in Nottingham, I assumed I wouldn't be playing again. England were leading the series 1–0 and victory in the next Test at Headingley would seal the series. I was included in the squad. I thought I was just turning up at Headingley either to find out when my operation was going to be or for them to have a look at me and rule me out of contention, but that was not the case. The management made it clear that they wanted me in. We sat on the grass talking about my fitness and I ended up having yet another injection in my backside to get through it. So instead of watching Steve Harmison and my other mate Robert Key, who was making his debut after Marcus Trescothick broke his thumb, I was playing alongside them. I remember being very nervous for Key in that Test, almost more nervous for him than I was for myself. He's such a fine player and I wanted him to do well so badly.

Looking back on it now it was a big mistake for me to play in that Test on a lot of counts: I wasn't fit, didn't take a wicket, failed to score a run and I was in agony. Even in the nets beforehand I remember Graham Dilley asking me how I was and I told him I wasn't good. It hurt me when I batted and bowled because I couldn't open my legs properly, which inhibited me even when I tried to run. As well as the massive anti-inflammatory jabs in my backside I was also taking painkillers orally and if this episode taught me anything it is that I will never, ever do that again. We were now nearing the end of August, so I had been playing over two months since I first felt the injury playing for Lancashire in that semi-final. I think there was unreasonable pressure put on me to play and it didn't turn out well for me in any way.

That didn't stop me bowling 27 overs, most of which were

bouncers because I was really struggling to bowl anything else, as India piled up over 600 runs in their first innings. That Test also continued my disappointing record at Headingley, although I did get what I thought was a bad decision in the first innings to get out for nought. John Crawley had got out to the previous ball from spinner Harbhajan Singh, trying to work the identical delivery around the corner and got caught. I saw the ball coming again and thought I'm not going to do what Crawley has just done so I let it go and padded up to it. This was on a wicket that was turning and bouncing and I thought it was going down legside by about a foot. I remember trying to get in as big a stride as my injury would let me but I was given out to suffer my third duck in as many Test innings at Headingley! I suffered an identical outcome in the second innings to record successive pairs at the ground and England lost the Test convincingly.

Afterwards I had a further chat with England's management and it was then decided I had better have an operation, possibly because they didn't think they would really miss me that much for the Final Test after my performance at Headingley. I went in for a double hernia operation just before the Oval Test and had staples put on either side of my groin, where they cut me open and made me immobile for a couple of days. I then went down to London with Rachael and watched one of the days of the Test from a box, had a couple of beers and came back home ready to begin my rehabilitation.

Shortly after that final Test I was named in the squad for the forthcoming winter's Ashes series and I began my rehabilitation under the supervision of Lancashire's physio, Dave 'Rooster' Roberts. But after working well with Rooster, for some reason I was then instructed to go to the National Sports Centre at

Lilleshall and continue my rehabilitation there. I worked hard there for around a month, under England supervision, before I was told I could go away for a week, so I headed off to Dubai for a break with Rachael. Immediately following that holiday I was checked over by Dr Mark Ridgwell at Lilleshall, who had come to check on the progress of myself, Mark Butcher and Darren Gough in the build-up to the Ashes tour. He had a look at me and said he could guarantee I would be fit for the one-dayers in Australia, which started in January, but he couldn't say anything about the Ashes Test series beginning in November. It was not what was thought when I had the operation, but I had done my bit. I had done everything I'd been asked to do and worked hard at Lilleshall. The schedules we were working to were just too tight. I didn't feel like a guilty party, except perhaps for not answering my phone. I know Dean Conway, who was now the England physio, tried and failed to get hold of me while I was at Lilleshall, but that was because I hate phones and don't like answering them.

So I went to Australia not being able to run. I hadn't run since the operation and England were aware of that, but once we got to Australia there was a meeting and Duncan Fletcher said he didn't realise that I couldn't even jog. It was around this time that Lord MacLaurin, the ECB's former chairman, also started having a go at me, claiming I hadn't been doing my training properly. All I could say to that was that he's not a medical man or a physio and I knew myself that I had done everything that had been asked of me. It hurt me that everything seemed to be my fault and all the blame seemed to be with me. I'm a cricketer and I don't know anything about rehabilitation programmes – I do what I'm told to do. There seemed to be a lot of people covering their own backs and a lot of people looking after themselves. I was an easy target and I had a very unhappy time in Australia.

It was awful. The side weren't doing very well, I was a spare part and I wasn't getting any sympathy. It was a very frustrating time for me. Once again I hung around with Steve Harmison and Robert Key a lot. We didn't tend to go out much, but stayed in our rooms instead watching DVDs of *The Office* and *The Royle Family* – I think we watched just about every episode of those series. I couldn't run, but I could bat and I don't think I've ever worked as hard as I did then on my batting. I remember staying behind with Key at Brisbane until eight at night in the indoor school and working on it, but I was still getting criticised.

There I was in Australia, due to play in my first Ashes series, not knowing if I was going to be fit. It is obvious to me now that I should have had the operation much earlier. That is the blatant fact that stares you in the face – it should have happened a lot sooner but because that didn't happen, we were playing catch-up towards the end of my rehabilitation. I went to the Academy for a week to try and increase my fitness and when I returned I played against Queensland in Brisbane to try and prove my fitness for the First Test a week later. I don't think I was ready for that. I bowled 26 overs and that knackered me completely. It was clear I wasn't going to be fit for the First Test, but I did do a little of the 12th man duties. I was asked to go on and I told them if they needed a slip I could do that, but instead I was banished to the boundary. I tried chasing after one shot and simply couldn't do it. They sent me off the field after that.

After Brisbane we moved on to Tasmania and some of the things I was going through during this period were horrible.

I had a jab in my pubic area which was the worst pain I have ever experienced, all to get me fit for the Second Test in Adelaide. There is nothing worse than being on a tour and not being able to play because you are injured and there wasn't much sympathy coming in my direction from England. They all seemed to have forgotten the jabs I had endured to play at Headingley. It was a very unhappy time for me and all I wanted was just to get home for Christmas and to see Rachael. I couldn't be doing with it any more. It was supposed to be the biggest series of my career and all I wanted was to be sent home, which eventually I was. To make matters even worse, my mum and dad were flying out to Australia to see the cricket – our planes probably crossed in the air.

I got together with Rooster Roberts again on my return and trained with him every day. The idea was to get me fit for the World Cup in South Africa and we had six weeks to do it in. He had a look at me and told me he couldn't guarantee I was going to be fit, but we gave it a go and worked very well together. We worked hard, but it was enjoyable, even if he did treat me like a dog. He talks to me as if I'm a dog – and he's playing up to it a bit these days. He says things like, 'Fred . . . in here, now.' During that time we did a lot of different exercises strengthening my groin and a lot of running. We were doing things which I didn't do on my previous rehab programme like running up hills and by the time that six weeks were up, I was in unbelievable shape. He was very tough on me and wouldn't stand for any messing about, but I enjoyed working with him. He is a real straight talker, calls a spade a spade and takes the mickey out of anyone and everyone.

One of Rooster's favourite torture routines was to take me running up a big hill called Rivington Pike in Bolton. We used to start with a two-mile run up to the reservoir where there is an embankment about 50 foot tall which I would have to run up and down about 30 times, as fast as I could. That would nearly finish me, but then I had to run another four miles around it and back. Rooster would always set off like a shot, leaving me trailing behind among all the ramblers and walkers, while he would shout back something along the lines of, 'Come on, Fred, you're supposed to be an athlete. Look at me, I'm 45 and running faster than you.' The onlookers weren't to know how many times I'd run up and down that embankment hill.

Rooster taught me everything when we went running. He put me straight on mortgages, investments, marriage, Ian Botham . . . we spoke about almost everything. I was enjoying it because at last I was getting fit. I was also putting the Australian nightmare behind me. It keeps Rooster young as well, training with me – I think he's actually happy when I'm injured because he can get his weight off.

I was living with Rachael at the time in a flat in Altrincham because my flat was being decorated. Rooster gave me Christmas Day off and she and I had Christmas dinner together and my grandparents came up to see us. We had a really nice Christmas and after what had happened to me in the previous few months, it was good being around people I could trust.

Once those six weeks were up I flew back out to Australia, not really knowing what was going to happen. I went to Adelaide and had a couple of Academy games while the main England team played a one-dayer in Adelaide and after that I joined up with them and went to Melbourne for the second final of the one-day tournament. I got one for 56, which I wasn't that disappointed with. I was also quite pleased with my batting after such a long lay-off. We were in a position to win it and I was feeling good at the crease wearing my new England one-day kit for the first time. Then Brett Lee came back on.

I was standing expecting a yorker so close to the end of the innings. I was all set for it. I saw it, but I just didn't realise how fast it was going to come at me. The ball went straight through me. It was the first time I'd ever faced Lee. In my recent Academy games I had come up against Brad Williams who was a bit lively, but Lee was another level of pace again. The more you bat, the more you get used to pace and I had not faced a bowler that quick in some time. Disappointed as we all were to lose another game against Australia, the good news as far as I was concerned was getting through the game with nothing more than a bit of stiffness.

After that, we were given a few days off because for most of the boys it had been quite a long winter already. Steve Harmison went home to see his new daughter, Abby, and the rest of us flew to South Africa and on to Sun City, which is a Las Vegas-type resort, for a four-day break – and I'd only been back on duty for a week or so!

*Captain Nasser Hussain fielding even more questions
about our World Cup fixture in Zimbabwe.*

12

WORLD CUP POLITICS

While I was still at home recovering from my hernia operation at the end of 2002, the whole issue of whether we should be going to Zimbabwe the following spring to play our opening match of the World Cup became big news. We were due to start our tournament by playing in Harare, but it became a really big political issue. There were MPs going on radio and television to say we shouldn't be lending support to the regime by playing there. I saw a BBC programme on Zimbabwe which was enough to convince me they had a point.

It was a horrible experience once we got to South Africa. After the opening ceremony in Cape Town, we went straight into meeting after meeting on the Zimbabwe issue. We had everyone from David Morgan, the ECB chairman, to Richard Bevan of the Professional Cricketers' Association, to various high-ranking members of the ICC hauled in to address us. We also had Henry Olonga and Andy Flower, who had both stood up against the Zimbabwe government and won a lot of praise for their decision to wear black armbands during that tournament, smuggled into the hotel. They talked to us and were rightly worried about their own situations. We had a briefing from security experts as well. I don't think I was the only member of the squad who thought it was all a bit much, when we were supposed to be preparing for a World Cup, which was due to start the following week.

I didn't really get involved in the meetings because I had already made up my mind before rejoining the squad. Then we got a written death threat from a group calling themselves the Sons and Daughters of Zimbabwe and that settled things for a lot of people. The letter said that if we came to Zimbabwe we would be going back in wooden coffins and it also made threats to our families if we made the trip. Suddenly this was something different. It was all very well sitting in a room for three days talking about the rights and wrongs of going to Zimbabwe, but when death threats were being made, we owed it to our families and our loved ones back home to take them seriously. There was also a sense of genuine disappointment among the players that they had been put in that position by the authorities. As England players, it was not our job to make this type of decision – it was our job to play cricket. Why couldn't the cricket authorities and the politicians have got together sooner so this was all sorted out before we landed in South Africa? I felt sorry for someone like Jimmy Anderson, who had only been in the England squad for a few weeks but was expected to make a considered decision on such a serious matter at the age of 21. By the time a vote was finally taken and it was decided not to play our opening match in Zimbabwe, it was something of a relief to get it over with.

Having made the decision, it was clear our qualification for the next stage would be made more difficult. We were already in a tough group which included world champions Australia, India and Pakistan and by forfeiting the points against Zim-babwe, it meant we had to win at least two of our three matches against the other big teams if we were to be sure of qualifying for the Super Sixes stage of the tournament. It was understood by everyone that our decision made things difficult for ourselves, but at the same time that it should not be used as an excuse for our exit from the competition because we had developed a strong team spirit by the time the meetings had finished and we believed we could still do it.

The whole situation had been a shock to us all and was very hard to get our heads around. I know some people got emotional, but my decision had already been made, regardless of what was being said in the meetings – I was definitely not going to Zimbabwe. Whether we had got death threats or not, I was not going. Even if the rest of the squad had decided to go, I was not going to change my mind. It was the right decision for me and, even after that World Cup, I decided that unless something drastic changed in Zimbabwe, I was never going to go there again, which was why I was not available when England returned there the following year.

While we got on with finally preparing for the tournament, Tim Lamb and the rest of the ECB officials out in South Africa set about trying to appeal to the International Cricket Council to see if we could at least get some points for the cancelled first match against Zimbabwe. As the ICC had given us a hostile reception during all the meetings and tried to put a lot of pressure on both the players and administrators to fulfil the fixture, I don't think anyone was very optimistic the appeal would work. Sure enough, the appeal failed, but at least we knew what was ahead of us if we were going to make progress in the World Cup. I don't think anyone thought it was a task which was beyond us. We were without Gough, who had failed to recover from injury, but we had a good squad and if we played well there was no good reason we couldn't progress.

Once we started to concentrate on cricket again I took to talking with both Steve Harmison and Angus Fraser about my bowling as I was feeling a bit rusty. My major asset as a bowler is my control, particularly in one-day cricket. I'm not one of these bowlers who can move the ball around at will, but I have good line and length and talking to Gus and Steve helped get that back again. Harmison is good to talk to about bowling. He is one of the best bowlers in the world anyway, but he also has a good understanding of what to do and what not to do. He just simplified everything for me so I could run up and bowl without worrying. I also got Gus to have a look at the way I was bowling in the nets to see if he could spot anything I was doing wrong. Gus may be a full-time journalist now, but he is still very helpful. He is one of those people you can approach, who desperately wants England to do well and is keen to help. He is someone I have asked for help from time to time over the years and his input has always been appreciated.

Our tournament started with wins over Holland and Namibia before we completed our group matches with the three toughest games which would decide our fate. We returned to Cape Town to face Pakistan and before the game we had talked about Shoaib Akhtar and how best to combat his pace – he bowled at 100 mph to Nick Knight during the match. We also talked about the threat posed by spinner Saqlain Mushtaq and I was asked how to play against him. I was flattered to be asked, particularly as I had a reputation for not being able to play spin, but I had scored runs a few times against him for Lancashire against Surrey and was pleased they had asked for my input – apparently I was someone he didn't like bowling to.

Of course, come the match, I came down the wicket to him and got stumped! I did pick what delivery he was bowling, which was why I came down the pitch and went for it, but I didn't quite get there and he spun it past me. The conditions were very much in our favour during this game. We batted on a flat wicket and then it turned into good conditions to bowl in once the lights came on. I remember bowling to Wasim who couldn't believe what was happening because I swung one back into him which nearly cut him in half and I'm not normally known for swinging that much. That match has since become famous for Jimmy Anderson's great display and I wouldn't want to take anything away from him for the way he bowled, but conditions were definitely in our favour. I think we perhaps got a bit carried away with ourselves after winning that match. It was a great win, but perhaps not as good as it seemed.

One of the bonuses about playing international cricket in tournaments like a World Cup is meeting up with older players and talking to them about the game. I was lucky enough to do just that with one of my big heroes after the Cape Town match. I was sitting in the hotel bar after the match with Wasim when Viv Richards walked in and said hello to Wasim. Then he said, 'Hello, Fred.' We spent about 20 minutes talking about batting and when someone like that talks, you listen. He told me that I had to play myself in if I was playing one-day cricket. He said it doesn't matter if you've only got six off 25 balls, because once you're in you'll score at more than a run a ball and more than make up for the slow start. I took everything he said on board and I always remind myself of it when I go out to bat in one-day cricket.

Winning the toss is almost everything in day-night matches. You bat first unless it is absolutely obvious it is better to bowl first, because playing under the lights definitely favours the bowling side. We were confident going into the match against

India in Durban after our win against Pakistan. Conditions were similar and I don't think we could have expected what happened against India. I bowled my overs straight through and was very pleased with claiming two for 15 and we managed to limit them to a total of 250/9. When we batted, the ball was nipping around in a similar manner to the way it did for us against Pakistan and we lost early wickets. I remember being surprised how fast the bowling was when I went out to bat. I was facing Zaheer Khan and Ashish Nehra, who can bowl at a reasonable pace, but I was surprised because the way they were coming off the wicket was faster than Shoaib in Cape Town. With Viv Richards' wisdom in mind, my plan was to consolidate, bat for a bit and see where we were up to. We lost a few more wickets and Ronnie Irani came out to bat. He said to me: 'Stay with me, Fred, I think we've got a real chance here,' and was out first ball. But Andy Caddick and I managed to put a little partnership together. I remember thinking that realistically I was going to have to bat for a while and then, when it got to the last eight to ten overs, I was going to have to have a go. There was no point me batting and finishing unbeaten on 80-odd with England finishing well short of India's total.

The run-rate got up to around 11 an over, which was when I thought it was time for me to have a go and I hit their seamer Javagal Srinath for a few in an over. Then he bowled me a slower ball full toss which I also tried to hit, but was caught at mid-wicket for 64. If I had not been thinking it was time to get going, I'm sure I would have nailed it because Ganguly still had a few overs to bowl. It was probably a bit naïve of me not to be a little bit more patient. I could perhaps have tried to take advantage of his bowling, not because he's a bad bowler, but because he was probably the weakest member of their attack.

We fell 82 runs short, which meant we needed to beat Australia in our final group match at Port Elizabeth to guarantee our progress to the next stage.

During that tournament the wicket at St George's Park, Port Elizabeth, was quite easy to score off with the new ball, but as the ball got softer, the pitch got slower. We started off in this match like a train with Knight and Trescothick smashing it everywhere but then Australia brought Andy Bichel on and changed things. He wasn't swinging the ball that much, but he did put it in good areas and after losing a few wickets Alec Stewart and I had to consolidate the innings. We both got into our 40s, but all the time we were desperate to be more aggressive. I was particularly patient against Brad Hogg, their spinner, and I got out with seven or eight overs to go. Again, I was probably a bit naïve. I'd like to think if I was batting again now I would not have done that. Bichel came back on and I got my left leg out of the way to try and hit him over mid-wicket, which is a shot I play at that stage of an innings. There were still six or seven overs left, but if I was playing the innings now I'd like to think I would wait until the 47th or 48th over before trying something like that. It's amazing in one-day cricket just how much time you do have left; there's always more time than you think.

We got to 204/8, which wasn't a bad score on that wicket, and we were winning the game after reducing them to 135/8 when Bichel walked out to bat as their number 10 batsman and only Glenn McGrath to come. Sometimes teams get criticised for thinking they have won the game before it has actually happened, but I don't think that happened in this case. You can talk about not having a killer instinct and not putting people away, but I just think it was Andy Bichel's day. He got seven wickets and 34 to win the game. He was also batting with an absolute master in that situation in Michael Bevan who paced his innings unbelievably well. Whenever they needed a boundary he sensed it and hit one: it was an amazing display. In the heat of the moment you probably don't recognise it, but I look back on that game now and realise I learnt something just from watching Michael Bevan give a demonstration on how to go about a run chase – they don't call him the finisher for nothing.

Even in my last over I remember Bichel driving one back at me which I stuck my hand out to. It was one of those where it either sticks or it doesn't. If I had caught it there was every chance we would have gone on to win it. The big talking point at the end was Nasser Hussain giving young Jimmy Anderson the penultimate over instead of Caddick, which was a big feather in Jimmy's cap. He had the force with him in that tournament and everything he touched seemed to turn to gold but not on this occasion. We lost by two wickets.

The dressing-room was very flat because we'd come so close to beating Australia for the first time in years, but because we let it slip in the middle overs of our innings, we let them get away again. The whole dressing-room was shattered by the defeat, but we picked outselves up enough to go across the road from the hotel to an Italian restaurant. The Australians, who were staying in the same hotel as us, were also in there and we all had a few drinks that night.

That defeat meant we were relying on Pakistan beating Zimbabwe in Bulawayo a couple of days later to determine whether we would go through to the next stage. Come what may, whether we were going home or staying in the tournament, our next game was a few days away. As that was the case I didn't think there was any harm in myself and Steve Harmison going along to a Barmy Army six-a-side tournament, where they were raising money for charity. As soon as we got there someone put a Castle lager transfer on my forehead, but then I put a cap on for the rest of the day and had forgotten all about it by the time we got back to the team hotel, having had four or five beers during the afternoon. We had a team function that night and when I bumped into Phil Neale, the England Operations Manager, I assured him that I was all right to attend. I would probably have been all right too, but I chose that moment to take my cap off and reveal the transfer on my forehead. Phil and the rest of the management team decided I was not in a fit state to represent my country socially and I was fined for my behaviour. Maybe my timing wasn't the best just a day after being beaten by the Aussies and I can now see it from their point of view.

Steve Harmison, a great friend and a great bowler.

13

TIME TO DELIVER

I came home from the World Cup disappointed we had not gone further in the competition, but pleased with my own form, even if the fine at the end of the tournament put a bit of a dampener on things. I was feeling good about myself because I had scored runs against the Aussies and India and I had bowled well. I started in the nets at Lancashire early that summer, but my good mood came to a halt when I got hit on the shoulder by a beamer from Sajid Mahmood, our young fast bowler. He's a good lad, and it was a complete accident, but that didn't stop me having a right go at him at the time. For someone to earn a living out of bowling and still deliver a beamer I find incredible. Even if they are trying to bowl a yorker and misjudge it they are still nearly six feet out. It's like a darts player missing the board and hitting the announcer. Maybe if someone is learning to bowl a slower ball out of the back of their hand it can happen, but for a normal ball to hit you on the head or the shoulder is ridiculous. It hurt and my shoulder swelled up a bit but I played at Middlesex and got a century to continue my good run of form. I only really knew there was something wrong when I went to bowl and my arm was going numb, and I couldn't feel my fingers. It was clear I had a problem and it turned out that where I'd got hit had caused an internal bleed which sent the nerves in my arm haywire. I couldn't bowl and that meant I missed the two-Test series against Zimbabwe.

In some ways it helped me because I was able to play five first-class matches for Lancashire as a specialist batsman and scored consistently throughout this period, averaging more than a hundred. That run of form gave me the confidence to go on and play well for England later in the summer of 2003, as did working with Mike 'Winker' Watkinson in the nets on different parts of my technique. I always enjoy working with Winker. He has been involved in cricket for nearly 25 years and I'm sure, given the chance, he would strap his boots on again and get out there playing. I feed off his energy. It's not just the technical stuff I like about working with him, but the all-round package. Winker thinks nothing of bowling at me for an extra hour off 17 yards, trying to get the pace a bit quicker. The exercises we were doing were designed to make my game tighter so I wasn't reaching for the ball quite so much and could keep the shape of the shots better. After Winker had worked me over I knew where my off-stump was and I was playing like a proper batsman. He's a fierce competitior still and that showed in our practice sessions. He'd be up appealing every time he thought he'd got me out. There was none of the gentle bowling practice approach with Winker, he'd be trying to get me out.

It became something of a joke with the rest of the lads when they used to see us disappear off to the nets again for what became known as the Winker master classes. But they were invaluable for my preparation as I waited for the injury to heal and to get back with England. Playing regular international cricket often means you have little time to practise and I was delighted I used the time I had available properly. It was to be the first time I had gone into a series with England feeling really good about my game. It was also the first time I had consistently dominated at county level. I had gone through periods when I'd scored runs in the past, but I found a method of playing where I wasn't going out and just belting it. I was still scoring pretty quickly, but I began to play a lot more proper cricket shots and my technique was solid. I don't think I have ever played better than I did in those five matches for Lancashire against Surrey, Notts, Middlesex, Kent and Leicestershire.

My best innings during this period was against Kent at Canterbury and it was particularly satisfying because we had lost a few wickets early in the innings and were in a bit of trouble. Mark Ealham, whom I'd played alongside for England during the 1999 World Cup, was a decent bowler and got four of the first five wickets to fall. I remember taking him on virtually from the moment I got to the crease, driving him back over his head and thinking to myself that I was feeling good. Even the umpire John Holder commented on how good I was looking and perhaps it all went to my head because I tried to hit a ball in the next over out of the ground and missed it hopelessly. It was a horrible shot and I couldn't help but laugh after my conversation with the umpire just a few minutes earlier. I turned around to where he was standing at square-leg and, sure enough, he was laughing as well. On that occasion, I didn't get carried away and went on to hit 154 off 158 balls, confirmation I was playing well when I was called up for England for the three-match one-day series against Pakistan in June.

We started at Old Trafford. Playing for England there is always a strange experience for me. All my mates are in the crowd shouting and screaming, which puts me under a lot more pressure to perform. I also put pressure on myself because

I want to do well there for England. I started reasonably well and got 39, but Pakistan won it by two wickets in the final over in front of a highly worked up crowd. We got a lot of spectator abuse that day, it was like being the away team! I must admit I find it very disappointing that a crowd can behave like that to an England team at Old Trafford. We came back well to win at the Oval with Jimmy Anderson continuing the remarkable start to his England career by claiming a hat-trick and becoming the first England player to do so in a one-day International. That gave us the confidence to win the decider at Lord's, where I took four wickets, and enter the one-day triangular series with our spirits high.

I showed my new-found technique with a slow half-century against Zimbabwe at Trent Bridge on a horrible wicket. They won that match with a determined innings from Grant Flower, but we moved to the Oval to face South Africa and a further three wickets there, all with yorkers, took me to the milestone of 50 wickets. That match also underlined for me what close margins there often are in this game. Makhaya Ntini marked my arrival at the crease with a bouncer which I immediately tried to duck for self-preservation but then decided to take him on and hooked him for six just over the head of the fielder on the boundary. I got applauded for getting off the mark with a six, but if he had caught it I would have received a right slagging off from the press and television for getting out with such a shot. I was playing well, though I should have probably scored more runs during that one-day series.

The last three matches of that tournament started my amazing run of man-of-the-match awards, although I have to admit that my award against Zimbabwe at Bristol was perhaps a little fortunate. Darren Gough had bowled really well to knock over their top order and I nipped in to get their last three men out and corner the glory. I batted well and just missed out on scoring a half-century, but I still think I was lucky to win the award. We were in a bit of trouble at 25/4, but we were only chasing 90-odd and it came off for me. I got dropped on the hook, but I was just going for it around this time – and everything seemed to be going for me in return. An indication that luck was smiling on me was the shot that won the game, an attempted pull which flew over the top of the slips for six! I also got the award in the next match at Edgbaston against South Africa, which was another steal. I scored 54 and grabbed 1/47, but I bowled terribly. I think the viewers of Sky vote for the award and the votes are often collected before the end because Michael Vaughan won that game for us with a good innings under the lights with Rikki Clarke.

We went on to beat South Africa comfortably in the final at Lord's, where I was also voted man-of-the-series, which showed I was getting better and more confident at one-day cricket. It helped playing under our new captain Michael Vaughan, who had been given the captaincy of the one-day side that summer following Nasser Hussain's retirement from one-day International cricket after the World Cup. We weren't to know it then but he would soon also be leading the Test side.

The weather helped us a bit at the opening Test against South Africa at Edgbaston, because we were up against it after the first of several big innings from their captain Graeme Smith. His century there was a strange one because when I came on to bowl the ball was doing a fair bit and I thought I was going to get him out with every ball. The ball was nipping around and he went on to score 277 – so much for my confidence that I had him! He's gritty and he's got a method of playing that works for him, which is probably the most important thing for a player. People talk about having good technique, but he had a method that enabled him to hit us for double hundreds in successive Tests during that series. We managed to force a draw at Edgbaston.

When we all assembled for the Edgbaston Test there was no hint of what was to follow. We turned up ready to play for Nasser as captain and as far as I was concerned he didn't seem to be any different to normal. I didn't know what was going on inside his head and that he was considering his future as England captain. It was a big surprise to me when we were told at the end of the First Test that he was stepping down. Michael Vaughan had a very different style to Nasser. It was going to be difficult adapting. When Vaughan is in charge he is very relaxed and chilled out and encourages people to express themselves.

Nasser was totally different to that. He was a lot more animated, ruled with more discipline and was more like a schoolteacher with us. He was a very passionate captain and also very astute. But he did it with a style I didn't particularly like. He was confrontational and put a bit of undue pressure on the lads at times. He used to eff and jeff at mid-on and throw his cap around, but that's the way Nasser is. I don't think he could have changed. However, he would always back his team, and if there was any flak flying in the middle, he'd always be there for you. I don't think anybody can complain about his style because he was very successful with it. He made England hard to beat and by the time he finished, he passed on a decent side to Michael Vaughan. I had great respect for him and what he achieved.

It was interesting a couple of years ago when people were comparing the different styles of Steve Waugh and Nasser

Hussain during the Ashes series. Steve Waugh got a reputation for being a hard captain because he was hard on the opposition, but Nasser's reputation for being hard was because he was like that with his own team. He also played like the captain he was and played some fantastic innings for England while he was in charge. The one that immediately springs to mind was the century he scored in Christchurch when we were in real trouble and the ball was nipping around. He just refused to buckle and guided us to a good total which enabled us to win the Test. He was also good at surrounding himself with players of big character. He liked players who would not back down in a confrontation. England had been accused in the past of doing that, but Nasser led by example and encouraged players like Thorpe and Gough to stand up there with him.

So Michael Vaughan was thrown right in at the deep end with only two days to get himself together and captain the side in the Second Test at Lord's following Nasser's announcement. Typically of Vaughan, he took it all in his stride and picked up where he left off in the one-day series with the relaxed style which suits me better. He speaks to me about how I play and I think he likes the way I play and doesn't want to change that. He also accepts that every now and then I will have a howler but hopefully my better times come along more often than my worst. He likes me to play with a smile on my face and enjoy my cricket, which is the way I've always liked to play. I don't think it is any accident that I have played some of my best cricket under Michael simply because he encourages you to enjoy your cricket without fear of failure.

Now he is captain I suppose he has to detach himself a bit, but he has also made a conscious effort to remain one of the lads. He will come on nights out, but there are also times when he has to stand apart as captain; he's found a great balance. In my short experience of captaincy with the Under-19s I now realise I put too much pressure on myself. If there was hard work to be done, I always found myself doing it, be it bowling into the wind or bowling too many overs. I think I expected too much of myself as captain. I know Vaughan has very high standards, but I've been impressed with the way he's handled himself in the job. He is very keen on people speaking out in team meetings and not being afraid of telling somebody if they're not doing something right or not pulling their weight. He wants everyone in the side to be on the same level and I think that has showed in our performances since he took over.

Vaughan didn't exactly get off to the start he wanted as captain. We let him down as a side at Lord's. We batted terribly in the first innings and were bowled for only 173 with four of five of us getting out trying the hook shot. I told Vaughan I would bowl as much as he wanted me to when they came out to bat and he took me at my word. I bowled 40 overs for only one wicket in that first innings, but I bowled all right and there were a few dropped catches off my bowling.

There was a fair amount of criticism over the dropped catches at the time, but fielding at slip is anything but easy; I know because I field there myself. I've never had a go at anybody for dropping a catch at slip because it is one of the hardest places to field and your team-mates aren't exactly queueing up to go there.

South Africa forced us to follow on after declaring on 682/6. When you are going out to bat on the third day trailing by 510 you know it's going to take something special to save the match. The only thing that encouraged us was that they had got a big total and the wicket was still playing very well, but it soon became evident we were heading towards a heavy defeat.

In the course of that final day I scored my first century in a home Test match. That innings was also my first major partnership with Steve Harmison, who came out to bat when I was on 80-odd and told me he would stick around so I could get my century. Once he said that I started playing even more shots, including 20 in one over off Pollock. But at the time reaching 142 meant very little to me because we had lost the match. Looking back now I suppose it should mean more because it was a century and it got my name on the honours board at Lord's, but we still got beaten. We had lost early wickets and I was basically just teeing off, I wasn't batting properly. I would rather have got a hundred doing something that was going to help the side win a game. Instead I was throwing the bat at everything and the crowd loved it because, until then, we looked like losing without showing any fight.

I had a great battle with Ntini, who I enjoyed competing against all that summer. He's a bowler who keeps coming and coming when other players have taken a rest. He's a fine athlete and it was a real contest between the two of us. I hit him for six a couple of times, but he also hit me on the helmet twice – one of them caused a lump which is still there to this day! The one thing that innings did do for me was boost my confidence because I had got a century and I had imposed myself on South Africa, so next time they would have to think about me a bit more. But apart from that it was a hollow feeling – and I'd broken my best bat.

I've never been one to cherish my bats and knock them in, so I shouldn't have been too surprised, I suppose, when it split in half as I tried another big shot. I immediately waved the broken bat in the air, much to the amusement of everybody in the crowd, and signalled for the 12th man to come out with my other bats. When he arrived in the middle I didn't have a clue which one to use because they were all brand new. I told him just to give me one, I wasn't bothered which. People like Graham Thorpe cherish their bats and look after them but that's not me. Thorpe thinks that's the bowler's side of the allrounder in me coming out. There are some players who will have one bat when they use a bowling machine, another for the outside nets and another one again is kept for matches. I have one bat which I use until it breaks, which is not the end of the world, and then I pick up the next one. I have to put my hand up to bat abuse. Some of the lads get surgical spirit and clean all the marks off and make sure the grip's at the bottom near the splice and sand them and clean them. Can you imagine me doing all that?

My area of the dressing-room is always a mess and I'm usually fishing around for parts of my kit. I'm often found desperately searching for my box just as I'm about to go in to bat. Alec Stewart tried to influence me into having an immaculately tidy coffin like his, which had to be seen to be believed, but it didn't work. That's just the way I am. I could no more understand why he felt the need to have a coffin like that than he could understand why I have one that looks so chaotic. There have been a few occasions when I've come back from tour and just chucked my bag in the garage until I was ready to play again. Sports psychologists would probably argue that if you are organised off the pitch, you are more likely to succeed on it, but I've got a Filofax now – what more do they want?

We moved on to Trent Bridge and I was feeling good after my innings at Lord's. I received a great reception when I went out to bat and the inevitable happened – a duck in the first innings after getting stuck on the crease to a good delivery from Andrew Hall which I edged behind. It was a terrible wicket and James Kirtley cleaned up on his debut with six wickets in the second innings. He's a fine bowler anyway, he's deadly accurate and bowls wicket to wicket, and when the ball is keeping low and misbehaving that is exactly what you want. He was perfect for that wicket and brilliant during that Test. It was also the end of Graeme Smith's dominance over us. I had spotted on the videos that the South African captain took his guard way back in his crease, so I dug one in short to him when he was on 35 and he trod on his wicket. We were glad to see the back of him after two double centuries and we would have appealed for anything. Getting him out gave us all a big lift and winning that Test by 70 runs brought us back into the series as we headed for Headingley.

I was really nervous approaching the Fourth Test because of my record at Headingley. It had started to get embarrassing and I tried to make a joke out of it after four successive ducks there. I was telling people I already had an Audi badge and I was going for my Olympic rings. I remember being pleased that I wasn't facing Pollock, who had gone home for the birth of his child, or Ntini when I first went out to bat. After I took my guard I was determined to take the first chance I was given to get a run. I was in that much of a state that it didn't matter whether it was the first ball or whether I got a half-volley or a bouncer, I was going to hit it. I got a bouncer third ball and pulled it through mid-wicket for two and ran as hard as I could to the other end with a big grin on my face. I even considered raising my bat to the lads on the balcony, but thought better of it just in time. That first run out of the way, I achieved my maiden half-century at Headingley and we needed just over 200 on the final day to win the game.

Mark Butcher and I thought we were going to win it. We thought one good partnership would do the job. But Kallis got Butcher in the first over and then he got me after I had made another half-century with one of the best balls I have faced. It drew me into the shot and then moved away and I nicked it to slip. Kallis had not bowled much during that series and got a bit of stick about it but ended up with six wickets to win them the match.

I have every sympathy for him because it is extremely hard to bat in the top order and bowl. I have been batting at number 6 for the past year or so and find that difficult but it is even harder for him because he bats at number 4. Even in one-day cricket I find it really difficult bowling at the death and then coming off and having to get ready to bat at number 5, never mind trying to do it in a Test match. If you have bowled 35 overs you are really tired and it is very rare allrounders get both things going right at the same time. In the 2004/05 winter series in South Africa, when Kallis didn't bowl, he got a lot of runs and his low scores usually happened after he had bowled quite a few overs. To be honest, if I could bat like him I don't think I'd even think about bowling!

I wasn't happy batting at number 7 because I thought it was a place or maybe a couple of places too low. It was during this series that I badgered Duncan Fletcher to let me bat higher up the order, perhaps at number 4, but soon realised I couldn't have done it. At Lord's, after I had bowled 40 overs in their first innings, Duncan asked me how I'd feel if I had to bat number 4 that day and I admitted I couldn't have coped – the subject was closed. Still, before my recent improvement in form there were some people who would have said that number 7 was too high for me.

With South Africa ahead in the series once again we went to the Oval knowing we had to win and fought back really well as a team. Herschelle Gibbs played brilliantly to score 183 but we did well to limit them to 484. Trescothick gave us the foundation for an equally big total with a brilliant double hundred and at a team meeting on the third morning, when we led by just 18 with seven wickets down, we said we wanted to get as close as we could to 600. That was nearly 100 runs away and looked a very stiff task, particularly after we lost Martin Bicknell virtually straight away. He was replaced by Steve Harmison and the two of us old mates had a great time. It was a situation where I thought I could play my shots and on that day they came off.

Our partnership started off with me trying to help him and then it changed around. He could see some of the outrageous shots I was trying and he was walking down the wicket saying, 'What are you doing?' and telling me to get my head down. I started off trying to shepherd the strike away from Steve, but I wasn't going to do anything daft to try and get a single off the last ball of an over. Steve can bat, even if he does bat better some days than others, so I just let him. He only got three runs in that 99-run stand, but the runs weren't as important as the support he gave me and it helped us into a strong position. It was one of the most enjoyable partnerships I've had.

I also had a confrontation with Ntini when he bowled at me and the ball ended up at my feet. I let him come down the wicket and pick it up rather than throw it back to him. That really annoyed the South Africans and they were making all sorts of choice observations to me after that. But that's the way I bat and it's the way I was taught to behave when I first started with Lancashire. Naturally he dug it in short next ball and I pulled him for four and then drove him down the ground for six when he pitched it up to take us close to 600.

I was eventually out just five runs short of my century which, looking back, I was a bit disappointed with, but the way I was playing I don't think I could have just pushed singles to get my 100. Maybe that's what I should have done, but I wanted to hit Paul Adams for six and thought I could do it. I had already hit him for six off the previous ball and I was toying with whether to go running down the pitch at him or to try and slog-sweep him. I went for the slog-sweep when I should have run at him and was bowled, but his celebration was an absolute disgrace. He punched the air with his fist, he stared at me, he shouted at me. I thought to myself: Hang on a minute, I've just hit you for God knows how many and we are over 600 – it was a bit bemusing to say the least. From that moment we were on top in the game, but time also became an issue because in their second innings they were scoring at a good rate, Pollock was hitting a few and another half an hour of him may have taken the game out of reach for us.

That was when Steve Harmison came of age as a top-class bowler. He is a special talent and in some ways we have been quite similar in our development. It has taken us both a bit longer than we would have liked to do what we wanted, but this innings was the making of him. He got Pollock early on the final morning and went on to get four wickets and helped us win by nine wickets. It was a Test series which both sides felt they should have won. A draw was probably a fair result at the end of the summer between two evenly-matched teams. I was proud to be named man-of-the-series for scoring 423 in my eight innings, which included a top score of 142 at Lord's and three 50s, making an average of 52. I had also bowled 20 more overs than anyone else and taken ten wickets. My bowling average of 59 would have looked a bit more respectable if those who shall be nameless had held their catches!

We stayed in the dressing-room for some time after that win and after a few drinks we re-emerged on the outfield to have a game of football with those big Swiss balls we use for fitness. We played North against South and I can't remember who won, which is probably a reflection on the amount we had drunk beforehand. Then we went out as a team into London to some poncey bar which was the latest in place and where we paid £8 for a pint – great choice of venue that! At the next one I looked at Steve Harmison and we both walked around the corner to a normal pub and met the rest of the lads at the next trendy spot they found. The rest of the celebrations after that Oval Test were a bit of a blur, so much so that I got a call from Neil Fairbrother the following day asking me what I had been up to with Steve. I'd told him I had been out and had a few drinks but he had received a phone call from one of the papers claiming I'd been throwing eggs at the magician David Blaine, who was suspended in a glass box near the Oval going without food and water for some strange reason. I couldn't remember if I was guilty as charged or not after the celebrations we'd had, but I hope I was.

Surrounded by well-wishers during a trip to Bangladesh.

14

BACK DOWN TO EARTH

That winter we were due to tour Bangladesh for the first time, but my groin was getting tired and sore with the amount of cricket I had been playing. I needed a rest from everything and a few weeks of rehabilitation. I told David Graveney I was fit to go as a batter, but after a lot of dithering the selectors decided to have a look at other people rather than take me just to bat. My bags were in my hallway and I was toying with putting on my blazer ready to leave for the airport when I finally got the nod that I wasn't needed and they were taking Rikki Clarke instead. I spent the subsequent time training hard for the one-day series in Bangladesh that followed the Tests in November 2003.

The first one-day International at Chittagong was a bit embarrassing because I received three different awards for the same match – bowler-of-the-match for taking 4/14, batsman-of-the-match for an unbeaten 55 and man-of-the-match. I reminded myself that it was the only hat-trick I was ever likely to get for England. But I was slightly embarrassed about it because if I had bowled like that against Australia or South Africa I would have gone for 80 runs in my ten overs. I was bowling how I wanted to bowl, but it was a slow wicket and I was bowling around chest height and getting wickets because they couldn't hit me. They obviously were not used to having bowlers bowl it short at them. When I batted I just went out to play a few shots. A similar thing happened in the other two matches, which we won pretty comfortably and I got man-of-the-match in both games and won man-of-the-series again – I don't think I shall ever go on a tour where I will pick up as many awards as that one.

The standard of cricket in Bangladesh may not have been great, but they were on a learning curve and it was a good experience playing there. They proved they are a developing side over a year later when they beat Australia, the World Champions, in Cardiff. It was also a useful tour for getting the squad close together. Bangladesh is one of those places, like Pakistan and India, where there isn't that much to do in the evening and we spent a lot of time talking tactics and just generally about cricket. I'm sure that helped us as a squad later that winter because we were mentally stronger by the time we arrived in the Caribbean early in 2004. I also met up with Dav Whatmore again, who was now coaching the Bangladesh national side. We got on far better than we did while he was coach at Lancashire. Away from all the pressures at Old Trafford he was fine. Looking back to my relationship with Dav, I had my problems with him but I was hard work as well. I was young and I would imagine at the time I annoyed quite a few people at the club. Dav was also kind enough to praise my efforts publicly to the press, so he clearly had not borne a grudge from our fall-out at Old Trafford.

After Bangladesh we moved on to the far stiffer challenge of beating Sri Lanka on home soil when I would be facing my old mate Murali again. I had done reasonably well against him in English conditions, but this was a different matter altogether.

Facing him on dusty, turning wickets is one of the hardest things any batsman can experience in world cricket. I just couldn't play him during that series, but I was by no means the only batsman forced to admit that. I was all right with the other bowlers and I think I proved I could play spin on that trip. The only bowler I really had trouble with was Murali and that is because he is one of the greats of the game. Michael Vaughan played extremely well to help save the game for us in Kandy by scoring a century, but Murali was a different bowler this time to our previous visit to Sri Lanka.

When I first played with and against him I could pick Murali, but he was a much better bowler by the time we faced him on this tour. This was the first time we had come across his new delivery which goes the other way with no discernible change in his action. A couple of times I played back to him and was out lbw thinking it was the straight one. I will hold my hands up now and admit I couldn't play him until I had seen a bit of him and was able to score 77 in the last Test at Colombo. By then I had found a method to play him, but by then it was too late to influence the series. He is without doubt the hardest bowler I had ever faced at that stage. You have to resign yourself to the fact that you are not going to get a great deal to hit. You can try and use your pad and block and just try and score at the other end, which is when batsmen often get out. The only other thing is to hope he gets tired. With all that action he puts on the ball, even though he's a spinner, it's bound to take it out of him and we have seen that in the last few years with the number of shoulder injuries he gets.

Once again Murali was very friendly towards me, even in the middle. I would often be standing at the non-striker's end and he would say something and I'd mutter something back.

Sometimes when he was bowling at me and I played and missed he would have a big grin on his face and I couldn't help but speak to him. There were people in the England camp who thought I was a bit too pally with the opposition, but I look at it another way. Just because I know him well, it doesn't make me any less determined when I'm playing against him. In some ways you are determined to do even better because you don't want your mate getting you out. You want to be able to rib him like he did me every time we went out for dinner. That's one of the great things for me about playing cricket. When I first started in the county game at Old Trafford, no matter who you were playing against, you would play hard and then meet in the members' bar and have a pint, but that seems to be going now. I suppose I'm very much from the old school when it comes to that sort of thing. Even at county games I like mixing with the opposition and the umpires, which is a part of the game I like best. It isn't as common for the England team to do this, but I'm sure if we got to know our opponents better we would have a better understanding of how they tick.

Perhaps the most galling thing about that series in Sri Lanka was when Murali started getting runs. He scored 38 in the First Test at Galle using my bat! We are both sponsored by a company called Woodworm for our bats, so I told him he could use one of mine because he didn't have one. When he came out to bat he had his helmet on and his shoulders were up and his eyes were big and wide and he had a big grin on his face. As I walked past I asked him how he was going to bat and he replied, 'Slogging.' And that is just what he did. He hit his third ball over my head at mid-off for four and then I bowled it short to him and he spooned it over his head one bounce for another four and there he was, swinging and heaving, and every time

156

he made contact he had a massive grin on his face. I couldn't help chuckling just watching him because he is comical when he's batting. He went on to score more runs in the next two Tests.

Seriously, though, it was really hard work playing that series. The side showed a lot of character to draw the first two Tests in Galle and Kandy, slowing things down a bit when we needed to try and get the bad light which came late in the day. We battled so hard that both those draws seemed like victories to us. It is difficult to explain just how hard it is playing cricket in Sri Lanka and to come away with draws from the first two Tests was a fantastic effort. Sri Lanka is the toughest place in the world to play. It is humid, hot and you also have to contend with Murali.

We had a big party to toast the draw in Galle, but by the time we got to Colombo for the final Test we had just run out of steam. We are fit professional cricketers, but it takes incredible endurance out there to compete with Sri Lanka day-in and day-out, particularly in back-to-back Tests like we had on that tour. Defeat in the Final Test was disappointing and we regarded the series defeat as a setback, but we all believed we were going in the right direction. There were plenty of positives to come out of our performances. That Final Test finished unhappily for me when I injured my groin yet again bowling in their only innings. I had bowled a lot during that tour and my body just could not stand up to it. I'm a big lad and pounding down in those conditions did take it out of me. My action is a very hard-working one, it's anything but natural. I have modified it over the years of playing international cricket, but that is how I get them down the other end and it takes a lot out of me. I would love to have an action like Harmison, but that's just not going to happen. We returned home to England satisfied with our efforts if not the result. It underlined just how good a side Australia are to go to Sri Lanka and dominate them, because Sri Lanka are a really tough side to play on their home soil.

That was the winter that Michael Vaughan introduced the new keep-fit regime among the squad, which was something I had already become used to over the previous couple of years. It involved the whole squad going to a gym as a group. I do put on weight quickly and I still enjoy an occasional beer, which is not something that has been banned, but if you indulge it is harder to reach that level of fitness. Fitness these days is not a problem to me. There have been times in my career when it has, but it is part and parcel of what I do now.

Taking the wicket of Fidel Edwards during our memorable
Test match win in Barbados.

15

TRIUMPH IN THE
CARIBBEAN

E ngland's players had a very welcome and rare break that
year. We returned home from Sri Lanka before Christmas
and so had a few weeks' respite before setting off for the Caribbean to play West Indies in a series everyone seemed to be
talking about. OK, we had lost in Sri Lanka but we all felt there
were positive points to be taken from our performance; we were
happy about how we had stuck together and fought our way
through.

West Indies, we knew, would be a totally different proposition to Sri Lanka, but a team whose style would be more
familiar after Sri Lankan conditions. This time we would be
facing seam bowlers and quick bowlers, not batting for hours
on end for three runs on a wicket that was turning. What
neither team expected to see in the Caribbean was a hurricane
called Harmison.

We started out in Jamaica where there were good practice
facilities. The locals made it clear they loved their cricket and
promised us: 'King Lara is going to kill you boys.' People kept
telling us the West Indies would 'lick us down', whatever that
means. It was very aggressive there, quite intimidating in some

ways and probably not the sort of place to go walking alone at night.

The warm-up matches started OK and we got better as the Test series came nearer. Steve Harmison and I trained really hard and even imposed a drinking ban on ourselves, although we weren't sure how long it was going to last for. But we wanted to demonstrate to everyone that we were committed to being successful on that tour. A pair of laid-back characters we might be but we wanted to show a few people that we were there, we were up for it, we wanted to beat the West Indies in their own backyard and we were willing to make sacrifices to do that. Steve had had a bit of a rough time of it after returning home from Bangladesh injured and missing Sri Lanka. A lot of people had started to question whether he had it in him to succeed at the highest level, saying he was not tough enough, so it was a big tour for him.

As a result of the drinking ban, I turned up for the First Test feeling fit and refreshed. I had not scored many runs in the warm-up matches, but I felt all right with my batting and good about my bowling. In the first two Tests we showed the character the team had built from our experiences in Sri Lanka. Whenever we needed someone to do something they stood up and did what was required. We lost early wickets in Jamaica and both Tino Best and Fidel Edwards bowled with a lot of pace to Nasser Hussain and Mark Butcher. I didn't watch that period of play because I was due to be in soon and it is not great for your confidence when you see other batsmen getting hit all over the body!

Fortunately for me and for England, Hussain and Butcher put together a useful partnership so things were a bit easier when I went out to bat. I was going through a period around this time when I would do all the hard work and then fall to a part-time bowler. That was certainly the case in Jamaica where I battled to 46 only for Ramnaresh Sarwan to get me out. We managed a slender first-innings lead, but nothing could prepare any of us for what was to happen on the fourth morning.

I had seen Steve Harmison bowl fast before, but nothing like his performance that morning in Jamaica. It was something really special. At one stage we had eight men fielding in positions behind the bat, including a short-leg, which is a field you don't see very often in Test cricket. It looked like every ball was going to go to the slips, gully or short-leg. It was quite an amazing spell of bowling. To get 7/12 at any level of cricket is special but to do it in a Test match for England against West Indies in Jamaica was incredible. He was bowling 90 miles an hour with outswing – it was one of the great moments for me. Since that win in Jamaica – when West Indies were bowled out for 47 in their second innings – England have had a lot of success but for me that was probably the best spell of bowling I have ever seen in my England career. I thought Harmison had bowled well in the first innings, but in the second he bowled even better and was almost unplayable. He was seriously quick that day. Steve Harmison has two gears to his bowling usually, quick and rapid, but that day he found a third. He was extremely rapid. He was bouncing it, swinging it, seaming it – it is just not what you want to face – I certainly would not have liked to be out there batting against him.

After our win we sat around the dressing-room and it was clear Steve had no idea what he had just done. I kept telling him what a big achievement it was, but he simply shrugged his shoulders. When you are away on tour you become a bit detached from the reaction back home because you don't see the papers or watch television and I don't think he had a clue what a hero he had become. That's one of the great things about him. When he produces those special performances he is still very humble. His grin just gets a lot bigger.

The atmosphere at the Jamaica Test was good old-fashioned West Indies style, with loud reggae music pounding out all day, every day, and the crowd joining in with plenty of banter, telling us what West Indies were going to do to us – which made the win more sweet. But it was the last time the atmosphere was like that because after that win the England fans came out in their thousands to support us in the other three Tests. After that win as well, the West Indies press started talking up this new fast bowler called Harmison and, when they weren't talking about him, they were giving their own players a lot of stick.

Immediately after our win in Jamaica, a few of their players had gone into the party stand at the ground, where everyone was dancing to reggae music, drinking rum and beer and generally having a good time. We thought about going in there as well, which might have been more acceptable because we had won, but their players got a lot of flak for doing it after losing so heavily.

Instead of going to the party stand, we all returned to the hotel and the whole team sat around having a few beers. Steve and I were still supposed to be on our drinking ban, but after the way he had bowled, there was never any chance of us staying on the wagon. Then some England fans turned up and we had a few more beers and the odd rum and Coke in celebration. One or two of the lads strayed a bit too near to the pool that night and ended up in it!

Harmison's performance that day really kick-started our tour of the West Indies and also what was to happen over the next

year. We were becoming a bowling unit on that tour, with Troy
Cooley, our bowling coach, going out of his way to get us
thinking like a team within a team. If one of us was not getting
wickets we would try and block one end up to allow someone
else to prosper at the other. Troy has been really good for all of
us. He had been brought in to work with the bowlers the previous year. He doesn't try to impose himself. Some bowlers like
looking at computers and he does all that and has all that
technology, but he is equally happy just talking, if that's what
is required, or using any other methods that can help us. He
has a good knowledge of us now as a group and he knows what
works best for each of us. Working with us as a separate unit
has been tried in the past, but a lot of it also depends on
personality and, as a group of lads, we are a unit anyway. For
Troy it was easy to identify with this. We all go out for dinner
at times with Troy and talk not just about our bowling but life
in general and I have found that helps me more than anything
– talking about things in a relaxed environment among friends.

I have also talked things through a fair bit with Steve Harmison over the years, because he is very good at working with
other bowlers. He's got what I want in a bowler. His attributes
of pace and his ability to swing the ball away are what I have
been striving for all these years. He is better than me at bowling
and I want to improve, so who better to look up to? All four
bowlers in the Test side – myself, Hoggard, Harmison and Jones
– got on really well together, so there was a genuine desire to
help each other do well.

It was never a case of one being happy because he had bowled
all right if someone else hadn't. We all wanted us all to do well.
The great thing about our unit is that we can bowl on most
surfaces now because we are all very different types of bowler.

Harmison is just himself and is a threat most of the time; Simon Jones is one of the best in the world when it comes to reverse swings, he has pace and swings it away; while Matthew Hoggard is very accurate and I just try to hit the deck hard. Because of our differing strengths one of us might bowl more on a particular day and a particular surface than at other times; Michael Vaughan certainly has great options there.

After celebrating long and hard in Jamaica, we moved on to Port-of-Spain, Trinidad for the next Test and Harmison continued his purple streak by claiming six wickets in the first innings to stop West Indies building on a promising start given to them by their opener, Chris Gayle. He had scored quite freely and West Indies looked like they were going to come back at us strongly when they raced to 100 without loss before lunch on the opening day. We were fortunate the conditions changed, though, and after starting the match in blue skies and hot sun – ideal conditions for batting – cloud cover drifted over and helped us wrap up the rest of their innings pretty quickly. I was disappointed to get out when we batted because I had reached 23 quite comfortably but gave a leading edge back to the bowler when I was feeling good at the crease.

Trinidad followed on similar lines to Jamaica with Butcher and Hussain again having to withstand some hostile fast bowling to give us the platform to claim a first-innings lead of over 100. I think the whole team were delighted when Simon Jones got five wickets in their second innings, the first of his Test career, after everything he had been through during the previous year. A lot of us were in Australia when he suffered that horrendous injury and it was good to see Simon finally come through his terrible time to triumph on this tour. I first got to know Simon when I was captain of the Under-19s and he came and played a development game for us. I'd never seen him before, he was just this raw Welsh lad, who bowled really rapidly on a slow wicket. I didn't see him again until I played against him for Lancashire at Blackpool a few years later when he abused me as he is prone to do at times. But despite that, we've become quite close because of the time we have spent together with England and at the Academy. In Trinidad Simon's efforts helped us wrap up another convincing victory by seven wickets on the final morning of the match, despite losing a whole day to rain. By now the whole team were buzzing at the way things were going.

The match was finished by about 10.30 a.m. so, as part of the team celebration, we were invited aboard the yacht owned by Rod Bramsgrove, the Hampshire chairman, who was out following the tour. This yacht of his was unbelievable, like nothing I've ever seen before. It was a massive thing. We had a bit of food, a lot to drink and got the jet-skis and the rings out on the water. A few of the lads were jumping off the top of the yacht into the water. I didn't get involved too much with all that because I was concentrating on the rum and Cokes with Butcher. I remember going out to this miniature *QE2*, but still to this day I don't remember coming back!

Trinidad was a double celebration for me. As soon as the Test was over, I announced to the rest of the team that Rachael was pregnant and I was going to be a dad. Rachael had told me about six weeks before and somehow I'd managed to keep it a secret from everyone. Not screaming the news from the roof-tops was something which was incredibly hard for me because I was very excited about it, but you never know what can happen so we waited for the scan and all that before making it public. The lads were all really happy for me, although a few of them couldn't quite picture me pushing a pram and were taking the mickey, but it was a great double celebration for me – I think I packed two celebrations in anyway!

The next Test was one of the strangest I have ever played in abroad. The ground at Bridgetown, Barbados is nothing like an English ground and the weather was obviously different, but otherwise it was like a home match with thousands of England fans cheering for us. They had all been ripped off, with the West Indies authorities charging them many times more for their tickets than home fans, but they still came in their thousands and it was a major boost to the team. Walking out to the pitch during that Test was incredible because of all the England fans and the flags and the way they got behind us – they turned the ground into one gigantic party. It was special for us too because we had our families out there to see us win the series and the way Graham Thorpe played was spectacular.

That was the Test I got my first five-wicket haul. I bowled a 13-over spell during their first innings, which was a far longer spell than I would normally bowl, but we were on and off for rain, so that helped me a lot. It was during that Test that I began to swing the ball away, which was a bit of a collector's item back then. It was something I had been striving to do for a while, I was getting closer to doing it, and in Barbados it happened for me. I put the ball in decent areas and followed the plans we had for each batsman and it was great to get a five-for – it's something I never thought I'd achieve.

I was really excited and punched the air like a footballer scoring a goal. I do get a bit carried away with my celebrations when I take a wicket at times, out of surprise more than anything in some cases. I was getting better as a bowler and this

Test, with my 5/58, was evidence of that. When I was younger I couldn't really work on my bowling as much as it needed because of my recurring back problems, so that in some ways I'm still a bit of a novice as a bowler. It took me 32 Tests to achieve a five-for – I'm not usually that good at statistics but that one I remember because the press kept ramming it down my throat – and I'm still learning. I was pleased to get it, particularly with my mum and dad and brother in the crowd, although I'm not sure Chris would have seen much of it because he was so hammered on rum he probably wouldn't have known what was going on.

When we did the lap of honour at the end I sprayed some champagne into the crowd and my brother and another mate of mine managed to topple over the barriers at the side of the pitch and all mayhem broke loose with celebrations in the stands and on the field. Although that Test will be remembered fondly in the Flintoff family for my five wickets, everyone else will rightly recall Barbados as being the place where Hoggard got a fantastic hat-trick to wrap up the game and the series for us. He had already taken two wickets in two balls and I really wanted to contribute to his getting his hat-trick. Trescothick and I had been catching really well in the slips so I was willing the ball to come through to me and it was great when it did because Hoggard just went berserk. He was screaming and wagging his fingers and I was delighted for him because he had had a hard time in Australia the winter before, but come back strongly on this tour. He's an honest cricketer and keeps going to bowl his overs and never stops. As you can imagine, the whole team celebrated late into the night after that one and I think the entire island of Barbados turned into one big party. All the thousands of fans that had made the trip enjoyed the victory just as much as we did and there were a few delicate cricketers around the team hotel the following morning.

The Final Test will always be remembered for Brian Lara's record-breaking innings of 400, but I think most of the England team will also recall it for the strange hotel we were put in during our stay in Antigua. Normally our hotels have excellent facilities where we can relax after a day's play and spend time with either team-mates or our families. On this occasion we were put in a resort-type hotel by the beach, mainly because it had nets and a practice area right next door which we used in the build-up to the match. What we didn't realise was that it was also an official Barmy Army hotel. The team really appreciate the support we get from the fans at home and especially away. They spend a lot of money travelling to watch us and it gives the team a massive lift hearing their support, but on this occasion we were a bit too close to our fan base. Because we were all staying in the same hotel, some of the fans were knocking on our doors asking for autographs and wanting to talk to us, while they were also up into the early hours of the morning in the bar singing songs. They were all perfectly entitled to behave in that way and if I hadn't been playing in a Test match I wouldn't have minded having a drink with them, but it wasn't the best preparation for a big Test.

One of the key factors in our success during the opening three Tests had been our ability to restrict Brian Lara's impact on the series. As he was one of the best batsmen in the world, we had obviously concentrated on formulating plans to bowl at him and for the first three Tests it worked a treat. Until we got to Antigua, Lara had not even scored a half-century, which was one of the main reasons why West Indies had not been able to reach competitive totals. All that changed at the Recreation

Ground when he scored the highest ever individual innings in Test history. I know it was a flat wicket, but he still had Harmison bowling at him at the top of his game and it was some effort.

We had a theory that he had edged it behind on nought off Harmison, but I don't know if that was ever proved by television replays. Lara may have a reputation for walking when he thinks he's hit it, but not many do when they're on nought. After that he just amazed me with his endurance during that record-breaking innings. He kept going and going and going. I've seen people go on and get big hundreds at that level before, like Graeme Smith, but the concentration levels required for that 400 I just cannot comprehend. He kept going for nearly 13 hours without making a mistake – it was phenomenal. I'm just glad he saved it up until we were already 3–0 up in the series. He had broken the record before in Antigua, hitting 375 against England in 1993/94, and it soon became clear he was in the mood to take it back. He had only lost the record a few months earlier when Matt Hayden hit 380 against Zimbabwe in Perth.

You almost sensed he was going to take the record back virtually as soon as he got past his hundred. Sometimes when people get to a century they start changing the way they play, they get a bit free with their shots and much looser but he just kept on and on and never really looked like getting out. The way he got the record was remarkable. Most people would have just nudged singles or twos to reach such a landmark, but to hit Gareth Batty for a straight six and a fine swept four off successive balls demonstrated a top player at the very peak of his game.

We were all happy for him. Lara was popular with the England lads and I went up and shook his hand after he broke the record and told him I was pleased for him and I meant that. You have to take your hat off to a bloke who has scored 400 runs in a Test match, no matter what the conditions or who they are playing against.

The word genius gets bandied around a lot, but in his case I think you can call him that. I would say Lara and Sachin Tendulkar are the two best batsmen I've faced, although you always think you have more of a chance when you are bowling at Lara. Tendulkar has a very simple technique, whereas Lara has a lot of movement at the crease and looks very flashy, but his hands are so good. I bowled 35 overs during that innings, mainly because Harmison had been taken out of the attack for continually running on the pitch. I kept reminding him I was bowling his overs as well as my own throughout Lara's innings, but everything I tried on behalf of both of us Lara seemed to have an answer for.

Before that Test I had gone off with Chris Read and worked on a bowling machine. I was getting out playing shots, so I practised defending on the back and front foot and tidied my game up a bit. As for Chris, he had just been told that Geraint Jones was going to take his place in the Final Test. I felt for him when he was left out, but in this day and age keepers have to score runs. I think most sides now select a batter first and a keeper second and Chris had not scored enough runs, no matter how good he had been behind the stumps.

The work on the bowling machine paid off for me. It was still a flat wicket when we made our reply but I had to get my head down and it was probably one of my most disciplined innings for England. The situation dictated I had to get in because we had lost our first four wickets relatively cheaply and we were a long way behind West Indies' massive total of 751/5 declared.

The unusual thing about that innings is that I was dropped three times on the way to my century. It's very rare for me to be dropped when I'm batting. Normally fielders start catching flies when I'm at the crease but on this occasion it worked out in my favour. Because of the way I had been out in the other Test matches I was determined not to give my wicket away. I had done all the hard work in Jamaica and got out to Ramnaresh Sarwan, the same again in Trinidad to Dwayne Smith. Now I wanted to get my head down and bat. They had bowled well to us and put us in a bit of trouble at 98/5 and I played the situation. It was the sort of knock I knew I could play because I had done it for Lancashire, though I had not really shown it until now on the international stage.

I was at the crease for five and a bit hours and faced 224 balls, which is easily my longest innings for England. We needed to get runs from the lower order otherwise we would have been in big trouble and I batted with Geraint Jones for the first time to add 84 in his first Test. He took the attack to the West Indies a little bit more than I was doing and after he got out I batted with the tail for long enough to add 103 for the last five wickets. England's tail bat a lot better now than many people give them credit for. I have put runs on with Harmison before and I would trust him to bat against all but a couple of bowlers in the world. He has proved what he can do, so I never have any worries about having him at the other end. I used to get carried away in my early days when I batted with the tail and would start teeing off when there were only seven wickets down. I have a lot more confidence in my ability and that of the people lower down the order now and I will bat properly right through to the last batsman. You have to give bowlers the confidence to believe they can bat. They don't believe they can if you keep pushing singles all the time to take the strike away from them. Look at the way someone like Hoggard has improved his batting through practice. It shows you what they can do at the bottom end of the innings.

Despite those efforts we were forced to follow on, but I don't think any of us really thought we were in danger of losing the Test because it was such a flat wicket. Trescothick and Vaughan put on a big opening stand which effectively ended West Indies' hopes of victory and we saw out the draw pretty comfortably. We were disappointed not to finish off the tour with a victory because we wanted to claim a series whitewash, but the 3–0 triumph showed our team were progressing in the right direction as we prepared for what would become a record-breaking summer against New Zealand and then West Indies again at home.

Before we could start preparing for those challenges ahead, though, we had a long one-day series to consider which finished the tour. Why would anyone ever want to play seven consecutive one-day internationals against the same country one has just played a Test series against? I think we all found the schedule amazing and having a few of these games washed out was a bit of a blessing in disguise. The Test series had been hard on many of us and I felt it, not just because of the batting but because I had bowled a lot as well, especially in Antigua. Most of us were tired going into that one-day series which never really got going for any of us. From the first game to the last it seemed like a lifetime, even though it was only three weeks or so. We ended up drawing the series 2–2 by winning the final match in Barbados, but by then I think most of us just wanted to get home.

Attempting the splits in midair as I appeal for a wicket against New Zealand at Lord's.

16

BUILDING MOMENTUM

We had barely had time to get back from the Caribbean and re-introduce ourselves to our families when the next Test series started against New Zealand at Lord's in May 2004; you could tell we hadn't had much of a break because we still all had suntans when we played that First Test. We had only had about ten days off, but I felt quite recharged, partly because the rain in the West Indies meant I hadn't played as much cricket during the one-day series as I thought I would. I shudder to think how I would have felt if we had played all seven one-day internationals and then come back and gone straight into a Test series against New Zealand! That rain in the Caribbean was a big blessing because it gave me the rest I required to start afresh for the English summer.

It was a bit of a strange start for the team with Michael Vaughan missing after injuring his knee batting in the nets two days before the opening Test. He does get some strange injuries occasionally, but this time it worked out well for the team with Andrew Strauss coming in and enjoying a debut to remember. I knew Strauss from the one-dayers in Bangladesh the previous winter and had spent a little time with him at the Academy a few years before that. From that experience I knew he could play, but it was also probably a good moment for him to launch a Test career. New Zealand had lost Shane Bond, their quickest bowler on the tour, through injury, so they didn't have an awful lot of firepower and Strauss exploited that to the full. You have to take your hat off to someone who scores a century on their Test debut and if Nasser Hussain hadn't run him out in the second innings, he could even have made two!

His great start was a further sign of what the confidence was like in the side. People were now coming into the side and doing well straight away and a lot of that was down to the captain and the lads already in the team. Michael Vaughan had created an atmosphere of enjoyment without any fear of failure. He wanted players to come in and express themselves as people and players and as a team. When a new player came in they were usually known to the rest of the team because most of us would have spent time with them at the Academy and, because everyone was secure in what they were doing, they were welcomed into the dressing-room.

While I'm sure Strauss was delighted with his start to Test cricket, I was also pleased with my start to the new season. I got two important wickets in New Zealand's first innings to remove Nathan Astle and Chris Cairns, two of their players I rated very highly. It's always more gratifying to get the wickets of better players than tail-enders, but particularly so in this Test because both of them were going well when I got them out, so they were important wickets for the team. That was particularly so in Cairns' case because he was playing an unbelievable innings at the time. He just kept teeing off and the ball kept disappearing and he broke Viv Richards' record for the most number of sixes – 84 – in Test cricket off my bowling. He hit some absolutely amazing shots during that innings. There was one point when I saw him backing off to try and give himself room when I was running in. I put the ball right where I wanted it, but it still disappeared over extra cover for six. In the end I got him caught at fine-leg trying to hit me for another six, which was a big relief to us all after he had hammered us for 82 off only 47 balls.

That innings helped New Zealand to a respectable 326 in their first innings, but I began a run of partnerships with Geraint Jones, this time adding 105 in only 19 overs to help us claim a 55-run lead. Geraint and I seem to complement each other well when we are batting. He takes the bowlers on, he's a positive player and once we get going together it makes it hard for the bowlers because we hit the ball in different areas. There is a big difference in height between us for a start, so that changes the bowler's length all the time and if you are facing the spinners, Geraint likes to sweep, whereas I like to drive down the ground or over the top. During that summer, we enjoyed several good partnerships and we both tried to put the onus on the bowler to take the attack to us by putting them under pressure. Geraint is also very quick between the wickets and we attempt to make the fielders feel the heat by running as many quick singles as my legs will allow. That sometimes depends on whether we've bowled first or not – if we have, you'll often see me try and walk the singles. I'm not the quickest between the wickets, but I've got a good idea about my runs and I usually know when I've played a shot how many runs I should get for it.

Just like in the West Indies, where I kept getting out after doing most of the hard work, I was disappointed to get out for 63 because I was playing really well. I was batting with the tail again and I probably tried to go for big shots a little too soon. I had already faced a few balls from Chris Martin and the way he was bowling, I thought I could get the better of him. It was sod's law because the first time I tried something it ended up backfiring on me. I had come down the wicket to try and hit him over the top and the ball was exactly where I wanted it to be, but the execution of the shot was poor and I sliced it straight to mid-off. I was annoyed with myself because it was there to be hit. I've always said I'd rather be caught on the boundary than in the slips, because if you get caught in the slips you've been found out a little bit – I'd sooner get out on my terms!

That Test ended with Nasser Hussain shocking us all by announcing his retirement from cricket. I could never work out what Nasser was going to do at the best of times, so I had absolutely no idea this was going to be his final match. I don't think I'd have been the first one he'd have confided in about his plans anyway; he was someone who gave me my chance and I respected him greatly as a captain, but we were never close friends.

The build-up to the Second Test at Headingley was again dominated by talk about the captain, but this time not about his injury. There seemed to be a lot of fuss about how much of the Test he would miss to attend the birth of his first child, which was due some time during the match. I don't know if Vaughan was more nervous than normal because of that, but he didn't seem to show it. As captain you try not to convey something like that to the rest of the lads, but having gone through the same thing later that summer when Holly was born, I can just imagine how nervous he must have felt inside. I don't know how he concentrated on leading the side in the Test. I know from my own experience how hard it is to think about anything else other than your family at times like that, never mind deciding whether we needed two slips or three and who should open the bowling. It was a bit of a strange situation in the dressing-room around that time because babies seemed to be one of the big topics of conversation. There was a bit of a baby boom.

Quite apart from all the talk about babies, it was a tough Test because we knew New Zealand would come back at us. They had scored a good first-innings total of 409 and when we made our reply we were in a bit of trouble at 240/4 when Geraint Jones and I came together again. The situation once again dictated that we put together some sort of partnership and Geraint played really well to score his maiden Test century, an innings which justified the selectors' decision to have put him in the team just a few months earlier in Antigua. I fell six runs short of also scoring a century, but I was happy with the runs I had got because I wasn't playing particularly well. It was the type of wicket which was very hard to bat on and I remember getting hit a few times with balls that flew up at you when you weren't expecting them. That partnership helped us establish an important lead and Hoggard and Harmison bowled them out cheaply in the second innings to complete another comfortable victory by nine wickets.

The momentum within the England squad was building nicely by now. The key was that everybody was performing. It wasn't the case of just the opening batters getting all the runs, we were now scoring down the order. If we needed a performance, someone always came forward and provided one which is always the hallmark of a good side. In the past that never happened, but people throughout the squad were starting to do things at the right times. That was underlined by the team scoring 284/6, the highest ever successful run chase in a Trent Bridge Test, to complete a series whitewash over New Zealand.

Graham Thorpe won the game with an unbeaten century, but that Test will be remembered by most of the squad for the return to form of Ashley Giles.

Ashley had been given quite a bit of stick during that period from the press and the crowd and when you spend as much time together as we do, you can usually tell how your team-mates are feeling. You can look around the dressing-room and tell when someone isn't right. I've been there myself and had my own bad times and dark days and it's very hard to deal with. You get a pat on the back from people and they try and help you out and that's what we tried to do with Ashley.

He had received a lot of criticism for what they call negative bowling by coming over the wicket to people like Tendulkar, but that was his job in the side at that time. If you look at where he bowls from around the wicket, he gets his front foot so close to the stumps it's like a lot of other spinners going around the wicket. Ashley has taken going around the wicket a lot further, he uses it as a wicket-taking option throughout the game. People began to see that at Trent Bridge because he bowled really well there and got crucial wickets in New Zealand's second innings before scoring 36 not out to help win the game with Thorpe. We were all pleased for him after that because he's a very popular member of the dressing-room.

That victory also completed the whitewash which was another big step for the team. We expected to win the series, but everyone was saying that New Zealand would be a test for us to see if we had improved and we blew them away. That's when we probably first started to believe we had a good side in the making. There was a lot of confidence in the dressing-room and everyone was sky high as we approached the one-day series.

Throughout that New Zealand series I had been troubled by

my left ankle. I had first noticed it a few months earlier when it started giving me a bit of pain during the Test match in Barbados, but I thought nothing of it and it went away. It came back again against New Zealand and that is when it became really sore and it was decided I should miss the start of the one-day series. With things going so well it was a disappointment for me, but there was nothing I could do about it. I had various options, to have it scanned or another injection, but I had had enough of those over the course of my career and it was not something I wanted to endure again. I had a long chat with Dave 'Rooster' Roberts, the physio at Lancashire, and I told him, and England, that I wanted to give it a chance to heal on its own, to see if the inflammation would go away if I rested. That didn't happen so I had to have another jab, which was due to put me out for around a fortnight.

I had a net during my spell on the sidelines and felt I was batting OK and in my absence England lost to West Indies and New Zealand. A few days before their next match, against West Indies at Headingley, I rang Michael Vaughan and said that I could play just as a batter if he wanted me. He didn't give me an answer one way or the other straight away, so off I went to a barbecue at Ian Botham's house in Yorkshire the day before the Headingley match, getting a lift with Rooster in his car. I was having my burgers when my phone rang – yes, in the end I succumbed to a mobile – and I was asked to meet the team at their hotel in Leeds that night because I was playing the next day! Fortunately I had only had three or four glasses of wine by then because if it had been a bit later, I would have had to have ruled myself out. I had already arranged to stay over at the Bothams', so I had to ring around and make all sorts of arrangements to get me to the team hotel. I got Harmison to pick me up on his way down to Leeds, I had to get Rachael to take my general kit to Leeds and I had to get Jim Cumbes, Lancashire's chief executive, to go into the dressing-room at Old Trafford to collect all my one-day international kit and bring it to the game. I practised the following morning and was selected for England's first win of the tournament.

I was extremely pleased I had managed to get back into the side as a batsman just a few days later when I scored my first one-day international 100 against New Zealand in Bristol. I wasn't at the races when I first went out to bat, I was a bit dozy. But I got hit on the head by Ian Butler, one of their seamers, which helped a lot. It was a big hit, flush on the helmet, and it woke me up a little. After that I got my head down and played properly, although I think New Zealand were convinced I had edged Chris Harris behind in my 40s, but I got away with it. It was my 73rd one-day international for England so it was about time I scored a century. Even so, we lost the match, which took a little of the shine off it.

It was a bit of a monkey to get off my back and I think it showed the improvement I had made in all areas of my game, including my batting, in one-day cricket. That wicket at Bristol was quite tricky to bat on first up and, although it will go down as my first one-day century, to be honest it was a bit of a scratchy knock. It was nothing like how I had imagined getting my first century, but I was really pleased when I got there. By coming back into the side early I was feeling under a bit more pressure to perform. Darren Gough seized on this and was taking the mickey out of me in the dressing-room, asking me: 'Are you going to ride out there on a white horse, Fred?' He was going around telling everyone that they were all right now because Fred was back! Pity we lost the match. That match also marked the one-day international debut of Sajid Mahmood, my Lancashire team-mate. It was a hard wicket to bowl on as well as bat: the type of surface which suited medium-pacers like Scott Styris and Chris Harris. Sajid probably had too much pace for the wicket and he ended up conceding 56 runs in his seven overs.

That innings at Bristol sparked off a good run for me. We moved on to Lord's to face West Indies and, unlike in my previous innings, from the first ball I faced in that game I knew I was going to play well. It was a big difference from a scratchy innings at Bristol to a full house at Lord's and a good wicket and the very first thing I tried came off. When I faced Dwayne Bravo in the West Indies I tried to move across my stumps and hit him through mid-wicket. I tried that again at Lord's and didn't quite get hold of it and for one horrible moment I thought I was going to pick out the man put back there for just that shot. Thankfully, it sailed over his head for six and as soon as that happened I thought it was one of those days when I was going to be all right. I enjoyed that innings and Andrew Strauss got a century as well. Together we put on 226, which we were told was the highest ever one-day partnership for England at Lord's. Our centuries still failed to get us the win we required to reach the NatWest Series final, though. Chris Gayle totally upstaged us with a brilliant innings of 132 and brought our one-day series to a halt. Little did we know then that both teams would meet again in the ICC Champions Trophy final later that summer.

Raising my bat after reaching a century against
West Indies at Edgbaston.

17

MAKING HISTORY

Despite the disappointment of the one-day series, we approached the Test series against West Indies with plenty of confidence, despite Mark Butcher being ruled out of the side after suffering whiplash in a minor car crash. I really felt for Butcher, who is one of my best mates in the England side, but I was pleased that it gave a further opportunity to another of my closest friends, Robert Key. It turned out to be quite a comeback for him. He played absolutely brilliantly to score 221 after we had lost an early wicket. Steve Harmison and I were really nervous for him because we wanted him to do well. In my opinion he is one of the best batsmen around. When it is not challenging for him he tends to struggle, but if he has the best bowlers in the world bowling at him I would back him every time. When he first went out to bat the wicket was doing a fair bit and it was not straightforward batting at all, but it flattened out as the game wore on and he really took advantage of that. The same could be said of Andrew Strauss and Michael Vaughan, who both scored good centuries and maintained our momentum from the New Zealand series.

That gave us a healthy first-innings score of 568 and then I shocked quite a few people in the crowd and in the media by bowling a few overs for the first time since having the injection in my ankle. When I was asked about the prospect of bowling in the build-up to the Test I had been quite defensive and told everyone it was unlikely. In fact, I had begun to feel much better by then, but I told everyone it was unlikely to stop expectations being raised. I wasn't bowling at anything like my full capacity, probably only around 70 per cent, but it was enough to get three wickets, while Ashley Giles continued his good run of recent form to claim four wickets, including Brian Lara as his 100th Test victim – he's not a bad one to have for that!

Another player back in form was the captain, who had done some one-to-one batting sessions with Duncan Fletcher in the run-up to the Test and that seemed to have worked wonders. Vaughan followed up his century in the first innings with another in the second, while I went out and scored a quick 50 off 38 balls, chasing quick runs to help us declare 467 ahead. Only Chris Gayle, Shivnarine Chanderpaul and Lara provided any resistance and they quickly collapsed to earn us our fourth Test victory of the summer.

Before their collapse was complete came a comical moment with my old friend Tino Best. We got off to a bad start in the Caribbean when he played a trick on me in the Second Test at Trinidad which I didn't find very funny. I had just walked out to bat and took guard ready for him to run in. He came charging in, like he does, and bowled and at first I thought it must have been a beamer because I didn't see it come out of his hand. I was expecting to get hit on the head at any moment because I just hadn't picked it up. But he thought it was a huge joke because he had run in without a ball in his hand. I'm the first one to enjoy a laugh and a joke on the field and there are some things you can do, but that was just not one of them. I didn't find it funny at all. At Lord's it was payback time. I was standing at slip and he was trying to hit Ashley Giles out of the ground and swiping and missing. I couldn't help myself saying: 'Mind the windows, Tino!' And he just couldn't resist. He had to try and smash Giles again and of course missed altogether and was stumped by a mile. Now that *was* a good laugh. It worked perfectly for us.

The big win at Lord's instilled us with even more confidence as we moved on to Edgbaston, one of our favourite venues. The crowds there are always very loud in their support and it gives the whole side a lift. That applied to me more than anybody because everything seemed to be going right. I had felt good with my batting for most of that summer. I had scored runs in the one-day series and I had got a Test half-century in the second innings at Lord's, although the situation dictated that I went out there and started slogging before the declaration. When I went out to bat in the first innings at Edgbaston we had once again lost a couple of quick wickets so I needed to consolidate the innings to make sure we got to a decent total. It was one of those days when everything I tried seemed to come off. Everything just clicked and when that happens you don't need to think about anything, you just bat. My innings was split over two days and there was a huge expectation that I would go on and get my century after reaching 43 overnight. As a batsman you always go out to try and score a hundred, but cricket is never that simple.

Once again I was batting with Geraint Jones. We both got off to a good start the following morning and that gave me the momentum to convert my overnight score into a century. I was happy with the timing of my shots and the pair of us took the attack to the West Indies. The moment everyone remembers from that innings, though, is that Flintoff dropped catch.

I had just had a few heaves at balls and Geraint came down the wicket to calm me down and get me to bat normally. When I faced the next ball I remember thinking I'd played a strange shot to it and got away with it. Jermaine Lawson had bowled me a length ball but because I was playing so well it became an extension of my shot. I might have been trying to drive but I wasn't quite there. It just flew off the bat and kept going.

At every Test venue you play at, you are aware of where your family are sitting because the tickets are the same every year. As the ball flew towards the Ryder Stand I thought: No, it can't do . . . can it? I could see my dad getting up to try and catch it and it landed straight in his hands and bounced out into the lap of Michael Vaughan's mum! People have said since that I tried to pick him out in the crowd – I only wish I did have that degree of ability to control where the ball goes when I'm batting! It was later voted one of the sports moments of the summer, but I think my dad would rather forget it. All he kept saying that night was: 'I can't believe I dropped it!' His nickname at work used to be 'Colin Big Hands'. He prides himself on his catching and he's always telling me about these blinders he's taken. His excuse was that he's never had to take a catch so far away and so high up before; I suppose he's going to claim he lost it in the crowd. If you ask me it's a betrayal of the sort of standard of cricket my dad plays now on a Sunday. I'm sure he got a lot of stick from the league team he plays in.

I should have known from my dad dropping me that my luck was in that day and I tried to cash in against Omari Banks, West Indies' offspinner. He'd got me out in the first innings at Lord's, but I had hit him a few times in the second innings and he was someone I thought I could get after. I was getting a bit carried away by the crowd at this point and I was trying to hit nearly every ball out of the ground. I hit him for 19 in one over, including three sixes, to take me to my highest ever first-class score but ended up getting out for 167 when Dwayne Bravo got me lbw to his slower ball. By then I was trying to be aggressive and he beat me all ends up. It was a good piece of bowling. I had also made the mistake of starting to think about scoring my first double hundred.

West Indies also batted well in their reply and I was delighted to be able to get Ramnaresh Sarwan, although only after he had scored a century, and Lara out. It was a sign of a steady improvement in my bowling, which had begun during the tour to the Caribbean. I had bowled well at the left-handers and Lara in particular in the West Indies and because we had only played them a few months before, it was still fresh in my mind how I was going to bowl at them and how I intended to get them out. It was inevitable that a player of Lara's class was going to get runs at some stage in the series. He had got to 95 and it was really important to get him out at that time because they were just starting to get going. I must have been doing something right during this period because I ended up getting Lara out three times in the next 20 balls I bowled at him during that Test and the next one at Old Trafford.

That was a further sign that I had gone from being a quite defensive bowler who didn't try much, relying on bowling dot balls and building up pressure, into someone who had started to think like a bowler. I was getting more confident in my ability, I was doing a bit more with the ball and I was thinking about how I was going to get people out. I got to that stage through working with Troy Cooley and talking to Steve Harmison. Up until then I had never really taken my bowling that seriously. I had always regarded myself as a batter who bowled.

One of my worst nightmares would be to turn totally into a bowler because I just don't want that. I have always enjoyed batting, but bowling is hard work, it's doing the really hard yards. I've always told the lads in the dressing-room that I hate bowling, which I don't really, but it does affect your batting just because you are more tired when you start your innings if you've had a long bowling spell. But now I was starting to think like a bowler and even behave like one, I was practising my bowling every day and trying to work on different deliveries.

After winning comfortably at Edgbaston, where I was declared man-of-the-match, we had a chance of winning the series at Old Trafford, my home ground. Playing a Test at home has always brought with it extra expectations with all my family and friends in the crowd. I'd only played one previous Test at Old Trafford and that didn't go very well for me, but this Test went almost perfectly. I continued my success against Lara from the previous Test by getting him out twice this time. I thought he kept moving across his crease towards off stump. Everything we bowled was going across him and he kept getting farther and farther over. The plan was for me to try and drag him out there. I was going to bowl wider and drag him farther and farther out there and then try and knock his leg stump out. You build up through two or three overs to try and surprise the batsman with one ball. Often the plan may not work out, but on this occasion it worked perfectly. It was spot on against Lara. I was so excited I think I ran off to square-leg and started jumping up and down. Those plotted-for wickets are always the most pleasing. You keep nagging away at something and finally it works out – it's a great feeling. The only other time I can think of a plan working that well was against Graham Thorpe, who I was playing against for Lancashire. Once again everything was

bove: Steve
armison delivers
he first ball in the
pening Test of the
unning 2005 Ashes
ries. I don't think
ve ever known an
tmosphere like that
rst day.

ight: Kevin
ietersen has been a
evelation since
reaking in to the
ngland team. He is
special talent.

After the dismissal of Adam Gilchrist in the first Ashes Test at Lord's, the intensity of my reaction gives an indication of how much pressure I put on myself.

Winning an appeal for LBW against Jason Gillespie as England draw nearer to victory at Edgbaston to level the series. None of us knew just how close that win would be.

Hitting out against Australia in the second innings at Edgbaston.

Brett Lee's performance in trying to get Australia over the line on that final morning at Edgbaston was brilliant and I went straight over to tell him so.

Jubilation after just edging victory at Edgbaston. The captain is as relieved as I am.

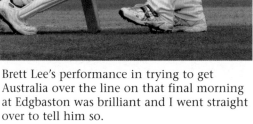

The moment we snatched victory. Steve Harmison has Michael Kasprowicz caught by Geraint Jones to bring an end to the greatest Test ever at Edgbaston.

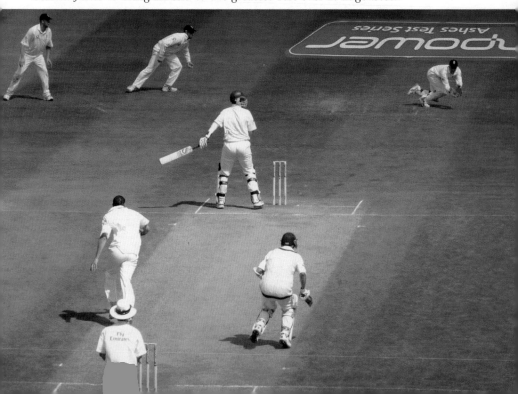

ractising hard at Old Trafford
efore the Third Test.

Stretching during the warm-up before the start of
the Old Trafford Test.

Michael Vaughan showed what a good player he is at Old Trafford. His 166 helped us to
decent total and put us in control of the match.

Simon Jones is relieved to see me catch Michael Clark off his bowling.

Attempting a back flip in celebration at getting Shane Warne out at Old Trafford.

Shane Warne claimed his 600th Test wicket at Old Trafford – what an incredible achievement.

Giving Matthew Hoggard a lift after he had made an early breakthrough to remove
Justin Langer in the second innings at Old Trafford.

Bowling one of my twenty-five overs on the final day at Old Trafford. I was exhausted mentally and physically after back-to-back Tests.

Ricky Ponting battled brilliantly on that final day at Old Trafford. His 156 saved the game for them.

Left to right: Ian Bell, me, Kevin Pietersen, Matthew Hoggard and Simon Jones – all of us looking dejected after Australia secured the draw.

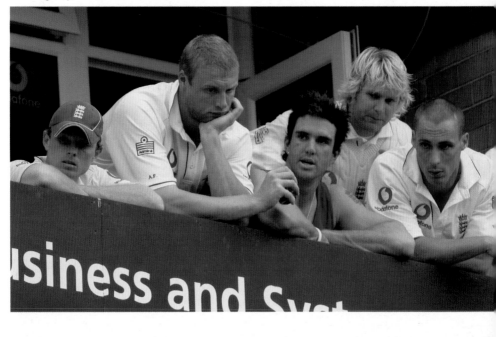

going across him and he kept leaving everything. I had a man out in the deep, planning to bounce him, but it was a question of timing it right, which I must have done because he took it on and got caught.

There was a fair amount of talk going on in the middle when I went out to join Robert Key. It was one of those wickets that suited the skiddy type of bowler like Fidel Edwards and I was a bit of a sitting duck. I couldn't get under a lot of his short balls because of the trajectory and I also struggled to get out of the way. I managed to hook him away for four early in my innings and then got hit a few times, so he came down the wicket and started having a go at me. Once he did that, they all joined in and also started having a go at Key. All that did was ensure Key and I stuck together and started having a go at all of them back. It got a bit fiery at one stage, but whenever I have batted with Key it's always been the same – if you have a go at one of us, you have to take on both of us. It got quite interesting for a while. It wasn't nasty, just the odd comment of the 'fat bastard' variety – we weren't sure which one of us that was aimed at! They picked on the wrong bloke with Robert Key. He's very sharp and I've never seen anyone get the better of him when it comes to sledging.

I couldn't think of a better way to finish any Test than the way that Old Trafford match ended up. After conceding a first-innings deficit, we were set a target of 231 to win the game which would have been a new record score to win a Test at that ground. We lost a couple of early wickets but Robert Key steered us home with a superb unbeaten 93. I also chipped in with an unbeaten half-century, my seventh in as many Tests, and hit the winning runs. I was batting on my home ground, scored the winning runs to win the series and I was batting with one of my best mates – how could it get any better than that?

The only thing that I was disappointed with about the way it finished was that Key missed out on a century. There was a point during our partnership when he could have got a hundred if he had been left to score all the remaining runs. I went down the wicket and asked him if he wanted me to block Sarwan out so he could get to three figures. It was typical of Key to turn around and say: 'Fred, if we can walk off together after winning the match then it won't get any better.' He told me to finish the game so we could get off and have a drink; it was one of the special moments of my career to do that at Old Trafford.

We were forced into changing the winning line-up at the Oval because Graham Thorpe had hurt his finger, prompting the selectors to call up Ian Bell for the Final Test. Once again he was someone I knew well from my time at the Academy. He is a good player who reminds me a lot of Michael Atherton in the way he plays and, like Strauss before him, he was successful straight away with 70 on his Test debut. That Test took on a great significance as it offered another opportunity to make history by equalling England's best ever run of seven successive Test victories. We had said the previous winter that we wanted to go to the Caribbean and win our first series there since 1969, which we did. We had wanted to whitewash them, which we failed to do. Then our next objective was to win every Test of the following summer. We wanted to whitewash New Zealand, which we did, and we wanted to do the same to West Indies on home soil. It seemed we were creating history with every match we played that summer and we wanted to carry on doing that. We were so confident by this stage that we were turning up expecting to win cricket matches. That was underlined by the way we wrapped up the Final Test on the third day to complete a memorable summer for us all and our celebrations matched our historical achievement that night.

In normal circumstances, the Final Test of the summer would be the signal for a bit of time off to relax before the winter tour, but this summer we had the ICC Champions Trophy tournament in England so there was no time for rest or recuperation. No sooner had we recovered from beating West Indies than we were facing a three-match one-day series against India as preparation for the ICC event. The first game at Trent Bridge was important for me if only because I got runs against Anil Kumble for one of the first times in my career. I had really struggled against him in India a few years earlier and he kept getting me out, but I was batting that badly at the time I think anyone could have got me out. It was a big cloud hanging over my head and when I went out to bat at Trent Bridge we didn't need many to win. I could have just knocked it around, but I purposely went out there to try and impose myself on the bowling. I wanted to prove that although Kumble had had the better of me in the past, I wasn't that bad a player. The second ball I faced from him I hit him back over his head for six and then finished the game by hitting him for another six. I wanted to make a statement and I think that's what I did.

In the second match at the Oval England were in a bit of trouble when I went out to bat. It was spinning quite a lot and Harbhajan Singh was bowling well. I had to try and bat for some time. I had been in a similar situation in the final one-day game in Bombay a few years earlier so I decided to try and see Harbhajan off and see where we went from there. Ganguly wanted to take him off after seven or eight overs, but he begged to stay on and finish off his ten. By this stage, Paul Collingwood and I had been batting for a while against him and we were happy for him to finish his overs, play him off and then get after the others. It was another of those days that summer where everything I tried came off apart from when I got out on 99 going for my century. It was a ball which I could have knocked to the legside and got my ton, but I was playing shots. A century is a century, but I didn't want to change because it would have been so obvious I was playing for the 100 and not for the team. To get out for 99 is only one off after all. I walked off laughing because I was pleased with the way I had played and I was happy with what I had done. That one run doesn't mean all that much to me because as a team we scored over 300. On my statistics it might say I didn't get a hundred that day, but I was man-of-the-match again and I'll remember how I played and how I enjoyed playing that innings.

I was due to play in the final match at Lord's two days later, but instead I was forced to withdraw because of the birth of our daughter Holly. Rachael had come with me to London and stayed at the hotel while we wrapped things up at the Oval. Instead of going out celebrating our winning lead in the series with the rest of the lads, I decided to stay in the hotel bar on the Friday evening with Steve Harmison and three of his mates from Ashington. I woke the following morning at around eight with a bit of a hangover and Rachael telling me it was all happening. My first reaction was to say: 'It can't be, there's another month to go!' But situations like that tend to bring you around pretty quickly. The hotel rang us a taxi and, with neither of us knowing where to go in London, we ended up at the Whitechapel Hospital, which was ideal because we didn't want to be bothered by press or photographers. Everybody thought we were up in Manchester. Once we got settled in at the hospital nothing happened. Holly was clearly not ready to take the field and the following evening they told us nothing was likely to happen for a further two weeks. I got kicked out of the hospital at around 8 p.m., so rang the lads to find out where they were and joined them in a bar in Chelsea.

Just as I had got used to the idea that nothing was likely to happen for a couple of weeks I got a call around 11 p.m. that evening to tell me to drink water for the rest of the night. I went back to the hospital around midnight and everything was happening. Because the baby was early we were totally unprepared. We didn't have baby clothes, blankets or a pram or anything. I had to ring Neil Fairbrother to ask him to bring our family car down with everything in it and take the two-seater, which we had with us in London, back home. Holly finally arrived on the Monday and I went out with the lads that evening to wet the baby's head and carried the celebrations into the following day after a few of the Lancashire lads flew down to raise a glass to Holly.

The following night I had to attend the ICC Awards dinner, a big affair with all the teams in the tournament attending. Because I hadn't seen most of the lads since Holly's arrival, they all wanted a drink with me. All the other teams were drinking mineral water, but the England table was awash with empty beer bottles! When my name was called out because I had won the one-day player-of-the-year award, my heart sank because I knew the state I was in. I think I just about coped OK with the interview on stage with Mark Nicholas, but I couldn't stop grinning in the press conference afterwards. I had this daft smile on my face as I tried to hold myself together sitting there next to Ricky Ponting and Jacques Kallis. Luckily I was only asked one question. In normal circumstances I wouldn't have dreamt of getting sloshed on duty, but I thought I had a reasonable excuse. It was a great time for me both on and off the pitch, but everything came swiftly down to earth again with the first match of the ICC tournament against Zimbabwe at Edgbaston.

Rachael had gone home with Holly and, although we were practising in Birmingham, I was going home every day. I would drive to Birmingham and then drive home after practice and then return the following day. It took a lot out of me and in that first game I just wasn't with it. I got three wickets, but when I batted, my mind was elsewhere and I was caught out in the deep for six. At least the team won by 152 runs and got off to a good start. Because I had been spending all day in the car driving back and forth to Birmingham, Rachael decided to come down to Southampton with the baby for the next game because otherwise I'd have been tempted to go back home after practice. It was great having them around and probably helped with my performance against Sri Lanka. I began playing really badly but somehow managed to finish unbeaten on 21 when the rain washed out any further play and took the game into a second day. The following day I played much better and confirmed my run of good form by scoring my third one-day century of the summer.

That win set up a semi-final game against Australia at Edgbaston. We hadn't beaten them in a one-day international for five years. I had only played them twice before, but there always seemed to be a different atmosphere in the dressing-room when we faced the Aussies. We knew they were the best team in the world and they knew we knew that. There was a nervous excitement in the dressing-room. We knew we were in a semi-final, we had a chance so we might as well have a go.

They got 259/9 in their innings, but we never thought we were not going to get them and Paul Collingwood and Andrew Strauss combined for the winning partnership. The atmosphere in the dressing-room afterwards was absolutely buzzing. We had beaten them for the first time in years and also reached our first major final for years. We'd have liked to have celebrated as a team, but Collingwood and I had to get off to London to attend the Professional Cricketers' Association dinner. Paul was driving, but as soon as we got out of the ground I told him to pull over at the first off-licence so I could buy a few beers in celebration of our win. It was great – I got to have a couple of beers while poor old Paul kept his eyes on the road!

For the final against West Indies at the Oval I was feeling OK, but I was glad it was the final game of the season. My form had started to dip and my luck had started to change as well. That was illustrated by the way I got out when I pushed hard at Wavell Hinds and Lara took a brilliant catch just off the ground to remove me cheaply. It really was a game we should have won. We had it in our grasp when they slipped to 147/8 chasing a victory target of 218. I thought I had a good shout turned down for lbw against Courtney Browne early in his innings, but after that you have to take your hat off to them. To win from that situation was some effort. According to the speed gun Harmison was bowling over 90 mph in the pitch black and Ian Bradshaw was getting nicely in behind it and hitting it all over. We gave it everything we had, but it wasn't good enough. The only thing that disappointed us was at the end. When we walked towards them to congratulate them, they ran off for a lap of honour without shaking hands. It was a slightly sour note to end a long summer, but none of us could really begrudge them their victory after the way they had played.

Lifting weights in preparation for the Second Test against South Africa in Durban.

18

SETTING NEW STANDARDS

Almost as soon as the last ball of the Champions Trophy was bowled, the controversy over England's trip to Zimbabwe reared its head once again. We were due to travel to Namibia to play a few games before facing a one-day series in Zimbabwe only a year after all the fuss about us going there for a World Cup match. A few of the players were uneasy about making the trip and Harmison had already revealed in his newspaper column that he was not going to go the day after we beat Sri Lanka in Southampton. I wanted to wait before I made the same announcement because we were playing Australia in the week and then we had the final coming up, so I didn't think it was the right time for me to also come out and say I wasn't going. As it was, Harmison's statement didn't affect the team at all. If anything, it lifted a weight from his shoulders because there was a lot of speculation about which players might refuse to go. Everyone else had this thing hanging over them about whether they were going or not and he just came out and ended the speculation.

After what we had gone through the year before there was never any chance of my going to Zimbabwe. I had made my mind up during the World Cup that unless things changed I wouldn't go. It's a great shame because I do love Zimbabwe the country: it used to be one of my favourite trips. The people were great to me when I was there on both the Under-19s tour and the A tour and the facilities were great. But what is happening out there is just not right and it left me with a simple decision. All the players had an appraisal with Duncan Fletcher in Southampton before the Sri Lanka game and he asked me then about Zimbabwe. I told him my decision and I also told Michael Vaughan at the same time. John Carr, who is the Director of Cricket Operations at the ECB, rang me up after that and said I had been given the chance to rest for the tour and wanted to know if I would like to exercise that option instead, but I told him no, I wasn't available. I didn't want to do that. I had spoken about it with Harmison earlier in the summer and we had decided we weren't going and I didn't want Steve going out on a limb in the press only for me to turn around and say I'm resting. I announced my decision shortly after that in the column I have in *The Sun* newspaper and it was not a decision I regretted after what went on when the England team got out there, staying in Johannesburg, deliberating for two days before deciding to go ahead with the tour; I was pleased to be back at home.

I took my decision for what I believe were good reasons, but at the same time it was also great being at home just spending time with Rachael and Holly. It was not all rest for me around this period, though, because I wanted to get much fitter before I flew out to South Africa for the Test and one-day series. I had toyed with boxing before and sparred with Iain Sutcliffe in the Lancashire dressing-room. We had even gone to Oliver's boxing gym in Salford together once. I wanted to train while I was off, but I didn't want to go to the gym on my own, so through Warren Hegg I contacted a promoter called Steve Wood and he arranged for me to go down and train at Oliver's. For six or seven weeks I went there every morning. I must admit that the first time I was a bit nervous. I got to the area early, but sat in my car waiting around the corner because I didn't want to appear too eager. It's quite an intimidating place to walk into and I was a bit shy when I first walked through the doors, but they were absolutely brilliant with me. I found it tough right the way through.

There are a few parallels between boxing and batting in that both sports are mainly side on and rely on footwork and the ability to transfer your weight quickly from foot to foot. You also need good hand-to-eye co-ordination, like in cricket. I was getting found out quite a bit to start with just because I was doing things I had never done before. They had an exercise called the bar which involves a bar set at the height of an average couch which you have to keep jumping over for a minute and then you go onto the bike for a minute and then back to the bar for a minute. It doesn't sound too difficult, but it is the hardest exercise I have ever done in my life. I think I impressed Oliver doing that. I wasn't as fit as some of his boxers, but I showed him that I never give up. Any exercise he asked me to do, I would finish, and I'd like to think I earned their respect in the end. Everyone involved in that sport has tremendous respect for each other. I really enjoyed my time there and Oliver's developed my interest in boxing, since when I have watched a few of the lads in the gym box and have been to watch Amir Khan and Ricky Hatton fight.

That time in the boxing gym helped my fitness when I flew out to South Africa with the other Test specialists not on the tour to Zimbabwe at the start of December. We only had a couple of weeks before the First Test and with hindsight I probably had not done enough bowling beforehand in the nets. We only had one game before the Test series began. This was against South Africa A in Potchefstroom, which is the place where a lot of British athletes go to train because it is at altitude and has good sports facilities. I think all the bowlers were a little under-cooked in that match. We started quite slowly and, as a result, slipped to a seven-wickets defeat just days before the First Test at Port Elizabeth. Defeat in the match immediately prior to the Test was not the best preparation for us. It was the first time we had lost a warm-up game since Duncan Fletcher became coach so that didn't go down very well at all! It was a bit of an eye-opener into the series for us. We had played a lot of good cricket through 2004 and been found wanting in one game, so in some ways it wasn't a bad wake-up call for us, even if it was regarded as a nightmare at the time. At least my bowling improved as the match wore on and I picked up three wickets in their first innings, but I was concerned about my batting after scoring just 25 runs in the match.

I had played well that summer, playing the way I play, but I wanted to get better to take myself to the next level and I think I became a little too technical about my batting on the South African tour. I started to hit hundreds of balls every day and tried to be technically perfect with every shot. I wanted my feet in the right position and to have a straight bat with every shot and that's just not the way I play. I have a basic sound technique but I also have my method of playing on top and I probably lost sight of that throughout that trip. I wanted to improve, but I was probably already improving doing what I was doing through the summer anyway. I was trying to take my game to a different level, but not in the way I should have done. Every player strives to be technically correct, but you have to learn the best way to play for yourself. If you look at a player like Graham Thorpe, he knows how to score runs the best way for him, and that is a lesson I learnt on that trip.

My concerns about my batting were justified when we got into the Test. I was playing really badly and I felt awful about my game. I was doing everything wrong which was typified by my dismissal to Ntini. He always bowls wide on the angle so I got across my stumps to try and hit him over mid-wicket, but dragged it straight to the fielder. It was terrible. It was one of those shots that you just don't watch the replay of, you hide from the television. Fortunately, the rest of the team were not playing as badly as I was and, with Strauss continuing the impressive start to his Test career with a century and an unbeaten 94, we wrapped up a convincing seven-wicket victory. I had already had a brief word with Geoff Boycott before the start of this Test about my batting. Geoff was out there doing some television and radio work and came up to me and asked: 'What's it going to be in this series then? Are you batting or slogging?' I told him we would have to see, but I ended up having a much longer talk with him before the Final Test.

My struggles continued in the next Test at Durban when Pollock got me out for a duck. He had already bowled me a bouncer which went through quite slowly and I left it, but he had set me up because he bowled me a quicker one which I went for and was caught at square-leg. We were right up against it in that Test after being bowled out for 139, but we showed our character by batting much better in the second innings. Strauss and Trescothick set the tone with a 273-run opening stand, while Thorpe also showed his class with a century. That put us into a position to win the game after South Africa lost early wickets before lunch on the final day. We were eventually denied by A. B. de Villiers and Pollock holding out for over an hour with a ninth-wicket stand when bad light arrived to save them. It ended our winning run after eight successive Test wins, but we travelled to Cape Town for the New Year Test knowing we were an improving side.

The start to 2005 was a bit of a disappointment to say the least with South Africa winning the next Test quite easily by 196 runs. Kallis showed us just what a fine player he is by batting on and on for an unbeaten 149. We were totally outplayed throughout the Test with not a single England player scoring a half-century. To make matters worse, I started having problems with my left ankle once again and it just got progressively worse during the back-to-back Tests in Johannesburg and Centurion and ended my tour early for the second successive time in South Africa. I was bowling a lot of overs during this tour and a common theme of my career is that every time I have a big bowling workload I end up getting some sort of injury. That could stem from the size of me. I've slimmed down from my younger days but I've still got a heavy frame which doesn't make it easy. My bowling action could also have something to do with it as well. I don't have a classical action like Steve Harmison, who is so smooth when he runs in to bowl. My action takes a lot of effort and it takes its toll on the body. If you look at the injuries I have had over the years, they are bowler's injuries. They are nothing out of the ordinary for bowlers because they have all had ankle spurs or hernia problems in their time. If I started to get a stress fracture of my back or I had problems with my discs, then I would probably worry a little bit more, but the things I have had are all bowler-related injuries.

For a long time England had been trying to cut down the number of overs I bowled to 12 or 15 in a day, but it is easy to say that when you are sitting in a room talking about it. It's totally different when you are out in the middle and circumstances dictate how much I am going to be used. Vaughan kept throwing me the ball during that series. He is wary about it, but there is not a lot that can be done. I must admit at times I am my own worst enemy because if we are struggling to break a partnership or get a batsman out I'll often say to Vaughan: 'Why don't you give me a try? I'll have a bowl.' Even though I keep complaining that I don't like it, I am quite a willing bowler.

It was touch and go whether I was even going to play in Johannesburg. I went to see a specialist who suggested a jab. I was a bit reluctant to go down that route again, so I told England that I would try to get through the next week and the Test in Johannesburg and, if it wasn't right then, I would have a jab before the Final Test at Centurion. I only just got through the week because I was in a lot of pain.

As it turned out, Johannesburg was the crucial Test with Hoggard swinging the ball at pace against their left-handers to win the game for us. Matthew Hoggard is one of the unsung heroes of our side. A lot of people don't recognise the job he does. There is always an end, no matter where you play, which is uphill or where you have to run into the wind or an end where someone doesn't want to bowl from and that's usually the end that Hoggard gets. People sitting at home watching on the television or those in the crowd don't appreciate that. A lot of his good work gets forgotten, so it was really great for Hoggard to come in and play like that and take seven wickets in the second innings to win the game. He is massively valued within the team. You only had to watch his performance at the Wanderers to see what a good bowler he is. He just kept going and going until he had won the game for us. I like the way he has also improved his batting. He is such a proud batsman now, he doesn't want to get out – he's a champion.

His performance that day effectively won the series for us and was another big step for the team as a whole. Everyone kept saying that each new series was a bigger test for us, but this was our biggest test by far. No England side had won in South Africa since they were re-admitted to international cricket and we did it without really playing as well as we can. We could have won even more comprehensively because we came very close to winning in Durban as well. In some ways our win out in South Africa was one of our best results because we had not played well but the side showed its character and kept on fighting, kept scrapping and never lay down to accept defeat. Even then people were looking ahead to the summer's Ashes series, it was almost as if the series in South Africa was forgotten. We didn't want to go into an Ashes summer in 2005 having been unable to win in South Africa so it was an important hurdle for us to clear.

Before we could celebrate our series win in South Africa, we had the Final Test in Centurion to get through. I was still worried about my batting after scoring only 9 runs in Johannesburg, so I had a longer chat with Boycott about the way I was playing. Rain had washed out the first day of the match and I was standing near the dressing-room with my pads on when Geoff approached and we started talking about all sorts of things and eventually about batting. He told me what he did when he was playing and what he thought about me as a batsman. He thought I was a batter, not a slogger. He said I had a basic technique and I should use it and not keep getting caught on the boundary or fishing at balls outside off stump. Geoff suggested I should make them get me out and not the other way around and it proved a very useful chat. I've always been a big advocate of using the expertise of former players. People like Geoff Boycott and Ian Botham are the greats of the game and if they have something to offer me, then I'll listen. I know some players are reluctant to talk to them because they are critical on television, but they are still great cricketers with useful things to say. That chat with Geoff helped me sort out my game. There was a bit of pride involved in that last Test because I wanted to show people that I could play. I had almost said to myself that I wasn't bothered what position my feet were in, I was just going to watch the ball so hard that nothing else would matter. I was determined to hit the ball despite where it was coming from and that is exactly what I did.

The 77 I got in that first innings was my best performance of the tour with the bat. I was batting with Graham Thorpe and it was hard work for a while, but I got a pull shot away, it triggered something in me and I began to feel much better about my batting. I got out in the end just wafting at one: it was a bit of a nothing shot, but it was quite an important knock in the context of the game because it enabled us to get a first-innings lead. Thunderstorms on the third day took further play out of the match and we were happy to complete the series victory with a draw in the Final Test.

Almost as soon as that Test was over I saw another specialist about my ankle and surgery was recommended. They were prepared to do it out there in South Africa, but if I had it done there it would have meant I would not be able to fly and I would be left sitting in Johannesburg on my own. I suppose I could have got through the one-day series with jabs and then had it sorted out when I got home, but that would have meant the summer getting closer and I didn't want to miss another Ashes series through injury. The other option would have been to struggle through the summer, with no guarantees of my being fit for the whole season, and then having the surgery done the following winter when we were due to tour Pakistan and India. I had a chat with Vaughan about it and we both agreed that in the sub-continent my bowling might be useful, so it was decided the best way forward was for me to go home and have the operation.

There was also the Ashes to look forward to and by going home when I did it gave me a window of five or six months before the First Ashes Test at Lord's for me to complete my recovery and rehabilitation. I came out of that meeting happy I was going home. I was disappointed at missing the one-day series and I knew I would be facing an operation to remove a bone spur on my left ankle when I got back, but it would mean I could spend two or three months at home with my family, which is a bit of a rarity for an international cricketer.

*Having a happy home life with Rachael and Holly
helps me concentrate on my cricket.*

19

MARRIED TO THE JOB

The operation took place almost as soon as I touched down at Manchester Airport and once it settled down I was reunited with Dave 'Rooster' Roberts and began the long road back to recovery. I had come out of the operation with just a sock on my ankle, but Rooster wasn't happy with that because he knows what I'm like. There would have been every chance I'd have bumped it or knocked it about, so he organised a light cast similar to the one which David Beckham used a few years earlier. We worked on the upper body to begin with, but once the stitches came out I started doing hydrotherapy to try and speed up the healing process.

Another reason to get fit was Rachael and my wedding in March. I kept my bootcast on and carried my crutches on my stag weekend in Budapest, which Rooster thought would be a wise precaution. Even with my movement restricted I had an absolutely brilliant weekend. There were 55 of us ranging from old Preston mates to some of my Lancashire and England team-mates. Budapest is a beautiful city and, even better, nobody knew who we were, we were just another stag party. I came back with my head shaved, which caused Rachael to have a second take when she saw me again and I think my phone was last seen floating down the Danube. The trouble was the lads only shaved down the middle of my head and I had little choice but to have my head totally shaved for the wedding. After I had dried out for a week we all departed to London for the big day. The wedding was just perfect. We had a lovely venue in Knightsbridge and enjoyed a great day. We had had a lot of interest from various magazines, but Rachael and I didn't want to do any of that. It was our wedding day, not a money-making exercise. It was a fantastic day with all my mates around and Georgie Fame and Bill Wyman and his band entertaining us later in the evening – I never knew getting married would be that much fun.

We had decided not to have a honeymoon, so after the wedding I started to build up my fitness. My stag weekend had interrupted my rehabilitation and I didn't want any comeback from anyone if I wasn't fit in time for the Ashes Tests. It was important I got back on the pitch as quickly as possible.

I came off my crutches after the wedding, but I had a slight setback when I went down to Loughborough and was put through a spinning session which caused my ankle to swell up nicely and I was back on crutches for another week. Other than that, my rehabilitation went quite smoothly, mainly because this time we took it nice and slowly. Dave Roberts was liaising with England all the time and I think they were cautious in their timespan so they didn't raise expectations of my return. I was given sheets of what I should be aiming to do by what week but I was always hopeful of returning before then.

They had things on it like 'Week 16 to 20: Light bowling'. I said to Dave that we should be doing better than that. I wanted to start the season with Lancashire playing as a batter, which I didn't quite make, but I wasn't far off. As part of the process I was driving up to Blackburn Rovers every morning to continue the hydrotherapy, which was set up by Dave through some mate of his who worked at the football club. I was starting to get a little frustrated during this period because I wasn't getting a break. My rehabilitation was taking all day and I was travelling all day. I spent my whole time rushing from one place to another, charging around all the time because if I was late for one thing it would set my whole day back. I was driving 1,000 miles a week just to get to all my rehabilitation classes. There were several times I thought about telling England or Lancashire that I'd had enough, I was fit and I wanted to play. I had worked hard in the nets during this period, but I was just so much looking forward to playing cricket again.

The frustration of it all caused me to blow up in the dressing-room at Lancashire the week before I finally made my return. The Seconds were playing a game and I wanted to play in it, so I turned up and asked Gary Yates, Lancashire's second team coach, what he wanted me to do. He told me I wasn't playing, so I went back into the dressing-room and began screaming and shouting. I just exploded. I was at my wits' end. I thought I was playing, but I didn't have clearance to play. It wasn't anybody's fault, but I had geared myself up for this match. Two days before I had played in a practice match between two Lancashire sides at Old Trafford and as far as I was concerned I was fit to play after that, which was why I exploded in the dressing-room. I did apologise to Gary later on that afternoon because I knew it wasn't his fault, but I was having a bad time of things.

My comeback date was finally booked at Lord's of all places in a Totesport League match against Middlesex, where I got to 17 before getting out lbw to Scott Styris. The first proper match came three days later for Lancashire in their championship match at Worcester and inevitably I fell to a fifth ball duck. I think I was just a little too eager to begin playing again. It was a decent ball from Kabir Ali and I probably chased it too much and edged to slip. I couldn't believe all the attention I was getting. There was a ridiculous amount of media present at both my matches, but all I wanted to do was have a bat. It was on the front page if I blew my nose, it was incredible. I even ended up doing a press conference after I got my duck, although there wasn't an awful lot I could say about my innings because it didn't last long enough. The bizarre thing was that most of the press had gone by the time I got 83 in the second innings: there were only about three of them left. The ball was doing quite a lot for the seamers when they were bowling and then Gareth Batty came on and it sometimes works against you as a bowler if you know someone well. I had batted against him every day in the nets during practice during the England tour that winter. I knew what he was going to try and do and there were small boundaries, so I had a go at his first ball and it flew for six. I enjoyed being back with the lads, it was just great playing cricket again.

I soon realised how frustrating the game can be as well just two matches later when Durham, who were top of the second division table at that point, arrived at Old Trafford. I got out to Mick Lewis, their Australian seamer, in the first innings when I got stuck in my crease, so I had a chat with Neil Fairbrother and we decided I should do a bit more work on the bowling machine to try and get my feet moving a bit more quickly. I was more upset about my dismissal in the second innings because I thought I was playing as well as I had done for a while. I had reached 55 when Harmison dug one in short which hit me on the chest and was caught behind. Durham went up for a big appeal, which was rejected. I played and missed the next ball and I thought I knew what Harmison was going to do with the next one; bowl wide of the crease and pitch it up. I made a big stride down the pitch but I was given out. I couldn't believe it. Harmison started his appeal, then stopped, and then just started laughing when I was given out. I was upset, possibly because it was Harmison, but I wanted more time at the crease.

The one bonus about that match was that I bowled for the first time in a match since South Africa. I had been bowling in the nets, but I was taking it slowly. I turned up against Durham to be told I was going to bowl and got through five overs. That was a big relief. But with the Test series due to start against Bangladesh, I still felt a bit under-cooked with my batting. All the contracted players were due to miss the next round of games prior to the First Test at Lord's, but I asked if I could play at Somerset for Lancashire. It turned out to be a total waste of time because it rained solidly for most of the game and I only got out in the middle for a brief innings.

As it happened, that innings would be my only one for some time because we dominated the Test series against Bangladesh so much that I didn't get in to bat. I did manage to claim five wickets in the opening Test but, because Bangladesh were collapsing quickly, I was only required to bowl 15 overs in the First Test and 22 in the Second at Chester-le-Street. It was another frustrating time for me because of my lack of practice. After the Durham game I was getting to where I wanted to be with my batting, but after that Test series I thought I had gone backwards again. You can go on the bowling machine to practise, but it is not the same as batting in the middle in match conditions. It felt like my season hadn't started and meant I was going into the one-day series without having batted properly for nearly three weeks.

From the very start of the summer, when the media were not talking about my injury, the talk was all about the Ashes. Everyone was waiting for the arrival of Australia to see if we could match up to them. Our first meeting with them was in a Twenty20 match at the Rosebowl, which turned into everything we hoped it would be. The atmosphere was electric and produced a great night. I had only played a couple of Twenty20 games before, so I wasn't quite sure how to approach it. County sides have got better by playing it regularly but most of us had hardly played it and I think the Aussies had played even less. As a spectacle it was fantastic and the Rosebowl was a fine venue for it. The wicket was good and it turned out to be a great night. To win by 100 runs is a big margin in any form of cricket, but there were an awful lot of people reading far too much into that result. It was a Twenty20 friendly and we played very well to bowl them out for 79, but there was also a fun element to the game. If it did nothing else it proved to ourselves and everyone else that we were not a bad side.

We saw that Twenty20 night as a night to enjoy, though everyone made a lot of me hitting Brett Lee on the shoulder with a short-pitched delivery which ended up ruling him out of the first couple of one-day games and began a rivalry with him which lasted for the rest of the summer. I wasn't consciously trying to target Brett, it was just the way I bowl at tail-end batsmen. That match really began the build-up to the Ashes for all concerned. The Ashes had been the main talking point for months before then, but our early Twenty20 victory seemed to spark off the excitement even more. Everywhere I went at the start of that summer more and more people were coming up to me asking me if we were going to win the Ashes and all the grounds had sold out well in advance.

Before we began thinking about that, though, there was the one-day series to get through and, after losing to us in the Twenty20 match, Australia also lost to Somerset and then to Bangladesh, which surprised us all. We all watched their defeat to Bangladesh from our hotel in Bristol, where we were due to play the Aussies the following day. It was an amazing result, but Bangladesh have played a lot of one-day games and the law of averages would suggest they were going to get it right sometime. We certainly didn't think we were going to walk all over Australia when we played them the following day and that was just how it turned out. They had posted a reasonable score and we were struggling in reply. I had got to 19 when they brought Brad Hogg on and I tried to hit him over long-off. I was trying to hit it over his head, but I didn't catch hold of it properly and was caught on the boundary. We looked like we were going to lose until Kevin Pietersen came in and played an incredible innings. He really is some player, very special. I had got to know him briefly in South Africa when he flew out for the one-day series just before I went home and he fitted into the dressing-room well that summer. He comes across as being very confident and he is, but he's a nice lad and he's good to be around. I was very impressed with the way he had played in South Africa because he was under extreme pressure to perform. That victory in Bristol gave us some momentum, which we kept going with another big win over Bangladesh at Trent Bridge when I again got out at long-off. My luck with the bat didn't improve when we returned to Chester-le-Street to face Australia again and this time I got out caught at long-on. I had been batting quite well, trying to rebuild the innings, and had reached 44 when I again mistimed a drive down the ground and was caught. Australia ended up winning by three wickets, a possible sign they were now starting to rediscover their best form.

After we both beat Bangladesh again and had our meeting at Edgbaston washed out, it was all set up for another contest with the Aussies in the NatWest series final at Lord's and what a way to finish the tournament. We seemed slow to start as a team and allowed them to get off to a good start in the first six or seven overs. It took the dismissal of Matthew Hayden, mistiming a drive, to spark us off. After that we bowled well as a unit and restricted them to 196, which was a total we thought we could chase down. Like the Test which followed a few weeks later, it was a wicket which suited the taller bowler and Glenn McGrath bowled magnificently well to reduce us to 34/5. I remember sitting on the balcony saying that if Collingwood and Geraint Jones could put a partnership together and get the deficit down to less than a 100 then we had a chance. They did just that and if it hadn't been for a couple of run-outs we could perhaps have won the game. Instead we had to settle for a tie after Ashley Giles scrambled a two off the last ball. It was exciting stuff, but once the result had sunk in I sat in the dressing-room a little disappointed we hadn't won. Having restricted them to 196, our failure to knock them off was a big let down. If we are being honest we should have won that game.

I think all the team were pleased with the way we bounced back from that disappointment to win the opening game of the three-match Challenge series which followed at Headingley, which was an important victory for us after missing a big opportunity at Lord's. It was an isolated victory, however, with Australia winning the last two matches at Lord's and the Oval. It is a measure of how closely the two sides were matched that we kept coming back at each other. They had arrived in England a little rusty and from our point of view it would have been better to have started the Ashes there and then. After losing that opening Twenty20 match, though, they got better. They dominated the last match at the Oval with Adam Gilchrist finding form to take the game away from us and there was no doubt they had the momentum going into the Ashes series.

The tension of the incredible 2005 Ashes series is obvious.

20

PRESSURE OF
THE ASHES

The biggest worry as we approached the Ashes series was that some of their batsmen were getting into form. Australia had played well in the final two matches of the Challenge series. As for us, we were mostly relieved by the end of that series because it meant the Ashes were finally upon us. The whole country seemed to have been waiting and waiting for the action to begin, the build-up had been going on for months and now it was here.

What worried me personally was that because of the way the Test series against Bangladesh went I had not batted a great deal, and with the Tests followed straight away by the one-dayers, I had not had a first-class innings in some time. It would have been reassuring to have been able to fit one in before going into the First Test but, as the series went on, I was glad I had not played that much cricket because it was mentally and physically exhausting enough as it was. I'm sure it is always a tricky situation for people like Duncan Fletcher, trying to balance giving his team enough first-class practice against not playing them too much. I thought I was under-cooked at the time, but it turned out they got it pretty much spot on for me the way my form picked up during the series.

The one thing I was encouraged about as we prepared for the Ashes was my bowling. I had found some extra pace from somewhere at the start of that summer, probably an extra five miles an hour, consistently. This came largely from being injury-free after sorting my ankle out. It had taken ten weeks to get over the operation, mentally more than anything. I did a lot of work with Rooster Roberts too before the start of the season, strengthening different parts of my body. We worked on my arms, we worked on my shoulders and we strengthened my core. I put some weight back on and as a result felt stronger coming into the crease.

We seemed to have found a balance between just being fat, as I was, and at one point – don't laugh – possibly being too light, which meant I was not able to use my strength. I was starting to find my feet with my new pace towards the end of the one-dayers, but it was in the Test matches that I really started to show it. No matter how much time you spend in the gym, there's nothing really like bowling. We had tried to simulate certain bowling actions in training and tried to strengthen those areas but, as the one-day series went on, I started to settle in and find the rhythm. I felt I got better and better throughout that series and it was perfect timing for me for the Tests. I'm not saying I used the one-dayers as a warm-up, but for me they provided perfect preparation for the Ashes.

I don't know whether the Aussies were taken aback by the speeds I was bowling – all I know is that I certainly was when I looked up at the speed gun register on the odd occasion during that First Test at Lord's. I was getting well into the 90 mph range, which was as big a shock to me as it probably was to them. I had always been able to get into the upper 80s and took 90 mph now and again, but at the start of that series I discovered I could bowl over 90 mph consistently.

Amid the inevitable pre-Test hype everyone enjoyed pointing out I had never played in an Ashes Test before. This was true, and I had waited impatiently since my 1998 Test debut to do so. People were saying that players can only really be judged against the best and I even heard myself coming out with remarks like that in interviews. It is probably true, but in saying it I put too much pressure on myself and forgot how I normally go about things. I had to remind myself that I enjoy playing cricket, but it is also not a matter of life and death and I lost sight of that.

Once the First Test arrived, the buzz around the ground at Lord's was like nothing I had ever encountered before. There is always an atmosphere at the start of a Test match, no matter where in the world you play, but particularly at Lord's. When we walked through the Long Room that morning, we emerged onto the pitch to a roar more approaching Eden Gardens than NW8. That Test started so well for me with Justin Langer spooning one up in the air off a ball which was just short of a length. I started celebrating as soon as I saw who was under it – my old mate Steve Harmison. By lunch they were in some trouble at 97/5, a position we could only have dreamt about before the Test began.

My good start continued after the break when I also dismissed Adam Gilchrist edging behind. I was putting it outside off stump as part of the plan we had for him. I had seen left-armers have some success against him bowling out there, particularly Alan Mullally, bowlers who came around the wicket and hit an area he found difficult to deal with. He kept throwing the bat at it, he edged it down to third man and belted me through the covers a couple of times. I was getting a little fed up with him carving me over the slips and edging wide of fielders. But I had a gut feeling our cunning plan was worth persevering with. So when he did finally nick one behind I was delighted. I celebrated by standing there, nodding my head with this wide-eyed expression on my face. I had never done it before and I don't think I'll be doing it again. People said I was mimicking Courtney Walsh, but that certainly wasn't the plan. I simply did what felt natural at the time – after all, I had just got out one of the Aussies' most dangerous players.

Bowling them out for 190 on the first day, after they had won the toss, was a fantastic feeling. It was a great effort by everyone and when we went out to bat we were all full of it. The buzz around the ground was that the Ashes were coming back. We had won the first session, ended their first innings, so bring it on! Those high spirits were quickly ended by Glenn McGrath, who showed what a fine bowler he is. He is a strange bowler in some ways and in a lot of ways he reminds me of Shaun Pollock, putting it in the one spot all the time and always testing you. I went in at 19/4 and did not last very long. I have watched the replays of the ball that did for me and the experts will say I should have got a big stride in and I should have done this and should have done that. But it simply shot along the ground and hit my stumps. On the slow-motion replay you can watch it bounce with the seam up and swing onto off stump, so there was not an awful lot I could do about that one. The first or second ball I faced from McGrath I left off the same length and it went past me waist-high, so I don't think I did that much wrong. The ball I got out to I wasn't even thinking about playing initially. I only threw the bat down as an after-thought. You can always be hypercritical on television, but he is 6 ft 5 ins and he bowls in good areas.

I couldn't quite believe I had got a duck in my first innings in an Ashes Test. Once I got back to the dressing-room, my first words were: 'I've just waited six years for that!' Everyone was expecting so much and the crowd was behind me. There had been a huge roar when I went out to bat, so to toddle back in for nought was a strange feeling.

That amazing spell from McGrath enabled them to gain a 35-run lead, but we fought back well to get them at 139/3 when Kevin Pietersen missed a big chance at cover on his debut. Everyone can miss catches from time to time and I am not having a go at Kevin for missing this one, but it was a big drop because Michael Clarke had only scored 21 at the time and went on to make 91. His innings effectively batted us out of the game.

The one positive point we could take from their second innings was the way we clawed it back as a team from a really bad period of half an hour. The ball was going everywhere, there were overthrows, everything was going wrong but we got it back together and stuck to our task. Then I dropped a really simple catch in the slips to miss McGrath. It was an absolute sitter at second slip. There was only one wicket to go and all I was thinking about was getting back into the dressing-room and getting ready for batting. I don't know whether it was nerves or the expectations or what but we were more jumpy than normal. Maybe it took us a Test to settle down, but I think it affected the Aussies as well because they also seemed very nervous.

Those nerves certainly affected me in the second innings, possibly because I faced the embarrassment of a pair at Lord's. I wasn't in great form anyway because I still had not played that much, but sometimes the difference between playing well and not is when you look at the field. When you are not playing well and you look at the field, all you can see is fielders and when you are playing well you can see the gaps. All I could see that day were the fielders. I just could not see past them. I got off the mark with a leading edge and then got out to Shane Warne's slider. A lot of people were saying afterwards that I didn't pick it, which I did, but you still have to play the thing. It just kept coming at me and got fuller and fuller on me. The ball was probably too full on me to try and cut it and I ended up edging behind.

Before the start of the Test we had been introduced to a machine called Merlyn, which was supposed to replicate all the different deliveries we were likely to be confronted by when we were facing Warne. Before Lord's we had it outside in the nets but it wasn't working properly, so it wasn't much use to us. By the time the next Test came around at Edgbaston its boffins got their act together and I gave it a try. You can never replicate Shane Warne because the problem with a machine is that, apart from there being no earring and no stare, there isn't any arm to come over either. What it does give you are the angles the ball is going to be coming at you and where you are going to look to score and how you are going to look to play it. In that respect it does serve a purpose, but the guys who were running it were claiming it could bowl a slider, it could bowl a googly and it could bowl a leg-break. The problem with that is you have no chance of picking it with no arm coming over and no hand to watch. The ball just pops out of a hole and the two guys who invented it stood there laughing while we tried to figure it out. They are obviously very proud of their machine, but I did not find it really helpful and there were a couple of times I came running down the wicket trying to hit the ball as hard as possible and get my own back on the machine! Merlyn has been helpful to a few of the lads, however, but you do wonder what is going to come next. Are they going to invent a machine that bats like Ricky Ponting?

We ended up losing comfortably on the Sunday afternoon after being totally outplayed. A lot of us had never experienced what the Ashes Tests were all about because we had never played in one before. After Lord's we were sadder and wiser. None of us needed telling how good the Australians were, but after that Test we knew what we were up against and what we needed to do against them. In some ways it was like a learning Test and we had to learn pretty sharpish if we were not going to lose the Ashes series again.

I got into my car after the end of the match and drove straight to Devon to escape from everything for a few days. I just wanted to spend time with my family and reflect on how I had played and how the Test had gone. I really enjoyed the time away. We stayed at a lovely hotel on Dartmoor and the other guests seemed to be there to take things easy too. They were really nice. A couple of people came up and said hello, but otherwise I wasn't bothered much. It was great. I had a body wrap and a massage and just got away from it all. I had promised Nigel Stockill, England's fitness trainer, I would go to the gym but it was so relaxing that I'm afraid I didn't make it! I had also planned to do a bit of fishing one day and a bit of golf the next, but I didn't do any of it. I just sat about, pushed the pram around, and went to have a look at a couple of the villages nearby, which was perhaps just what I needed.

Those few unwinding days helped me a lot because the Test series got bigger and bigger as it unfolded and, though the attention I was receiving was all very flattering, it became harder and harder to have my own life. Spending time with Rachael and Holly after the disappointment of Lord's also put things in perspective to a degree and helped me relax. But there was also a sense of embarrassment about the way we played at Lord's. We all wanted to win the Ashes and we had not performed anything like we were capable of doing. A lot had been written prior to the series about how good we were and we ended up playing like that. It put extra pressure on us to come back strongly in the next Test at Edgbaston and prove we were a good team.

I returned from our break in Devon on the Thursday after the Test defeat and I worked hard on the bowling machine with Neil Fairbrother for the rest of that week. He was building me up and telling me how well I was playing, but I didn't feel totally right. I didn't believe that I was doing what I do well. We had three sessions lasting around four hours apiece and eventually I got to the stage where I was feeling better about the way I was playing. The strange thing about batting is that sometimes you forget the things you know how to do and I am particularly bad for that. I will hit the ball and wonder why I didn't pick the bat up like that the previous time I tried that shot. It is all about grooving your game and getting back into the groove and that is what I was trying to do in those sessions.

My preparation for the next Test also included seeing a guy called Jamie Edwards, who describes himself as a 'mental coach', and has helped golfers like Lee Westwood. Chubby Chandler told me if I didn't rate him I didn't have to see him again, but he thought it might be a good idea. Michael Vaughan also saw somebody from the same company.

The main thing I got from my session was to remember what I do when I do well. I had to focus on how I went about things and not just the way I played, but my demeanour, the way I carried myself. I had probably lost a bit of that. It was like a reminder to myself of what I needed to do to get back there. The session consisted of Jamie asking questions and from the answers I gave, the penny finally dropped. At Lord's I was probably thinking about things far too much, instead of relying on my instincts a bit more. Jamie got me to try and stop over-complicating things and just go out there and play. He broke me down into two people; there is Andrew who goes home and is a father and a husband, and on the cricket pitch there is Fred who just goes out there and has a crack. I took that on board and for the rest of the series I tried to go out there and just play and enjoy my cricket. I wasn't going to get out bowled pushing forward or nicking a soft one to the keeper. I was going to get caught on the boundary if I was going to get out – I was going to get out on my terms.

Earning the congratulations of Kevin Pietersen and Michael Vaughan after claiming a wicket in the 'Greatest Test' at Edgbaston.

21

THE GREATEST TEST

When we assembled at Edgbaston for the next Test, I had been studiously ignoring the papers so was totally unaware of all the talk in the media during the previous week about the need to change the side. We had been a good side for two years and after one bad performance they suddenly wanted changes. As it was, the selectors backed us by naming an unchanged squad and everyone seemed to have a renewed determination when we turned up for nets. Whether it was the bowlers bowling for a long time in the middle or the batters going and working on Merlyn, everybody practised with a real intensity. It seemed that everybody had learnt something from the way we performed at Lord's. I went into the nets and worked with Merlyn on my angles for when I faced Warne. I expected him to come around the wicket and over the wicket and worked out a gameplan for what I was going to do in each case and how I was going to try and score off him. I prepared well.

The first signs of things starting to change in our favour was the morning of the Second Test when word filtered through that Glenn McGrath had trodden on a cricket ball in the warm-up and was out of the match. I know people were saying that no matter who Australia fielded they would still be good, but you just cannot replace Glenn McGrath. It was a massive boost to us all not having the guy who knocked over the top order at Lord's in their side. We were also a little surprised when Ricky Ponting won the toss and decided to field, because we were always going to bat if we had the choice. We had played on a similar Edgbaston pitch against South Africa a couple of years before when Graeme Smith scored a double 100. I remember bowling quite early in that match when it nipped around a little and I beat him on several occasions, but once he got set and the ball a little softer it was a great wicket to bat on. We thought this wicket would be similar, so we were happy they were bowling – particularly with no McGrath in their ranks.

Once we got started it was a bizarre Test from start to finish. To score 407 runs on the first day was unbelievable, but the tone was set by Trescothick and Strauss at the top of the order. I think Marcus took 12 off one of Brett Lee's early overs and then Warne came on and, unlike at Lord's, the lads got after him a bit. Everyone in the dressing-room gained confidence from the way the openers played. We were looking at Trescothick and Strauss attacking Warne and thinking: If they can do that, then maybe I can do it as well. By the time I came in we were still in a good position, but both Vaughan and Bell had gone in quick succession and the innings needed rebuilding. After my experiences at Lord's, I wanted to take the aggressive route to rebuild rather than trying to grind it out and bat for time. Coaches will always tell you to bat for time or bat for an hour and then have a look, but I don't think I am at my best when I bat like that.

I could have been out for another duck after trying to hit Warne over the top. I lined the shot up and decided I was going to go for it, but something made me check at the last moment and I only just got it over Michael Kasprowicz's head at mid-off for four. Once I had got off the mark, my nerves eased and I felt a little bit better about the way I was playing. I decided that if he bowled in certain areas I was going to go after him. I had a definite gameplan. Even when Lee was bowling at me and had a man out to cover the hook, I was confident of taking him on. I was determined they were not going to tie me down. The venue probably helped me play with a bit more freedom as well. It was a very similar day to the previous year when I had scored a century against West Indies. It was a full house, plenty of people were shouting and it was another good wicket – the only difference this time was I failed to pick out my dad in the crowd in order to give him some more catching practice.

It was also my first proper partnership with Kevin Pietersen, which was what everyone had been wondering about since the start of the summer when Kevin broke into the side. Like me, he is a very positive player and we scored quickly for the hour and a half we were together. We hit the ball in different areas and we are different types of players. I tend to be fairly relaxed when I am at the crease, whereas he is absolutely hyperactive, so it's quite a contrast. I remember playing against him years before in Durban on the first England tour I went on when he was batting number 8 or 9. In his early days I don't think anyone worked with him on his batting. The way he bats reflects that, because he has figured out a method that suits him which is why you will see him play a few unconventional shots. But that is the best way for him to go. He has figured it all out for himself. He's unorthodox and he must be very hard to bowl to because he can hit the same ball through mid-wicket or point. Sadly, neither of us went on to get big hundreds, but after Lord's my 68 came as a relief to me and I felt much better for it.

As a team we had managed to score 407, which was a good total after being put in to bat. People were saying we had played too recklessly and if we had applied ourselves better we could have scored more runs. But to score 407 in a day is a lot of runs in a Test match. We also knew that because of the aggressive way we had got them, Australia would want to match us by coming out and being just as positive, as the Aussies always do, which would give us a chance.

We got off to a good start with Hoggard removing Hayden with his first ball to a field Vaughan had set for him out in Australia. He had mid-off set back, a straight drive man and a slightly wider drive man and it worked a treat when Hayden drove straight to Strauss at extra cover.

Harmison had set the tone with a great first over to Langer when he kept hitting him and unsettling him. The key to us getting such a good first-innings lead of 99 though was the ball starting to reverse swing very early in their innings. It started going from around the tenth over and for me that is absolutely ideal because the ball is hard and it enables me to swing it away from the right-hander. I had almost given up trying to do this with conventional swing and was just attempting to hit the seam and an area, and most of the deliveries would come back in to the right-hander. But both at Edgbaston and Old Trafford, where the surfaces were abrasive and scuffed up the ball, it reversed nicely for Simon Jones and for me.

Australia showed what a good side they were by coming back strongly from that position and putting us in a bit of trouble by the time I walked out to bat. Warne and Lee had once again gone through the top order and at 72/5 there was a need to stabilise the innings if we were to stay in the Test. I felt the first innings had served its purpose. I had hit myself back into a bit of form in it and I wanted to play with the same intent in the second innings, but now I had to bat properly and circumstances dictated I get my head down a little bit. In some ways the loss of wickets while I was out there helped me reconcentrate and get in again and then, when we slipped to 131/9, I switched back into the other mode of going after it. When you are playing positively like that, it is a lot more instinctive. You just go out there and hit it and I enjoy doing that.

I was trying not to think about the series situation too much. If we had crumbled and lost the Second Test, who knows what would have happened at 2–0 down with three to play. But we did have a lead and ideally we could have got that up to 350 runs going into the final innings. That was the target I was working towards and we almost reached it with Simon Jones hanging around and adding 51 for the last wicket. We were given great support during that stand. Saturdays at Edgbaston are always loud and it doesn't take much to spark the crowd off. The moment it swung in our favour was when they brought Michael Kasprowicz into the attack after Lee had bowled a big spell. Without Lee's express pace, you have slightly more time to play your shots. I was able to get two sixes away in one over and that was when I felt a big shift in the momentum towards us. Because of that over, they didn't bowl Kasprowicz again and brought Lee back on. But he was slightly tired after bowling a big spell, and by then I thought he was someone I could get after.

Throughout my partnership with Simon Jones I tried to give him two balls an over. I was happy with him facing the seamers rather than taking on Warne. He is an aggressive batsman and he can hit the ball so I didn't want to suppress that totally. I just told him that when he hit the ball, he had to go wholehearted at it, really try and hit it and not get out by not going one way or the other. He hit one over the slips, which at that stage I thought was a decent shot, and another over mid-off. The balls he left were good, but the ones he went for, he went hard at. The runs, as it turned out, were vital to us winning the Test, but it also gave us a belief we were going to win. By getting 73 in that second innings, my confidence was high and I'm sure Simon and the rest of the team felt the same. We just didn't have any idea of how close it was going to be. At one point we would have taken a lead of around 230, but to come off 281 ahead on a pitch that was spinning and wearing gave us plenty of confidence.

That was certainly reflected in the way we bowled and by the end of that momentous day, Australia had slipped to 175/8. I had never known a day like it in my life. I was told at the end that I had been on the field for 77 of the 95 overs and had contributed 141 runs, six wickets and two catches to the match. It was certainly my best day for England and I don't think I have had a better day in any match if you take into account the opposition and the occasion. I should perhaps have known it was going to be my day because I was called on to bowl with them going well in their second innings and got a wicket with my second ball. I was brought on in the thirteenth over and it was a nice time to come on because the ball had started to reverse early.

One of the things I pride myself on now is not needing a warm-up ball. I try to hit my stride as quickly as I can and that first over was probably one of the best I have ever bowled. Langer blocked my first ball, but he got an inside edge onto his stumps with the next, which brought out Ponting. I had what I thought were two good lbw shouts rejected against him, he left another, edged one to gully and then edged one behind off the seventh ball of the over – it was one of the few occasions I was happy to have bowled an earlier no-ball. I was asked time and again that night about that over and I probably would not have been able to bowl it if I hadn't batted the way I did earlier in the day. I was still on a high from my batting and just ran in as fast as I could and tried to hit the areas I bowl in. With Harmison claiming a wicket off the last ball of the day to remove Michael Clarke, our hopes were high for a victory to level the series.

Everybody was saying we had already won, but we knew we must not get ahead of ourselves. Warne had scored runs in the past and Lee is also no mug with the bat. They needed 107 to win next morning and we arrived at the ground determined we weren't going to be complacent about it. The really worrying thing was the rate at which they were scoring during the early stages. Warne is a tricky batsman to bowl at because he squirts it here and there and he was scoring really quickly. I tried to push him back by bowling a few bouncers at him. I could see he was getting back close to his stumps and I went for a leg stump yorker. I know he trod on his stumps, but I'm going to take some credit for it! When we got him out with Australia still needing a further 62 to win, we all thought that was it. I reckoned I had Kasprowicz leg-before at one point and he also skied one down to third man, but Simon Jones missed a difficult chance. When they got down to needing less than 20, we started thinking to ourselves: Surely not. By the time they needed less than 10 there was almost a feeling among us that this could not be happening! I remember standing next to Marcus Trescothick at slip with both of us saying: 'They can't get this, can they?' We kept smiling nervously at each other.

The one thing we were clinging on to was the hope that pressure would get to them. When tail-enders are chasing a total and they need around 30 they can play how they want, but by the time they get into single figures they are suddenly expected to win and they try and play a lot tighter, rather than relying on the method that got them there in the first place. But with only three runs needed by the Aussies, Steve Harmison came up with the goods with a short ball into Kasprowicz's ribs which he nicked down the legside for Geraint Jones to take the catch and earn us an amazing victory. It is incredible to think that just one shot edged past the field would have done it for them and one ball did it for us. To win by only two runs after almost giving it up for dead at one point was incredible. I don't think any of us could believe what had happened. It had been a bizarre game from start to finish and it will probably go down as the most exciting cliffhanger of a Test match ever.

Everyone started celebrating all around the place. In the stands, on the field, everywhere. I went straight over to Brett Lee because I really felt for him. He had tried everything to get Australia over the line and to hit an unbeaten 43 in those circumstances was unbelievable. I remembered what it felt like to lose against the West Indies in the ICC Trophy final and how, when we went to shake hands with them at the end, there wasn't one of them anywhere to be seen because they had all set off on their lap of honour. I told Brett that he should be proud of the way he had played because he was absolutely brilliant, and then I went over and said the same to Kasprowicz who had sunk to his knees after being given out.

A lot was made of my conversation with Brett Lee out on the pitch because of the battle we had had, but I thought he was tremendous that day. In every Test series there are always a few personal battles going on and there was certainly a duel developing between Brett and me. It was great to be involved, particularly with someone like that. I liked the way he plays his cricket, with a smile on his face, but still giving everything for his team. I also like him off the pitch. He's a really nice lad. But when you get out there in the middle he will give you everything. He has the odd smile at you and has a word from time to time, but he goes about his cricket the way it should be played.

The good thing about this series was the way the two teams had a drink with each other after each Test and, despite the tense circumstances, this was no different. The Aussies quickly joined up with us for a beer and every one of us was proud to be involved in such a match. I certainly was. Getting the man-of-the-match award in a fantastic Test like that has to rank as a major highlight.

Steve Harmison prepares to bowl the final ball at Old Trafford.

22

TAKING IT TO
THE BRINK

The victory at Edgbaston gave us an extra day off to recover between back-to-back Tests, something players on both sides were grateful for after the drama of that Sunday morning. Going to Old Trafford the anticipation was even greater. Could we live up to the performance we had just given? Edgbaston seemed to have captured the attention of everyone and a much wider interest in cricket was developing; we were getting clapped out onto the field just to warm-up.

I spoke quite a lot in the team meeting before the game, because England had not played a Test at Old Trafford for a couple of years and they wanted what local knowledge I had on the way the wicket was performing and the best way to approach batting and bowling.

At Old Trafford Tests I always feel the added pressure of being a Lancashire player with all my friends in the crowd and every-one expecting big things of me. What I had not reckoned on was being the focus of critical attention – by myself! When I went out for the warm-up I happened to glance up from the crease and saw a life-size 6 ft 4 in cardboard cut-out of me on the balcony of every box. There were 20 of the things in all, wagging encouragingly, courtesy of my sponsors, Thwaites Beer. I just couldn't believe it. If there was any doubt I was the centre of attention that morning, that ended it. Even a little ceremony before the start of the Test to present me with a special cap to celebrate my fiftieth Test did not affect me as much as I thought it would. I must have been so focused on the game, I didn't really think about reaching such a landmark at my home ground. Maybe if I reach that very select club with 100 caps it will be different, but at this time I was just keen to get out there and try and prove we could repeat the performance we delivered at Edgbaston a few days earlier.

Winning the toss is always important at Old Trafford and we knew if we posted a reasonable score in the first innings we had a decent chance of winning the game. The captain showed how good he is with a brilliant 166 in the first innings and guided us to a very respectable total at 444, one which we believed gave us control of the Test. The only disappointment for me was falling just four runs short of a half-century on my home ground, although it could have been much worse had I gone out the night before. It was decided to send Matthew Hoggard out as a night watchman instead when Kevin Pietersen fell just a couple of overs before the close and I was very grateful it wasn't me. There were 20,000 beered-up Mancunians all shouting for me and Brett Lee was in the middle of a fantastic spell, so I was in no hurry to get out there! The ball that did for Hoggard just before the close would have probably got me out too, swinging away late to take his off stump – Hoggard was a bit of a sacrificial lamb on that occasion.

By the time I started my innings the next morning things had settled down and I felt satisfied with my batting after Edgbaston. Once again I enjoyed a good partnership with Geraint Jones, adding 87 in only 17 overs to take us past 400 – a score we knew would take some getting when Australia replied. Both of us missed out on our half-centuries, but we were happy with our total and felt confident of putting the Aussies under pressure.

We knew our score was good because it was the type of Old Trafford wicket which would get harder and harder to score on as the game wore on. That became even more evident when they began batting as the ball started reversing almost straight away. It was made for Simon Jones and he responded with a six-wicket haul, which earned us a 142-run lead. People were talking about the possibility of us enforcing the follow-on at one stage of Australia's innings, but you don't enforce that at Old Trafford. The one thing you want to do is bowl last on that wicket. It gives the bowlers a rest and the wicket starts to break up, so you never give away the opportunity of bowling last. We were held up by rain on the Saturday, but when we did bat again we batted really well, especially Strauss. He had taken a lot of stick at the start of the series, particularly from Warne saying he was his bunny, and he thought his ear was hanging off after being hit a couple of times by Lee. But he battled through all that to score a fine century to enable us to declare 423 ahead with all the final day to bowl at them.

The scenes before we even got to the ground on that final day were enough to inspire us. There were queues outside the ground and we found out later there were over 10,000 locked out – I had never seen anything like it. We had 98 overs to go at them and I knew we had a chance, but we would have to bowl very well to do it. Hoggard sparked us off by getting Langer in his first over. Hayden kept nicking me over the slips and into gaps, but he moved too far across his stumps and I bowled him around his legs. It was a strange sort of day because every time you thought we weren't going to do it, something would happen again to spark us. Through it all Ricky Ponting came out and played with great purpose. He looked very good from the start and we all knew it would take something special to remove him. We all bowled well. I had claimed a five-wicket haul in the West Indies a couple of years earlier, but I would rate my efforts on that final day at Old Trafford as one of my finest bowling displays. I know I only got four wickets not five, but against that opposition I was really pleased with my return. I had to change my action at one point because I was so tired I couldn't get my arm to go over like it normally does. I was just getting by with pure strength. I was absolutely knackered by the end of the day after bowling 25 overs.

I was particularly pleased with the way I was bowling to the left-handers because the reverse swing was helping it swing both ways and let me remove Simon Katich and Adam Gilchrist in one spell. I was dragging them into playing a few more balls than they would have liked. Katich, for instance, played at a wide one which he may have left in the first innings. I came back on just before the close as we pushed for victory from the Brian Statham End, which is normally the end I would bowl at for Lancashire but I didn't tell anybody because it's the dog end, the one where you usually have to run into the wind. It was reversing again and I considered I was back in it when I got Warne. I thought I was going to get Lee and Ponting too, but it just was not to be. They hung on again and, fair play to them, because they batted really well again. I really believed we were going to do it with four overs remaining after Harmison had Ponting caught down the legside for a brilliant 156. But even Glenn McGrath has improved his batting and is capable of hanging around and that is what he did.

There was massive disappointment in our dressing-room afterwards because we had given everything to try and win on that final day. To get so close to winning only to fall short in the final few overs was incredibly disappointing, but we told each other that we should walk out with our heads held high because we had been the better side for the last two Tests. We had proved to Australia that we could compete with them. We had shown them that we could beat them and that we could get on top of them. The crucial thing was to return from our week's break and perform with the same intensity when we assembled at Trent Bridge for the next Test.

I left Old Trafford absolutely shattered physically and mentally from two incredible back-to-back Tests. I was also picking up little injury niggles, so in the break in between Tests I disappeared to the South of France with my family to try and get away from the Ashes and recuperate. In my absence there was a row about England preventing the England players from appearing in the C&G Trophy semi-finals, where Lancashire were due to play Warwickshire at Edgbaston. I was unaware of it all in the South of France, but I couldn't have played even if I had been allowed to. There is only one way I can play for Lancashire and that is flat out and I wouldn't have been able to do that after those two Tests.

I enjoyed my French leave. Paul Beck, the Lancashire sponsor, had rented a villa with a pool on the top of a hill two miles from the beach. I didn't move from the pool, apart from one day when we had a trip to St Tropez, which wasn't my idea of fun. It was full of posers and people with massive lips, who have had every form of cosmetic surgery known to man, a side effect of which seems to make them incredibly rude. After that I was happy just to sit by the pool all day.

Meanwhile, back home the massive increase in the interest in cricket was snowballing. The *Daily Mirror* ran a front page cartoon of me as Mr InFredible. Even in non-cricketing France people recognised me when we went for a meal at night. Once I bumped into a bloke wearing a Preston North End shirt – what are the chances of that in France? I knew everyone was talking about the Ashes back home and it was very flattering to be noticed so often. People were always nice when they approached, wishing you all the best and urging you on to go and win the series, but I needed to get away after two hard Tests. Just relaxing with family and friends was what I needed.

*The century I scored at Trent Bridge was my best yet because of the
opposition and importance of the match.*

23

CHASING THE DREAM

G oing away after Old Trafford did me the world of good. I had felt really tired after the back-to-back Tests, but I came home from France refreshed and looking forward to the next Test at Trent Bridge. I had had time to reflect on what happened at Old Trafford because we saw the papers every day while away and I was eager to get going again. It was quite strange going into the Third Test because there was a lot of talk in the press and on television about who had the momentum Everyone seemed to think Australia had it after Old Trafford, which I could not quite understand because we had come within one wicket of winning there and going 2–1 up in the series. It was Australia who were clinging on at the end, not England, and it was they who were celebrating getting a draw. And when was the last time you saw the Aussies celebrating a draw? We had come within inches of winning, but somehow people thought we had lost momentum and I didn't understand that.

At 1–1 both we and the public realised this was the key match in the series. If we lost, the Ashes were gone for another series and if we won it would give us a massive advantage going into the Final Test at the Oval. Despite the importance of the match, the team were determined to do what we had done at Edgbaston and Old Trafford. The side met up on the Monday and we practised well. We had practised with a real intensity before Edgbaston and did the same in the build-up to Trent Bridge. We went in with the same attitude, to go out there and play and enjoy the occasion rather than become tense and intimidated by it.

There was a strange atmosphere around the dressing-room because it was almost as if everyone had forgotten the enormity of the occasion. By this stage of the series every Test match was getting bigger and bigger and bigger, but if anyone had spent any time in our dressing-room they would never have thought it. After what happened at Lord's, when the side was really tense, we had determined to go out at Edgbaston to enjoy our cricket. I think the penny had at last dropped for most of us. It was a realisation that we need not be intimidated by Australia. They had come over for the series with deserved reputations as the best players and the best team in the world, but we knew we could play against them and we could beat them. We enjoyed being in that position. Once the team accepted that and began to believe, it gave us a confidence and that was reflected in a new relaxed manner on the field. People have said to me since that the whole team seemed to do a lot of smiling, which was a further indication of how much we were enjoying our game and playing in the series.

Our smiles probably got a little wider once we discovered that McGrath would again not be playing. He had injured his right elbow in a tour match at Northampton, but everyone was expecting him to play, so it was a nice surprise to hear he wasn't. Once again Kasprowicz came into their side, a fine bowler and not someone to be underestimated, but he is not Glenn McGrath. Trying to replace a bowler of McGrath's calibre, someone who has taken over 500 Test wickets, is just impossible. Australia were still a very tough proposition without him in the side, but there was no doubt it made our jobs a little bit easier and I am sure we were all hoping his absence could be the factor which might help us take an advantage in the series. We were given a further lift by winning the toss, which enabled us to bat first. Trent Bridge is another of those grounds where you are looking to bat first because you are not quite sure what the wicket is going to do later. That certainly proved to be the case because it was far from easy batting last on it to win the game.

Trescothick once again gave us a flying start and played really well with Strauss to provide a century opening stand which gave us the foundation for a good first- innings score. We were hoping Marcus would go on to make his maiden Test century as had been playing well for a couple of Tests and taking the game to Australia's attack. We were all disappointed when he was bowled for 65 by young fast bowler Shaun Tait, who had been given his debut at the expense of Jason Gillespie.

The efforts of the top order helped those lower down the order like me because it is always easier to walk out to bat when there are plenty of runs already on the board. I went in to bat shortly after Vaughan had edged Ricky Ponting behind, which is the sort of dismissal all batsmen hate. Ricky is by no means the worst bowler in the world and he was getting it to swing a bit, but I am sure he only brought himself on to try something different. Getting the wicket of the England captain must have been a big bonus for him. I am sure Vaughan was furious at getting out to Ponting, but I never really found out as we crossed on the outfield, he trudging back to the dressing-room and I setting out to the middle.

I felt confident because I believed I had got myself into a

good rhythm. I had struggled early on in the series through a lack of match practice. At Edgbaston I just went out there to try and hit myself back into form. That worked because when we moved on to Old Trafford I felt I was batting properly again. Something just clicked at Old Trafford and it gave me great confidence going into the Trent Bridge Test.

All the same I soon began to understand how Vaughan had got out to Ponting because those first couple of overs from him were some of the hardest bowling I had faced all summer. It was a really testing period for me, probably the hardest throughout the Ashes series. He was swinging it both ways and it was also different to everything else I had previously faced. You can get used to the pace and types of deliveries when you are facing Brett Lee or Glenn McGrath all the time, but Ponting was a rogue element. It took time to get used to his style of bowling. It was a struggle. Once he took himself out of the attack I felt much more in control of my innings. I had turned the corner and was playing well and everything that happens when you are playing well was happening for me. I was relaxed at the crease, when I hit a shot it usually found the gaps and I just didn't think I was going to get out until I did with probably the first false shot I had played. An illustration of my confidence was when I reached my half-century by sweeping Warne for six, which was not at all what I had intended. He had started bowling around the wicket and it was early enough in the game for there not to be an awful lot of rough for him to aim at. With that in mind, I thought the sweep shot was a safe option, hoping I could get it through square-leg for four but I hit it better than I had planned and it sailed over the boundary for six. It took it as a sign that I was in the groove.

I was fortunate that once again I was batting with Geraint

Jones. Whenever we bat together we seem to complement each other's strengths and weaknesses and bowlers do find it hard bowling at the pair of us, having to adjust their lines and lengths constantly. We are also both naturally attacking batsmen and we were able to exploit that when Australia took the new ball. Sometimes you are not quite sure what to expect with the new ball. You either score faster because the ball is a bit harder and travels faster or it all becomes much tougher going. On this occasion it was a combination of the two. I think we both got better value for our shots, but you also have to graft with Tait and Lee tearing in at you. The pair of us were in full flow when the new ball was taken and a combination of the harder ball and the attacking fields enabled us to add 73 in the first 14 overs with it. I was particularly pleased for Geraint because he had take a bit of stick during the summer, but that 85 he scored was an invaluable contribution towards reaching a challenging first-innings score of 477.

He and I are close on and off the pitch and having him out in the middle helped me progress to one of the major moments in an already incredible summer. I'm sure every kid in the country, particularly after this summer, grows up dreaming of scoring an Ashes century and I was no different. I was incredibly proud to reach it, yet my celebration probably didn't reflect just how pleased I was inside. When I get wickets I am usually so excited I just can't contain myself, you may have noticed, but I have never done that when I have scored runs. I suppose part of the reason is that when you are bowling and you have got a wicket, that is the end of that batsman's innings but when you are batting the idea is to go and score as many runs as possible. I remember taking my helmet off and saluting the ground and also looking around to see where Rachael, Holly and the rest of my family were. But after that I wanted to go on and get a big score and help the team reach a major first-innings score, to put Australia under pressure. So I was really disappointed to get out a few overs later for 102, but once I got back into my hotel room that night I must admit to doing a little jig in celebration!

All centuries are special – I don't get enough of them not to feel like that – but that innings was probably the best of my career. When you look at how important the situation was and the standard of opposition it has got to be my best. When you are batting against players like Lee and Warne, it is extremely hard work scoring runs. To score a century against them without being dropped and being in control of the situation was something special.

We lost wickets pretty rapidly towards the end of the innings and some people were again saying that our score was not good enough, but we had scored over 400 runs again. It doesn't matter what type of wicket you are playing on, if you are regularly putting 400-odd on the board it has to put pressure on the other side. Despite losing those late wickets, I think we were all given a lift by our ability to get over 400 again. People were using the word momentum a lot by this stage and there was no doubt it was with us by then. As a group of bowlers, it gave us something to bowl at and it gave us the impetus to get five Australian wickets before the end of the second day.

The one thing that really worked in our favour was the ball started to reverse swing from an early stage of their innings because there was such an abrasive wicket. That brought myself and Simon Jones right into the game, and Simon did superbly to claim a five-wicket haul. Matthew Hoggard caused the early problems and was swinging the ball beautifully to claim three

Scoring a century at Trent Bridge – my finest innings for England.

It gives me a massive lift knowing Rachael and Holly are in the crowd giving support.

Andrew Strauss's brilliant catch to remove Adam Gilchrist really strengthened our advantage at Trent Bridge.

Ricky Ponting is run out, sparking another talking point in an amazing series.

Simon Jones exploited the conditions perfectly to give us the upper hand against Australia at Trent Bridge.

England's heroes Ashley Giles (*left*) and Matthew Hoggard walk off after clinching the close win at Trent Bridge...

...and Geraint Jones and I show how we feel about it.

Going 2–1 up in the series gives us all something to shout about.

Playing positively was a key part of my success against Australia.

Andrew Strauss has been a revelation since getting into the side. His century against Australia at The Oval was great.

Glenn McGrath (*left*) and Justin Langer fear the worst as they look at the gloomy sky.

Getting Matthew Hayden out LBW was an important factor in gaining a slender first innings lead at The Oval.

My second five-wicket haul in a Test match was made even better by Shane Warne's wicket being the fifth.

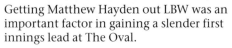

Matthew Hoggard and I walk off at The Oval after bowling out Australia in their first innings and leaving ourselves with a lead of just six runs.

Kevin Pietersen was Man of the Match at The Oval.

Holly comes to the Ashes party with her dad, Kevin Pietersen and Michael Vaughan.
Return of the Ashes, 2005.

wickets and, for the second time in the series Harmison took the wicket of Michael Clarke in the final over of the day.

It was not until we got back to the dressing-room that we were told Ponting had been furious at being run out by our substitute fielder Gary Pratt. Damien Martyn had called for a quick single and, before Ponting could reach the other end, Gary had brilliantly thrown down the stumps. As he made his way back to the dressing-room, Ponting had flung some choice observations up to Duncan Fletcher on the balcony about our use of substitute fielders. But Simon was genuinely injured at the time, so we were entitled to have a substitute. We were hardly going to use the worst fielder in the country to replace him, were we? I think that little outburst was a sign that Australia were getting frustrated and Ponting ended up with a fine from the match referee for his balcony scene, even though he immediately apologised.

That controversy could not distract us, though, and we were jubilant when we got back into the dressing-room with Australian on 99/5. It underlined our belief that we had a really good first-innings total. In our own domain we switched on the I-Pod and got some music going. At the Lord's game I had not been doing the things that I do to help me play well. I had been tense, uptight and not myself. When I spoke to Jamie Edwards, my mental coach, after Lord's we tried to find a recipe for things I did when I was playing well in the past. The first thing was always listening to music and enjoying the lads' company in the dressing-room and having a sing. Hence the I-Pod with the speakers turned up to a high volume, and Elton John's 'Rocket Man' being played again and again and again and again, and me singing along. There may have been people in the dressing-room who might have suggested a different song, but they couldn't be heard while I was in full flow. I'm not claiming I have a great voice, but I can't help but sing along to the songs I like and 'Rocket Man' became the song of the summer for the lads. When I have played it since in the car or at home, it always reminds me of the good times and puts me in a good mood and that all started that evening at Trent Bridge. It wasn't something we would do normally every night, but it seemed fitting that evening because of the way we had played that day.

The following morning Gilchrist came out with a real purpose. It is probably fair to say he was not playing at his best during the series, mainly because we had bowled at him well. He went after Hoggard a little bit, as he can against any bowler in the world, but when someone is doing that you have always got a chance. We were trying to bowl at him, as we had all summer, outside off stump and willing him to have a go. He hit a few boundaries during his 27, but I was happy to concede them because if he is swinging the bat and hitting fours and sixes then he is taking a risk and giving us a better chance of getting him out. The slips, the outfielders and the wicket-keeper are all in the game when he is playing like this and that proved to be the case when he did get out. I was the bowler who got him, but I take no credit whatsoever for the wicket – that was all down to Andy Strauss. He took an unbelievable diving catch at slip to dismiss Gilchrist. He was parallel to the ground when the ball hit his outstretched hand. I can't even remember celebrating that wicket because I had so little to do with it. For me, that was Strauss's first Test wicket because it was all down to him. Catches like that are instinctive, but you have to be able to get to them first and his athleticism was just incredible. Without Gilchrist, Australia lost their impetus and Simon Jones was able to demonstrate what a fine bowler he has become.

Everyone in the side was delighted at how well he was performing after the way his career had been stalled by that terrible injury a few years earlier. He really put it in to dismiss Australia for 218 and earn us a 259-run first-innings lead.

So we had the opportunity to make them follow on. Looking back, if we got into that position again I don't think we would have enforced it. But we did. Vaughan got all the bowlers together and asked us what we thought and whether we could carry on. I felt I could and so did Hoggard and Harmison, but the one thing we failed to acknowledge was that Simon Jones was not in the circle when we had the discussion. We were all taking it for granted he would come in and bowl, but he had hurt his right ankle bowling in the first innings and that proved to be more serious than we thought. It turned out that not only would he not be able to bowl in the rest of that Test, but he was also ruled out of the Final Test. We'd gone from four seamers down to three seamers and we were without the bowler who had taken five wickets in the first innings. The onus was really on the rest of us stepping up and giving that much more if we were going to win this Test. To make matters worse I had ankle problems of my own. On the Saturday morning the man who had operated on my ankle earlier in the year came to the hotel to give me another injection. I had had the ankle scanned the week before up in Rochdale and that showed there was nothing seriously wrong, but I was having a bit of discomfort all the same. The scan showed there was a build-up of inflammation caused by the workload during the series, particularly when I bowled 25 overs on the final day at Old Trafford on such an abrasive surface. I had struggled with my bowling in the first innings at Trent Bridge so we felt the best way to go was to have another jab.

The Aussies made a solid start to their follow-on, possibly because some of us had bowled a lot of overs and they started to get on top. It forced us to change our tactics a little bit. Someone like Michael Clarke loves to hit the ball and score boundaries so we tried to dry up his runs and make him come to us. We hung it outside off stump, not to the extremes we did when we bowled to Tendulkar a few years earlier, but we definitely tried to get him to play shots he wouldn't do normally. We were helped in this by Matthew Hoggard bowling a really good spell to him. People talk about bowling in the corridor of uncertainty and Hoggard was there every ball and it paid off when Clarke edged him behind. Even though we were not taking wickets regularly, Australia were not scoring at a great rate, so they were never taking the game away from us. When the wickets did come they came in a rush, just like they did all through the series. From being fairly comfortable at 261/4, they slipped to 387 all out to leave us chasing 129 for victory in the final innings. On paper it looked like a comfortable target, but the way this Ashes series had gone until that point suggested nothing was going to be easy and that is just how it turned out.

Trying to bat on a final-innings pitch with Shane Warne bowling was never going to be child's play, but I was praying we would win it with two or three wickets down. I was hoping my contribution to the match was over, but I should have known that nothing would be that simple in this series. Trescothick and Strauss got us off to a reasonable start and we had reached 32 without loss when Warne came on and the wickets started tumbling. It was extremely nerve-wracking watching from the boundary so it was almost a relief when it was my turn to go out and bat, even though we were 57/4 when I arrived at the crease. While I was out in the middle, I felt in control and I felt good. I thought I was going to see us home, but Brett Lee pulled a delivery out of nowhere. I don't know how fast it was timed at, but it nipped back and took my off stump out.

Nerves were starting to show by the time I got back into the dressing-room and there was incredible tension in there. It was a terrible feeling for me personally because I felt so helpless. My game was over. I couldn't do anything more to help the team except sit and watch. Normally I am not too bad in that type of situation, but I went through just about every emotion during this period. I felt sick, I felt excited and I didn't know what to do with myself. I was wandering around the back room at first and then I went to the toilets, to the middle room, and then onto the balcony. I was in a shocking state. I resorted to punching Strauss on the arm. I was grabbing him, anything to keep me busy. Poor Andrew probably got back to his room that night full of bruises. What his wife Ruth thought he'd been up to I don't know, but I promise you, it was me!

It came down to Ashley Giles and Matthew Hoggard in the end and what a performance they delivered. To go out there under such incredible pressure with the stakes as high as that was an absolutely magnificent display. I was always hoping we would get the runs, but I didn't think I would ever see Hoggard nailing a drive through extra cover off Brett Lee to almost take us there. I was particularly pleased for Ashley when he clipped off his legs for the two runs we needed for victory off Warne in the next over. He had had a lot of stick early in the summer and had come back yet again to play a big role. He showed the character he has and why we in the team rate him so highly. I cannot speak highly enough of how those two handled that situation when the heat was really on. When the pressure was on us during that series, every time they were there and delivered. When Ashley finally hit those runs I just exploded. I had totally gone, which is not like me. My eyes had gone, my head had gone – I was just so full of emotion I had lost it completely.

The party that followed was one to remember. Once again we sat and had a drink with the Australian players, which had become a bit of a tradition after each Test in the series, while the rest of the country seemed to go crazy. For the first time people started to believe we were capable of winning the Ashes. All we needed to do to was to avoid defeat at the Oval and the Ashes were ours again. It sounded simple, but we were all aware that nothing in this series had been easy and we faced another tough five days before we could begin to start thinking about celebrations.

Getting closer to the Ashes – another wicket falls at The Oval.

24

REALISING THE DREAM

I would have liked to have gone away again after Trent Bridge, just like I did after Lord's and Old Trafford, but had promised to play in a benefit match for Michael Vaughan at Headingley so I wasn't able to escape. The hype and hysteria surrounding the series had increased after the win at Trent Bridge and I arrived back home to discover photographers and news reporters outside the house, which wasn't the best of homecomings. Rachael and I were also starting to get followed by photographers when we went out in our cars. I could almost understand them following me, but I thought it was a bit much for them to start following Rachael when she had Holly in the back of the car – that was out of order. It seemed like the world had gone mad. By not going away this time I was obviously more aware of what was being written and said and it was almost as if people thought we had already got our hands on the Ashes urn before we turned up at the Oval. The players knew we were only 2–1 up and, if we got beaten, then the Ashes were going back on the plane with the Aussies, but the rest of the world seemed as though they were already planning how to celebrate.

Even before we had got to the Oval to start preparing for the Test, news leaked out about a possible open-top bus parade through the streets of London into Trafalgar Square if we won the Ashes. I'm sure we would all have preferred that sort of information to stay private. With everyone knowing that, there was almost no need for Ponting or John Buchanan, the Australian coach, to give a team-talk in their dressing-room before the game. They could just point to the newspaper cuttings to motivate them to spoil the party. Australia are such a good team they won't have needed much motivation anyway, but I'm sure it gave them that extra bit of determination when the match started.

There were all sorts of different pressures building up on us before the game. We knew we were favourites, being 2–1 ahead, but we were also aware there was a hell of a long way to go. We were also without Simon Jones, who had failed to recover from his ankle injury, which was a big loss to us and was bound to give Australia some encouragement, especially as McGrath had now recovered from his elbow injury and was fit to play. The selectors had included Paul Collingwood and Jimmy Anderson in the squad as possible alternatives. They offered different qualities to the side, Paul being more of a batsman than a bowler, whereas Jimmy is the opposite so there was plenty of speculation as to which of them was going to play in such a massive Test.

I had spoken to both Michael Vaughan and Duncan Fletcher during the week and assured them that the best way forward if Jones wasn't fit was an extra batsman who bowled. I told them I would bowl as many overs as they wanted me to in the last game of the season. If they had have wanted me to bowl from one end unchanged all day, that is what I would have done and so would Hoggard and Harmison. We were playing for the Ashes and were prepared to give everything we had got to try and win them back. We were a bowler light, but if I couldn't give everything for a match like this, then I never would. This was the biggest match of all our careers. It was a massive game and when I thought back to all the emotions I had been through previously in the series, I was not going to be fazed by the possibility of bowling 50 or 60 overs in one more game.

The important thing was to start well and not give Australia any encouragement that we were feeling the pressure and we did just that with Michael Vaughan winning the toss and allowing us to bat first. It was a good Oval wicket, but it was very dry for the Oval, verging on the crusty. The pitch was almost like a second or third-day wicket normally looks there. It was not the type of wicket where you could just stand there and belt the ball for boundaries like we had done in the past. So when we got 373 in our first innings, we were quietly confident. A lot of people were saying we should have got 450–500 but it was not that type of pitch. We had started well once again, but Shane Warne delivered an absolutely brilliant spell to dismiss our top five and after that it took a lot of hard work to take us to a good total.

Warne had bowled well all summer, but his performance at the Oval was the best he had bowled in the series. He was drifting it, spinning it – he was just awesome. Getting the top five on a first-day pitch was an incredible achievement. He had been one of my heroes for a long, long time and playing against him and getting to know him during that series was one of the highlights for me. Gaining the respect of people like Warne and Lee and developing a friendship with them has been really special. I may be getting soft after all the celebrations, but I don't believe Warne ever deserved to be on the losing side. To claim 40 wickets in a series and score crucial runs as well was an incredible performance and makes our victory all the more special because we have done it against great players like Shane Warne. His efforts ensured I batted for the first time in a Test with Strauss. We had batted together before at one-day level but for some reason he always got out before I got in – perhaps he thought I was going to start punching him again! He had battled through some tough times during that summer and took a lot of stick from the Aussies on and off the pitch and I was delighted for him when he got his century. He had played so well, it was just great to be at the other end when he did it. I came down the pitch and gave him a big hug because I knew he had been through it. The pressure was really on in that last Test match and one of our opening batsman had stood up to it, knowing early wickets for Australia could make it really difficult for us, and he had scored 127.

I was pleased with the way I supported Strauss and continuing my form from Old Trafford and Trent Bridge. I even began thinking of the possibility of scoring centuries in successive Ashes Tests, and that's probably why I got out when I did on 72. As soon as you begin thinking about what you could do rather than what you are doing you are in trouble and that is exactly what I did. The ball had begun to reverse swing and McGrath cramped me for a bit of room as I tried to play the ball down to third man. I tried to correct myself by playing straight and if I had gone with my initial shot I might have got away with it.

Despite not reaching 400 we were optimistic when they began their innings, even when Hayden and Langer got them off to such a good start. Their record together as openers suggested that at some time during the series they would enjoy a good partnership. We were just pleased we had kept them quiet for the rest of the series and they had only come good in the Final Test, otherwise they could have influenced the series more than they did. It was a bit like Lara's 400 in Antigua in that it came in the Final Test when it was impossible for them to win the series. As good as they were during that 185-run partnership, we always thought that if we got one wicket we might get a few. We also knew that to win the game they would have to bat through periods of bad light when the conditions were not that good for batting. That was exactly what happened with Harmison coming in with a fantastic spell which roughed up Langer and he got him out shortly after getting his 100. With Ricky Ponting falling before bad light ended play on that second day, we knew we were still in the game even with the Aussies on 272/2. I thought if we took three or four quick wickets in the morning, we would be right back in it.

We knew what was required from us and we showed the strength of character to do just that the following morning. As a collective unit we had shown the character of the side on numerous occasions during the last couple of years, bouncing back from defeat at Cape Town to win in Johannesburg the previous year and coming back strongly at Edgbaston against Australia. On those occasions we had all worked for each other and that applied again on that fourth morning when we dismissed Australia for 367 to claim a crucial six-run first-innings lead. I was given the job of bowling from the Pavilion End and produced what I consider to be one of my finest performances with the ball for England. It was a tight situation so all the bowlers knew they had to deliver and I found a really good rhythm. I was running in to bowl and it wasn't taking that much out of me and I was enjoying bowling. I wasn't even that aware I had bowled 14.2 overs unchanged either side of lunch to claim only my second five-wicket haul in Test cricket.

I was obviously pleased in getting 5/78, but the person who I thought should have received more credit that day was Hoggard. He bowled as only he can bowl, swinging the ball and making it difficult for the batsmen. I think he got Clarke out three times but we kept dropping him, myself included when I put him down in the slips, and he also got the key wicket of Gilchrist and mopped up Lee and McGrath. He was absolutely magnificent getting those four wickets and give us a lead, even though it was a slender one. We could have been facing a major first-innings deficit had we allowed Australia to bat on, but we all knew we still faced a massive effort to bat well in the second innings and keep Australia out of the game.

The light helped us to some degree and was turning the game into a draw and at that point I was quite happy with that. The stakes were so high I was happy for any help we could get from anywhere. We started the final morning having already lost Strauss the night before to Warne and it went pear-shaped for a while. Warne and McGrath reduced us to 127/5 and once again it looked like it was going to be another tense and close finish. Instead, we witnessed one of the great innings of all time that afternoon with Kevin Pietersen's century. He enjoyed a bit of luck early on and was dropped three times, but the way he played with the pressure he was under was absolutely brilliant. I've seen some really good innings from people like Lara, Astle or Kirsten but I think Kevin's performance that afternoon at the Oval was the best of the lot. When you consider what was at stake and what could have happened had he not played that innings, I don't think I've ever seen a better one. He took us from a situation where we were under massive pressure to a situation where we could finally begin thinking and believing we were going to win the Ashes. That knock, remember, was against players like Warne, McGrath and Lee who all kept running in, and doing their best for Australia, even when the game was obviously progressing towards a draw.

If Kevin's was the best knock I've ever seen, Ashley Giles's 59 that afternoon can't be far behind it. He had already made a massive contribution to the series by standing up under pressure to score the winning runs at Trent Bridge and there he was doing it all over again. To walk out to bat under that extreme pressure at number nine and hit your highest ever Test score takes some doing. This wasn't against Bangladesh, this was against Brett Lee, charging in at 95 mph, McGrath and Warne to produce one of his best ever performances. It was an incredible effort. At five wickets down there were quite a few worries in the dressing-room, but the longer Kevin batted with Paul Collingwood and then Ashley Giles, the more confident we became at getting the draw we needed. It was probably only when Ashley got out that our worries and nerves were finally settled and we all thought we were going to do it. When he got up the stairs after his innings, he was hugged by nearly every person in there. As the runs were going up, the overs remaining were going down. Our biggest fear was giving Australia 40 overs to bat because I think they could have chased nearly anything. They could have just gone out there and played their shots, but once it was down to 35 overs remaining we thought we were home and dry.

When the innings was finally over it was a real party atmosphere in the dressing-room and I just couldn't stop smiling. We were moments away from making dreams come true. People were high-fiving and hugging each other, it was a really special time. We went out to start Australia's reply knowing they only had a handful of overs remaining but their innings lasted only four balls from Harmison before they walked off again for bad light. We had purposely all gone out in our England caps which Vaughan had asked us to wear to mark the occasion. I always wear mine anyway, but some of the lads prefer the sun-hats. The only disappointing thing for all of us was the game was called off when we were off the field. We would have liked to have been out in the middle to see how the crowd reacted.

Once play was officially called off, the immediate aftermath became a bit of a blur. Everyone was jumping up and down in the dressing-room and there seemed to be more press and television than I've ever seen in my life. Winning the Ashes was special but winning man-of-the-series and the first ever Compton-Miller series award meant I had also made a contribution to it – it was a very proud moment for me.

Once the official presentation was completed, we did a lap of honour which will stay with me for a long time. We have done similar things when we've won other series, which are always special, but this was something else. Everyone in the crowd was going mad at what we had achieved and kept singing 'Jerusalem', which had been adopted as an unofficial anthem for England winning the Ashes. I lost count of the number of times the crowd belted it out while we made our way around the pitch. I suppose we should have known just by seeing the Oval crowd's reaction what a massive impact it had on the rest of the country. Straight after coming off the field, we continued our tradition of going into the Australian dressing-room to have a beer. The spirit between the two sides has been as good as I have ever known since I played for England and I had a really good time having a beer and chatting to their players. I sat with Hayden and

Langer and had a good laugh with them until we finally left the ground four or five hours later to go back to the hotel.

After that I think every move I made over the next twenty-four hours was well documented in nearly every paper. I had warned Rachael what was likely to happen if we won the Ashes and she went off to bed and left me to it in the bar. The thing I really enjoyed about that night was being surrounded by the people who really matter to me. A lot of the lads went off to some cabaret club, which isn't my cup of tea, but I was joined by some really good friends that night. Neil Fairbrother and Dave Roberts came back, Paul Beck was there and Geoff Durbin, the marketing manager from Lancashire, was also keeping me company at the bar. There were a few other people that I'd have loved to have been there like Paddy McKeown and my brother and my family, but I had most of my closest mates there and that was the important thing. I didn't want the night to end. I drank and drank and drank and drank and I could probably still be sitting there now. I was high on adrenalin and kept finding myself punching the air every so often.

I think I finally went up to my room around breakfast time and got ready for the reception we were due to have at Mansion House before we got onto the open-top bus. I had a bath and put my blazer on and went back down for breakfast, when I had another bottle of lager before we set off again. People who have seen pictures of my state for the rest of the day have asked me since whether I managed to take any of it in and I can assure them I did. I may have been a little unsteady on my feet, but what do you expect after drinking all night and having no sleep?

The reception we got while we were on the bus was something I'll never forget. All the lads were there with their families and there were crowds everywhere cheering and waving. A few of us were worried that nobody would turn up. It was arranged at such short notice. We could have turned the corner into Trafalgar square and seen nothing but a few tourists and some pigeons and a few old people waving a flag! We shouldn't have worried because when we did turn the corner into the square the number of people who had come to cheer us on was quite unbelievable. There were people hanging off the lampposts, others leaning out of the windows of offices. There were builders still in their hard hats. I don't think anyone in that area did any work that morning.

I was perceptibly a bit worse for wear by nowand we had Jonathan Agnew, the BBC's Cricket Correspondent, on top of the bus with us getting reaction from the whole team. He had spoken to most of the lads but was very wary of me. He spoke to everyone, Rachael, the other lads' families, no one was left out but me – I think he'd have even interviewed Holly before me if he could have done. I don't think he trusted what I might say and he was avoiding me like the plague. Although I am not usually that keen to give utterance to the media, I thought if ever there was a day to be interviewed this was the one. So I leered encouragingly. Finally he got around to me and I managed to just about get through my Ashes Regained interview, to the great relief of both of us.

That interview with Aggers was a good warm-up for David Gower asking me a few questions once we got to Trafalgar Square in front of thousands of people. He tried to get some sense out of me, but I was really struggling and I think the crowd sensed that by chanting: 'You're pissed and you know you are!' I managed to mumble a few words about my dark glasses hiding a thousand stories behind them and allowed

David to move on to interview one of the more composed members of the team – if he could find one. I couldn't really argue with the crowd's assessment, though, and just to prove their point I managed to get hold of a microphone and began singing Elvis' 'Suspicious Minds', which is a favourite song of mine. I'd only got a couple of lines out when they turned the microphone off so it didn't go through the tannoy and denied me my chance to seranade the crowd.

The whole day became a surreal experience because after being greeted by thousands of people in Trafalgar Square, we then went off to meet the Prime Minister in Downing Street. I didn't actually get to meet Mr Blair because I wanted to go for a tour of the house and had a nosey around in the Cabinet Room and things like that. People have said I fell asleep on a swing but that's a great exaggeration. I was given a tour of the house, had my photograph taken and kept out of the way. The only contact I had with Blairs was asking, Cherie where the toilet was – that was as near as I got to the Prime Minister.

From meeting government officials we were then driven to Lord's for another reception. We have these awards now when you get something for a 100 or five-wickets, so a few of us collected our trophies that day, which were particularly special because they were earned during a winning Ashes series. Of course more drink flowed at Lord's and a few of the lads went out again that evening, which I missed. By the time I got back to my room, I was ready to drop and conked out completely until the following day. With all the celebrations I hadn't really had chance to talk to my dad properly about it. He hadn't been happy about his ticket for the last day at the Oval, when he was moved to the other side of the ground and missed all the presentations, but other than that he was absolutely delighted.

If he can't play for England, winning the Ashes and seeing his little lad play a part must be the next best thing. He got quite emotional about it all because he knows what I have been through to get there.

It seems a long journey from then to the Oval and throughout that time I never dreamed I'd be involved in a winning Ashes series. Even just four years ago my prospects of playing in the Ashes didn't look great and it is going to take me a long time to sit back and take stock of what we achieved. No matter what happens in the future and what this England team can do together, it will be hard to eclipse winning the Ashes and those memorable scenes that followed.

ANDREW FLINTOFF IN TEST CRICKET

All records and statistics up to and including
England v Australia, 8–12 September 2005

Compiled by Vic Isaacs

TEST CAREER

Record

M	Inns	NO	Runs	HS	Avge	100	50	Ct	Overs	M	Runs	Wkt	Avge	5	10	Best
52	82	3	2641	167	33.43	5	17	34	1548.4	335	4621	143	32.31	2	–	5/58

Series by series

	M	Inns	NO	Runs	HS	Avge	100	50	Ct	Overs	M	Runs	Wkt	Avge	5	10	Best
South Africa in England 1998	2	3	0	17	17	5.66	–	–	1	35	5	112	1	112.00	–	–	1/52
England in South Africa 1999–2000	4	6	0	155	42	25.83	–	–	2	66.5	16	190	5	38/00	–	–	2/31
West Indies in England 2000	1	2	0	28	16	14.00	–	–	1	23	8	48	1	48.00	–	–	1/48
Zimbabwe in England 2000	2	3	0	33	16	11.00	–	–	–	13	5	35	0	–	–	–	–
England in India 2001–02	3	5	0	26	18	5.20	–	–	1	92	31	189	6	31.50	–	–	4/50
England in New Zealand 2001–02	3	6	0	243	137	40.50	1	1	2	93	20	313	9	34.77	–	–	3/49
Sri Lanka in England 2002	3	3	0	42	29	14.00	–	–	4	107	20	312	6	52.00	–	–	2/27
India in England 2002	3	5	0	99	59	19.80	–	1	3	112	25	357	5	71.40	–	–	2/22
South Africa in England 2003	5	8	0	423	142	52.87	1	3	–	182	44	592	10	59.20	–	–	2/55
England in West Indies 2003–04	4	5	1	200	102*	50.00	1	–	7	102.2	21	297	11	27.00	1	–	5/58
England in Sri Lanka 2003–04	3	6	0	143	77	23.83	–	1	–	97	20	221	9	24.55	–	–	3/42
New Zealand in England 2004	3	4	0	216	94	54.00	–	3	2	104.5	24	291	10	29.10	–	–	3/60
West Indies in England 2004	4	7	1	387	167	64.60	1	3	5	88.3	17	297	14	21.21	–	–	3/25
England in South Africa 2004–05	5	9	1	227	77	28.37	–	2	2	201.2	42	574	23	24.95	–	–	4/44
Bangladesh in England 2005	2	–	–	–	–	–	–	–	1	36.5	5	138	9	15.33	–	–	3/44
Australia in England 2005	5	10	0	402	102	40.20	1	3	3	194	32	655	24	27.29	1	–	5/78

Test record at each ground

	M	Inns	NO	Runs	HS	Avge	100	50	Ct	Overs	M	Runs	Wkt	Avge	5	10	Best
Lord's, London	8	11	0	362	142	32.90	1	3	3	225.1	54	712	21	33.90	–	–	3/25
Trent Bridge, Nottingham	6	10	0	299	102	29.90	1	1	3	206	36	671	13	51.61	–	–	3/60
Edgbaston, Birmingham	5	8	0	425	167	53.12	1	2	7	118	20	413	12	34.41	–	–	4/79
Headingley, Leeds	4	7	0	199	94	28.42	–	3	2	112	25	310	8	38.75	–	–	2/55
Old Trafford, Manchester	3	5	1	115	57*	28.75	–	1	4	129	25	384	13	29.53	–	–	4/71
Kennington Oval, London	3	4	0	247	95	61.75	–	3	1	84	20	275	9	30.55	1	–	5/58
Newlands, Cape Town	2	3	0	54	22	18.00	–	–	–	53.1	8	141	6	23.50	–	–	4/79
Kingsmead, Durban	2	3	0	65	60	21.66	–	1	1	70	19	178	5	35.60	–	–	2/66
New Wanderers, Johannesburg	2	4	0	83	38	20.75	–	–	–	60.1	15	181	3	60.33	–	–	2/59
St George's Park, Port Elizabeth	2	3	0	89	42	29.66	–	–	3	52.5	8	174	8	21.75	–	–	3/72
Riverside, Chester-le-Street	1	–	–	–	–	–	–	–	–	22	5	72	4	18.00	–	–	3/58
Sardar Patel Stadium, Ahmedabad	1	2	0	4	4	2.00	–	–	1	30	11	59	2	29.50	–	–	2/42
M Chinnaswamy Stadium, Bangalore	1	1	0	0	0	0.00	–	–	–	28	9	50	4	12.50	–	–	4/50
Punjab CA Stadium, Mohali	1	2	0	22	18	11.00	–	–	–	34	11	80	0	–	–	–	–
Eden Park, Auckland	1	2	0	29	29	14.50	–	–	–	39	7	157	6	26.16	–	–	3/49
Lancaster Park, Christchurch	1	2	0	137	137	68.50	1	–	2	28	3	123	2	61.50	–	–	2/93
Basin Reserve, Wellington	1	2	0	77	75	38.50	–	1	–	26	10	33	1	33.00	–	–	1/24
Centurion Park	1	2	1	91	77	91.00	–	1	–	32	8	90	6	15.00	–	–	4/44
Sinhalese SG, Colombo	1	2	0	107	77	53.30	–	1	–	18	0	47	2	23.50	–	–	2/47
Galle International Stadium	1	2	0	1	1	0.50	–	–	–	40	12	74	4	18.50	–	–	3/42
Asgiriya Stadium, Kandy	1	2	0	35	19	17.50	–	–	–	39	8	100	3	33.33	–	–	2/60
Kensington Oval, Bridgetown	1	1	0	15	15	15.00	–	–	2	29.2	6	78	7	11.14	1	–	5/58
Sabina Park, Kingston, Jamaica	1	1	0	46	46	46.00	–	–	3	16	3	45	1	45.00	–	–	1/45
Queen's Park Oval, Port-of-Spain	1	1	0	23	23	23.00	–	–	2	22	4	65	2	32.50	–	–	2/27
Antigua Recreation Ground	1	2	1	116	102*	116.00	1	–	–	35	8	109	1	109.00	–	–	1/109

Test record against each opponent

	M	Inns	NO	Runs	HS	Avge	100	50	Ct	Overs	M	Runs	Wkt	Avge	5	10	Best
Australia	5	10	0	402	102	40.20	1	3	3	194	22	655	24	27.29	1	–	5/78
Bangladesh	2	–	–	–	–	–	–	–	1	36.5	5	138	9	15.33	–	–	3/44
India	6	10	0	125	59	12.50	–	1	4	204	56	546	11	49.63	–	–	4/50
New Zealand	6	10	0	459	137	45.90	1	4	4	197.5	44	604	19	31.78	–	–	3/49
South Africa	16	26	1	822	142	32.88	1	5	5	485.1	107	1468	39	37.64	–	–	4/44
Sri Lanka	6	9	0	185	77	20.55	–	1	4	204	40	533	15	35.53	–	–	3/42
West Indies	9	14	2	615	167	51.25	2	3	13	213.5	46	642	26	24.69	1	–	5/58
Zimbabwe	2	3	0	33	16	11.00	–	–	–	13	5	35	0		–	–	

Wicket breakdown

	Batting	Bowling
Bowled	13	23
Caught	56	94
LBW	13	19
Run out	1	
Stumped	1	
Hit wicket	–	2
Not out	3	–
Total	80	138

Test centuries (5)

137	v New Zealand at Christchurch 2001–02
142	v South Africa at Lord's 2003
102*	v West Indies at Antigua 2003–04
167	v West Indies at Edgbaston 2004
102	v Australia at Trent Bridge 2005

Five wickets in an innings (2)

5/58	v West Indies at Bridgetown, Barbados 2003–04
5/58	v Australia at The Oval 2005

ANDREW FLINTOFF
IN ONE-DAY INTERNATIONAL
CRICKET

All records and statistics up to and including
England v Australia, The Oval 2005

Compiled by Vic Isaacs

ONE-DAY INTERNATIONALS

Record

M	Inns	NO	Runs	HS	Avge	100	50	Ct	Overs	M	Runs	Wkt	Avge	4	Best
90	78	11	2313	123	34.52	3	14	29	554.4	44	2358	96	24.56	1	4/14

Series by series

	M	Inns	NO	Runs	HS	Avge	100	50	Ct	Overs	M	Runs	Wkt	Avge	4	Best
England in Sharjah 1998–99	4	4	0	85	50	21.25	–	1	–	22.2	0	132	5	26.40	–	2/3
ICC World Cup in England 1999	5	2	0	15	15	7.50	–	–	–	18	0	96	2	48.00	–	1/28
Zimbabwe and West Indies in England 2000	6	5	1	70	42*	17.50	–	–	3	4	0	20	0	–	–	–
England in Kenya 2000–01	2	1	0	25	25	25.00	–	–	1	–	–	–	–	–	–	–
England in Pakistan 2000–01	3	3	0	111	84	37.00	–	1	1	–	–	–	–	–	–	–
England in Sri Lanka 2000–01	3	3	0	36	24	12.00	–	–	–	–	–	–	–	–	–	–
England in India 2001–02	6	6	0	147	52	24.50	–	1	1	49.5	2	217	7	31.00	–	3/38
England in New Zealand 2001–02	5	5	0	60	26	12.00	–	–	5	41.5	1	183	7	26.14	1	4/17
England in Zimbabwe 2001–02	5	3	1	108	46	54.00	–	–	2	30.3	1	143	6	23.83	–	2/12
Sri Lanka and India in England 2002	7	6	1	190	51	38.00	–	2	3	52.1	0	276	9	30.66	–	3/49
England in Australia 2002–03	1	1	0	16	16	16.00	–	–	1	10	0	56	1	56.00	–	1/56
England in South Africa 2002–03	5	5	0	156	64	31.20	–	1	3	48.4	9	140	7	20.00	–	2/15
NatWest Bank Series in England 2003	10	10	3	279	54	39.85	–	2	5	75.3	11	272	15	18.13	1	4/32
England in Bangladesh 2003–04	3	3	3	177	70*	–	–	3	1	29.4	9	63	7	9.00	1	4/14
England in Sri Lanka 2003–04	1	1	0	3	3	3.00	–	–	–	3.5	0	27	0	–	–	–
England in West Indies 2003–04	5	4	0	121	59	30.25	–	1	2	35	3	156	5	31.20	–	2/22
NatWest Bank Series and the ICC Trophy in England 2004	9	9	2	512	123	73.14	3	1	1	46.3	2	185	11	16.81	–	3/11
Bangladesh and Australia in England 2005	10	7	0	202	87	28.85	–	1	1	87	6	392	14	28.00	1	4/29

One-day international record against each opponent

	M	Inns	NO	Runs	HS	Avge	100	50	Ct	Overs	M	Runs	Wkt	Avge	4	Best
Australia	10	8	0	240	87	30.00	–	1	1	94.4	4	425	12	35.41	–	3/23
Bangladesh	7	5	3	216	70*	108.00	–	3	2	51.4	12	168	11	15.27	2	4/14
India	16	15	1	507	99	36.21	–	4	7	122.5	5	566	17	33.29	–	3/38
Kenya	1	1	–	–	–	–	–	–	–	–	–	–	–	–	–	–
Namibia	1	1	0	21	21	21.00	–	–	1	10	2	33	2	16.50	–	2/33
Netherlands	1	1	0	0	0	0.00	–	–	–	10	2	29	1	29.00	–	1/29
New Zealand	6	6	0	166	106	27.66	1	–	5	41.5	1	183	7	26.14	1	4/17
Pakistan	9	9	1	256	84	32.00	–	2	2	46.2	7	193	10	19.30	1	4/32
South Africa	6	6	1	129	54	25.80	–	1	3	42.4	3	186	8	23.25	–	3/46
Sri Lanka	9	8	1	220	104	31.42	1	1	–	33.3	0	156	8	19.50	–	3/49
West Indies	10	8	1	270	123	38.57	1	1	4	45	3	194	8	24.25	–	3/38
Zimbabwe	14	11	3	288	53	36.00	–	1	4	56.2	5	225	12	18.75	–	3/11

Wicket breakdown

	Batting	Bowling
Bowled	12	26
Caught	49	65
LBW	2	5
Run out	2	
Stumped	2	–
Not out	11	–
Total	78	96

One-day international centuries (3)

106	v New Zealand at Bristol 2004
123	v West Indies at Lord's 2004
104	v Sri Lanka at The Rose Bowl 2004

Four wickets in an innings (4)

4/17	v New Zealand at Auckland 2001–02
4/32	v Pakistan at Lord's 2003
4/14	v Bangladesh at Chittagong 2003–04
4/29	v Bangladesh at Headingley 2005

ANDREW FLINTOFF
IN FIRST-CLASS CRICKET

All records and statistics up to and including
England v Australia, The Oval 2005

Compiled by Vic Isaacs

FIRST-CLASS CAREER

Debut: Lancashire v Hampshire at Portsmouth 1995

Record

M	Inns	NO	Runs	HS	Avge	100	50	Ct	Overs	M	Runs	Wkt	Avge	5	10	Best
141	218	15	7347	167	36.19	15	41	149	15211	573	7381	229	32.23	3	–	5/24

Season by season

Season			M	Inns	NO	Runs	HS	Avge	100	50	Ct	Overs	M	Runs	Wkt	Avge	5	10	Best
1995	England	Lancashire	1	2	0	7	7	3.50	–	–	2	11	0	39	0	–	–	–	–
1996	England	Lancashire	1	1	0	2	2	2.00	–	–	1	–	–	–	–	–	–	–	–
1997	England	Lancashire	5	8	0	243	117	30.37	1	1	4	10	6	11	1	11.00	–	–	1/11
1997–98	Kenya	England A	1	1	1	2	2*	–	–	1	1	–	–	–	–	–	–	–	–
1997–98	Sri Lanka	England A	2	4	2	97	83	48.50	–	1	4	–	–	–	–	–	–	–	–
1998	England	Lancs/England	17	25	0	608	124	24.32	1	3	23	139	30	429	7	61.28	–	–	3/51
1998–99	Zimbabwe	England A	3	5	1	247	88	61.75	–	3	2	47.2	17	92	1	92.00	–	–	1/25
1998–99	South Africa	England A	2	3	0	295	145	98.33	1	2	2	52	17	111	1	111.00	–	–	1/19
1999	England	Lancashire	13	21	2	727	160	38.26	2	2	25	145.4	30	419	15	27.93	1	–	5/24
1999–2000	South Africa	England	7	11	2	396	89*	44.00	–	2	6	98.3	23	285	12	23.75	–	–	3/6
2000	England	Lancs/England	13	19	1	631	119	35.05	1	4	12	135.2	47	290	15	19.33	–	–	4/18
2000–01	Pakistan	England XI	1	1	0	0	0	0.00	–	–	1	–	–	–	–	–	–	–	–
2001	England	Lancashire	14	23	1	686	120	31.18	1	2	17	245.3	48	736	19	38.73	–	–	3/36
2001–02	India	England	4	7	0	66	40	9.42	–	–	1	126	42	263	12	21.91	–	–	4/50
2001–02	New Zealand	England	5	9	0	260	137	28.88	1	1	4	119	27	381	10	38.10	–	–	3/49

		M	Inns	NO	Runs	HS	Avge	100	50	Ct	Overs	M	Runs	Wkt	Avge	5	10	Best
2002	England	Lancs/England	7	10	0	284	137	28.40	1	1	8	251	53	768	14	54.85	–	–	2/22
2002–03	Australia	England	2	3	0	19	15	6.33	–	–	2	36	1	174	2	87.00	–	–	2/112
2003	England	Lancs/England	10	14	1	942	154	72.46	3	5	7	232	57	727	15	48.46	–	–	2/47
2003–04	Sri Lanka	England	4	7	0	190	77	27.14	–	1	–	111	22	262	10	26.20	–	–	3/42
2003–04	West Indies	England	5	6	1	204	102*	40.80	1	–	9	112.2	25	320	11	29.09	1	–	5/58
2004	England	England	7	11	1	603	167	60.30	1	6	7	193.2	41	588	24	24.50	–	–	3/25
2004–05	South Africa	England	6	11	1	252	77	25.20	–	2	3	219.2	44	634	26	24.38	–	–	4/44
2005	England	Lancs/England	11	16	1	586	102	39.06	1	5	8	250.3	43	852	34	25.05	1	–	5/78

First-class record for each team

	M	Inns	NO	Runs	HS	Avge	100	50	Ct	Overs	M	Runs	Wkt	Avge	5	10	Best
Lancashire	69	105	6	3672	160	37.09	9	16	94	717.3	170	2022	64	31.59	1	–	5/24
England	52	82	3	2641	167	33.43	5	17	34	1548.4	369	4621	143	32.31	2	–	5/58
England A	8	13	4	641	145	71.22	1	6	9	99.2	34	203	2	101.50	–	–	1/19
England XI	12	18	2	393	89*	24.56	–	2	12	169.4	34	535	20	26.75	–	–	3/6

First-class record against each team

	M	Inns	NO	Runs	HS	Avge	100	50	Ct	Overs	M	Runs	Wkt	Avge	5	10	Best
Australia	5	10	0	402	102	40.20	1	3	3	194	32	655	24	27.29	1	–	5/78
Australia A	1	2	0	16	15	8.00	–	–	–	10	0	62	0	–	–	–	–
Bangladesh	2	–	–	–	–	–	–	–	1	36.5	5	138	9	15.33	–	–	3/44
Cambridge University	1	1	1	80	80*	–	–	1	1	7	4	8	0	–	–	–	–
Canterbury (NZ)	1	1	0	1	1	1.00	–	–	1	19	4	56	1	56.00	–	–	1/45
Derbyshire	4	6	0	79	31	13.16	–	–	3	6	0	19	0	–	–	–	–
Durham	4	7	0	97	55	13.85	–	1	3	37	10	90	2	45.00	–	–	1/11
Durham UCCE	1	1	0	120	120	120.00	1	–	–	9	4	23	0	–	–	–	–
Essex	4	6	0	154	52	25.66	–	1	7	57	12	127	5	25.40	–	–	3/48
Free State/Griqualand West	1	2	1	102	65	102.00	–	1	–	–	–	–	–	–	–	–	–
Gauteng XI	1	1	0	145	145	145.00	1	–	–	24	8	45	0	–	–	–	–
Gauteng/Northerns	1	2	0	50	26	25.00	–	–	1	9.1	2	23	5	4.60	–	–	3/6
Glamorgan	2	3	0	114	68	38.00	–	1	6	29	4	114	1	114.00	–	–	1/79
Gloucestershire	1	1	0	158	158	158.00	1	–	–	–	–	–	–	–	–	–	–
Hampshire	6	10	1	302	117	33.55	1	1	7	63.5	13	184	12	15.33	1	–	5/24
India	6	10	0	125	59	12.50	–	1	4	204	56	546	11	49.63	–	–	4/50
India A	1	2	0	40	40	20.00	–	–	–	34	11	74	6	12.33	–	–	3/27
Kent	7	11	2	415	154	46.11	1	1	8	69	14	182	4	45.50	–	–	2/27
Kenya	1	1	1	2	2*	–	–	–	1	–	–	–	–	–	–	–	–
KwaZulu Natal	1	1	1	89	89*	–	–	–	3	22.3	5	72	2	36.00	–	–	2/47
Leicestershire	6	7	1	375	119	62.50	1	3	7	98	24	293	11	26.63	–	–	3/36
Middlesex	3	2	0	121	111	60.50	1	–	7	13	7	29	1	29.00	–	–	1/17
New Zealand	6	10	0	459	137	45.90	1	4	4	197.5	44	604	19	31.78	–	–	3/49

	M	Inns	NO	Runs	HS	Avge	100	50	Ct	Overs	M	Runs	Wkt	Avge	5	10	Best
Northamptonshire	3	6	0	239	124	39.83	1	–	8	28	7	85	1	85.00	–	–	1/58
Nottinghamshire	2	3	0	129	97	43.00	–	1	3	14	4	30	1	30.00	–	–	1/23
Otago	1	2	0	16	16	8.00	–	–	1	7	3	12	0	–	–	–	–
Pakistan Cricket Board	1	1	0	0	0	0.00	–	–	1	–	–	–	–	–	–	–	–
Queensland	1	1	0	3	3	3.00	–	–	2	26	1	112	2	56.00	–	–	2/112
Somerset	4	6	1	118	45	23.60	–	–	5	37.1	7	122	3	40.66	–	–	2/7
South Africa	16	26	1	822	142	32.88	1	5	5	485.1	107	1468	39	37.64	–	–	4/44
South Africa A	1	2	0	25	21	12.50	–	–	1	18	2	60	3	20.00	–	–	3/50
South African Board XI	1	2	0	150	80	75.00	–	2	2	28	9	66	1	66.00	–	–	1/19
Sri Lanka	6	9	0	185	77	20.55	–	1	4	204	40	533	15	35.53	–	–	3/42
Sri Lanka A	2	4	1	15	11	5.00	–	–	3	9	2	17	0	–	–	–	–
Sri Lanka Board President's XI	2	3	1	140	83	70.00	–	1	3	14	2	41	1	41.00	–	–	1/32
Surrey	6	11	0	375	137	34.09	1	1	9	115.5	28	316	10	31.60	–	–	2/32
Sussex	1	1	0	68	68	68.00	–	1	1	4	1	12	0	–	–	–	–
University of West Indies Vice Chancellor's XI	1	1	0	4	4	4.00	–	–	2	10	4	23	0	–	–	–	–
Warwickshire	2	3	0	122	70	40.66	–	1	2	6	0	31	0	–	–	–	–
West Indies	9	14	2	615	167	51.25	2	3	13	213.5	46	642	26	24.69	1	–	5/58
Worcestershire	4	6	0	206	83	34.33	–	2	6	33.3	5	122	6	20.33	–	–	3/27
Yorkshire	7	12	0	389	160	32.41	1	1	9	83.1	24	218	7	31.14	–	–	2/29
Zimbabwe	2	3	0	33	16	11.00	–	–	–	13	5	35	0	–	–	–	–
Zimbabwe A	2	3	1	170	88	85.00	–	2	1	40.2	17	75	1	75.00	–	–	1/25
Zimbabwe Union President's XI	1	2	0	77	61	38.50	–	1	1	7	0	17	0	–	–	–	–

Wicket breakdown

	Batting	Bowling
Bowled	40	34
Caught	132	167
LBW	26	26
Run out	1	–
Stumped	2	0
Hit wicket	0	2
Not out	15	–
Total	216	229

First-class centuries (15)

117	Lancashire v Hampshire at Southampton 1997
124	Lancashire v Northamptonshire at Northampton 1998
145	England XI v Gauteng at Johannesburg 1998–99
158	Lancashire v Gloucestershire at Bristol 1999
160	Lancashire v Yorkshire at Old Trafford 1999
119	Lancashire v Leicestershire at Old Trafford 2000
120	Lancashire v Durham UCCE at Durham University 2001
137	England v New Zealand at Auckland 2001–02
137	Lancashire v Surrey at The Oval 2002
111	Lancashire v Middlesex at Lord's 2003
154	Lancashire v Kent at Canterbury 2003
142	England v South Africa at Lord's 2003
102*	England v West Indies at St John's, Antigua 2003–04
167	England v West Indies at Edgbaston 2004
102	England v Australia at Trent Bridge 2005

Five wickets in an innings (3)

5/24	Lancashire v Hampshire at Southampton 1999
5/58	England v West Indies at Bridgetown, Barbados 2003–04
5/58	England v Australia at The Oval 2005

THE ASHES 2005

Scorecards

THE ASHES 2005
First Test, Lord's, 21–24 July

Australia won by 239 runs

Australia won the toss
Umpires: Aleem Dar and RE Koertzen
Man of the Match: GD McGrath

Close of Play
Day 1: Australia 190, England 92/7 (Pietersen 28*)
Day 2: Australia 190 & 279/7 (Katich 10*); England 155
Day 3: Australia 190 & 384; England 155 & 156/5 (Pietersen 42*, GO Jones 6*)

Australia 1st innings			Runs	Mins	Balls	4s	6s
JL Langer	c Harmison	b Flintoff	40	77	44	5	–
ML Hayden		b Hoggard	12	38	25	2	–
*RT Ponting	c Strauss	b Harmison	9	38	18	1	–
DR Martyn	c GO Jones	b SP Jones	2	13	4	–	–
MJ Clarke	lbw	b SP Jones	11	35	22	2	–
SM Katich	c GO Jones	b Harmison	27	107	67	5	–
†AC Gilchrist	c GO Jones	b Flintoff	26	30	19	6	–
SK Warne		b Harmison	28	40	29	5	–
B Lee	c GO Jones	b Harmison	3	13	8	–	–
JN Gillespie	lbw	b Harmison	1	19	11	–	–
GD McGrath	not out		10	9	6	2	–
Extras	(b 5, lb 4, w 1, nb 11)		21				
TOTAL	(all out, 40.2 overs)		190				

FoW: 1–35, 2–55, 3–66, 4–66, 5–87, 6–126, 7–175, 8–178, 9–178, 10–190

Bowling	O	M	R	W	
Harmison	11.2	0	43	5	
Hoggard	8	0	40	1	(2nb)
Flintoff	11	2	50	2	(9nb)
SP Jones	10	0	48	2	(1w)

England 1st innings			Runs	Mins	Balls	4s	6s
ME Trescothick	c Langer	b McGrath	4	24	17	1	–
AJ Strauss	c Warne	b McGrath	2	28	21	–	–
*MP Vaughan		b McGrath	3	29	20	–	–
IR Bell		b McGrath	6	34	25	1	–
KP Pietersen	c Martyn	b Warne	57	148	89	8	2
A Flintoff		b McGrath	0	8	4	–	–
+GO Jones	c Gilchrist	b Lee	30	85	56	6	–
AF Giles	c Gilchrist	b Lee	11	14	13	2	–
MJ Hoggard	c Hayden	b Warne	0	18	16	–	–
SJ Harmison	c Martyn	b Lee	11	35	19	1	–
SP Jones	not out		20	21	14	3	–
Extras	(b 1, lb 5, nb 5)		11				
TOTAL	(all out, 48.1 overs)		155				

FoW: 1–10, 2–11, 3–18, 4–19, 5–21, 6–79, 7–92, 8–101, 9–122, 10–155

Bowling	O	M	R	W	
McGrath	18	5	53	5	
Lee	15.1	5	47	3	(4nb)
Gillespie	8	1	30	0	(1nb)
Warne	7	2	19	2	

Australia 2nd innings

			Runs	Mins	Balls	4s	6s
JL Langer	run out (Pietersen)		6	24	15	1	–
ML Hayden		b Flintoff	34	65	54	5	–
*RT Ponting	c sub	b Hoggard	42	100	65	3	–
DR Martyn	lbw	b Harmison	65	215	138	8	–
MJ Clarke		b Hoggard	91	151	106	15	–
SM Katich	c SP Jones	b Harmison	67	177	113	8	–
+AC Gilchrist		b Flintoff	10	26	14	1	–
SK Warne	c Giles	b Harmison	2	13	7	–	–
B Lee	run out (Giles)		8	16	16	1	–
JN Gillespie		b SP Jones	13	72	52	3	–
GD McGrath	not out		20	44	32	3	–
Extras	(b 10, lb 8, nb 8)		26				
TOTAL	(all out, 100.4 overs)		384				

FoW: 1–18, 2–54, 3–100, 4–255, 5–255, 6–274, 7–279, 8–289, 9–341, 10–384

Bowling	O	M	R	W	
Harmison	27.4	6	54	3	
Hoggard	16	1	56	2	(2nb)
Flintoff	27	4	123	2	(5nb)
SP Jones	18	1	69	1	(1nb)
Giles	11	1	56	0	
Bell	1	0	8	0	

England 2nd innings

			Runs	Mins	Balls	4s	6s
ME Trescothick	c Hayden	b Warne	44	128	103	8	0
AJ Strauss	c & b	Lee	37	115	67	6	0
*MP Vaughan		b Lee	4	47	26	1	0
IR Bell	lbw	b Warne	8	18	15	0	0
KP Pietersen	not out		64	120	79	6	2
A Flintoff	c Gilchrist	b Warne	3	14	11	0	0
+GO Jones	c Gillespie	b McGrath	6	51	27	1	0
AF Giles	c Hayden	b McGrath	0	2	2	0	0
MJ Hoggard	lbw	b McGrath	0	18	15	0	0
SJ Harmison	lbw	b Warne	0	3	1	0	0
SP Jones	c Warne	b McGrath	0	12	6	0	0
Extras	(b 6, lb 5, nb 3)		14				
TOTAL	(all out, 58.1 overs)		180				

FoW: 1–80, 2–96, 3–104, 4–112, 5–119, 6–158, 7–158, 8–164, 9–167, 10–180

Bowling	O	M	R	W	
McGrath	17.1	2	29	4	
Lee	15	3	58	2	(1nb)
Gillespie	6	0	18	0	(2nb)
Warne	20	2	64	4	

THE ASHES 2005
Second Test, Edgbaston, 4–7 August

England won by 2 runs

Australia won the toss
Umpires: BF Bowden and RE Koertzen
Man of the Match: A Flintoff

Close of Play
Day 1: England 407
Day 2: England 407 & 25/1 (Trescothick 19*, Hoggard 0*); Australia 308
Day 3: England 407 & 182; Australia 308 & 175/8 (Warne 20*)

England 1st innings			Runs	Mins	Balls	4s	6s
ME Trescothick	c Gilchrist	b Kasprowicz	90	143	102	15	2
AJ Strauss		b Warne	48	113	76	10	0
*MP Vaughan	c Lee	b Gillespie	24	54	41	3	0
IR Bell	c Gilchrist	b Kasprowicz	6	2	3	1	0
KP Pietersen	c Katich	b Lee	71	152	76	10	1
A Flintoff	c Gilchrist	b Gillespie	68	74	62	6	5
+GO Jones	c Gilchrist	b Kasprowicz	1	14	15	0	0
AF Giles	lbw	b Warne	23	34	30	4	0
MJ Hoggard	lbw	b Warne	16	62	49	2	0
SJ Harmison		b Warne	17	16	11	2	1
SP Jones	not out		19	39	24	1	1
Extras	(lb 9, w 1, nb 14)		24				
TOTAL	(all out, 79.2 overs)		407				

FoW: 1–112, 2–164, 3–170, 4–187, 5–290, 6–293, 7–342, 8–348, 9–375, 10–407

Bowling	O	M	R	W	
Lee	17	1	111	1	(3nb, 1w)
Gillespie	22	3	91	2	(3nb)
Kasprowicz	15	3	80	3	(8nb)
Warne	25.2	4	116	4	

Australia 1st innings			Runs	Mins	Balls	4s	6s
JL Langer	lbw	b SP Jones	82	276	154	7	0
ML Hayden	c Strauss	b Hoggard	0	5	1	0	0
*RT Ponting	c Vaughan	b Giles	61	87	76	12	0
DR Martyn	run out (Vaughan)		20	23	18	4	0
MJ Clarke	c GO Jones	b Giles	40	85	68	7	0
SM Katich	c GO Jones	b Flintoff	4	22	18	1	0
+AC Gilchrist	not out		49	120	69	4	0
SK Warne		b Giles	8	14	14	2	0
B Lee	c Flintoff	b SP Jones	6	14	10	1	0
JN Gillespie	lbw	b Flintoff	7	36	37	1	0
MS Kasprowicz	lbw	b Flintoff	0	1	1	0	0
Extras	(b 13, lb 7, w 1, nb 10)		31				
TOTAL	(all out, 76 overs)		308				

FoW: 1–0, 2–88, 3–118, 4–194, 5–208, 6–262, 7–273, 8–282, 9–308, 10–308

Bowling	O	M	R	W	
Harmison	11	1	48	0	(2nb)
Hoggard	8	0	41	1	(4nb)
SP Jones	16	2	69	2	(1nb, 1w)
Flintoff	15	1	52	3	(3nb)
Giles	26	2	78	3	

England 2nd innings

			Runs	Mins	Balls	4s	6s
ME Trescothick	c Gilchrist	b Lee	21	51	38	4	0
AJ Strauss		b Warne	6	28	12	1	0
MJ Hoggard	c Hayden	b Lee	1	35	27	0	0
*MP Vaughan		b Lee	1	2	2	0	0
IR Bell	c Gilchrist	b Warne	21	69	43	2	0
KP Pietersen	c Gilchrist	b Warne	20	50	35	0	2
A Flintoff		b Warne	73	133	86	6	4
+GO Jones	c Ponting	b Lee	9	33	19	1 0	
AF Giles	c Hayden	b Warne	8	44	36	0	0
SJ Harmison	c Ponting	b Warne	0	2	1	0	0
SP Jones	not out		12	42	23	3	0
Extras	(lb 1, nb 9)		10				
TOTAL	(all out, 52.1 overs)		182				

FoW: 1–25, 2–27, 3–29, 4–31, 5–72, 6–75, 7–101, 8–131, 9–131, 10–182

Bowling	O	M	R	W	
Lee	18	1	82	4	(5nb)
Gillespie	8	0	24	0	(1nb)
Kasprowicz	3	0	29	0	(3nb)
Warne	23.1	7	46	6	

Australia 2nd innings

			Runs	Mins	Balls	4s	6s
JL Langer		b Flintoff	28	54	47	4	0
ML Hayden	c Trescothick	b SP Jones	31	106	64	4	0
*RT Ponting	c GO Jones	b Flintoff	0	4	5	0	0
DR Martyn	c Bell	b Hoggard	28	64	36	5	0
MJ Clarke		b Harmison	30	101	57	4	0
SM Katich	c Trescothick	b Giles	16	27	21	3	0
+AC Gilchrist	c Flintoff	b Giles	1	8	4	0	0
JN Gillespie	lbw	b Flintoff	0	4	2	0	0
SK Warne	hit wicket	b Flintoff	42	79	59	4	2
B Lee	not out		43	99	75	5	0
MS Kasprowicz	c GO Jones	b Harmison	20	60	31	3	0
Extras	(b 13, lb 8, w 1, nb 18)		40				
TOTAL	(all out, 64.3 overs)		279				

FoW: 1–47, 2–48, 3–82, 4–107, 5–134, 6–136, 7–137, 8–175, 9–220, 10–279

Bowling	O	M	R	W	
Harmison	17.3	3	62	2	(1nb, 1w)
Hoggard	5	0	26	1	
Giles	15	3	68	2	
Flintoff	22	3	79	4	(13nb)
SP Jones	5	1	23	1	

THE ASHES 2005
Third Test, Old Trafford, 11–15 August

Match drawn

England won the toss
Umpires: BF Bowden and SA Bucknor
Man of the Match: RT Ponting

Close of Play
Day 1: England 341/5 (Bell 59*)
Day 2: England 444; Australia 214/7 (Warne 45*, Gillespie 4*)
Day 3: England 444; Australia 264/7 (Warne 78*, Gillespie 7*)
Day 4: England 444 * 280/6dec; Australia 302 & 24/0 (Langer 14*, Hayden 5*)

England 1st innings			Runs	Mins	Balls	4s	6s
ME Trescothick	c Gilchrist	b Warne	63	196	117	9	0
AJ Strauss		b Lee	6	43	28	0	0
*MP Vaughan	c McGrath	b Katich	166	281	215	20	1
IR Bell	c Gilchrist	b Lee	59	205	155	8	0
KP Pietersen	c sub	b Lee	21	50	28	1	0
MJ Hoggard		b Lee	4	13	10	1	0
A Flintoff	c Langer	b Warne	46	93	67	7	0
+GO Jones		b Gillespie	42	86	51	6	0
AF Giles	c Hayden	b Warne	0	11	6	0	0
SJ Harmison	not out		10	13	11	1	0
SP Jones		b Warne	0	7	4	0	0
Extras	(b 4, lb 5, w 3, nb 15)		27				
TOTAL	(all out, 113.2 overs)		444				

FoW: 1–26, 2–163, 3–290, 4–333, 5–341, 6–346, 7–433, 8–434, 9–438, 10–444

Bowling	O	M	R	W	
McGrath	25	6	86	0	(4nb)
Lee	27	6	100	4	(5nb, 2w)
Gillespie	19	2	114	1	(2nb, 1w)
Warne	33.2	5	99	4	(2nb)
Katich	9	1	36	1	

Australia 1st innings			Runs	Mins	Balls	4s	6s
JL Langer	c Bell	b Giles	31	76	50	4	0
ML Hayden	lbw	b Giles	34	112	71	5	0
*RT Ponting	c Bell	b SP Jones	7	20	12	1	0
DR Martyn		b Giles	20	71	41	2	0
SM Katich		b Flintoff	17	39	28	1	0
+AC Gilchrist	c GO Jones	b SP Jones	30	74	49	4	0
SK Warne	c Giles	b SP Jones	90	183	122	11	1
MJ Clarke	c Flintoff	b SP Jones	7	19	18	0	0
JN Gillespie	lbw	b SP Jones	26	144	111	1	1
B Lee	c Trescothick	b SP Jones	1	17	16	0	0
GD McGrath	not out		1	20	4	0	0
Extras	(b 8, lb 7, w 8, nb 15)		38				
TOTAL	(all out, 84.5 overs)		302				

FoW: 1–58, 2–73, 3–86, 4–119, 5–133, 6–186, 7–201, 8–287, 9–293, 10–302

Bowling	O	M	R	W	
Harmison	10	0	47	0	(3nb)
Hoggard	6	2	22	0	
Flintoff	20	1	65	1	(8nb)
SP Jones	17.5	6	53	6	(1nb, 2w)
Giles	31	4	100	3	(1w)

England 2nd innings

			Runs	Mins	Balls	4s	6s
ME Trescothick		b McGrath	41	71	56	6	0
AJ Strauss	c Martyn	b McGrath	106	246	158	9	2
*MP Vaughan	c sub	b Lee	14	45	37	2	0
IR Bell	c Katich	b McGrath	65	165	103	4	1
KP Pietersen	lbw	b McGrath	0	3	1	0	0
A Flintoff		b McGrath	4	20	18	0	0
+GO Jones	not out		27	15	12	2	2
AF Giles	not out		0	4	0	0	0
Extras	(b 5, lb 3, w 1, nb 14)		23				
TOTAL	(6 wickets dec, 61.5 overs)		280				

DNB: MJ Hoggard, SJ Harmison, SP Jones

FoW: 1–64, 2–97, 3–224, 4–225, 5–248, 6–264

Bowling	O	M	R	W	
McGrath	20.5	1	115	5	(6nb, 1w)
Lee	12	0	60	1	(4nb)
Warne	25	3	74	0	
Gillespie	4	0	23	0	(4nb)

Australia 2nd innings

			Runs	Mins	Balls	4s	6s
JL Langer	c GO Jones	b Hoggard	14	42	41	3	0
ML Hayden		b Flintoff	36	123	91	5	1
*RT Ponting	c GO Jones	b Harmison	156	411	275	16	1
DR Martyn	lbw	b Harmison	19	53	36	3	0
SM Katich	c Giles	b Flintoff	12	30	23	2	0
+AC Gilchrist	c Bell	b Flintoff	4	36	30	0	0
MJ Clarke		b SP Jones	39	73	63	7	0
JN Gillespie	lbw	b Hoggard	0	8	5	0	0
SK Warne	c GO Jones	b Flintoff	34	99	69	5	0
B Lee	not out		18	44	25	4	0
GD McGrath	not out		5	17	9	1	0
Extras	(b 5, lb 8, w 1, nb 20)		34				
TOTAL	(9 wickets, 108 overs)		371				

FoW: 1–25, 2–96, 3–129, 4–165, 5–182, 6–263, 7–264, 8–340, 9–354

Bowling	O	M	R	W	
Harmison	22	4	67	2	(4nb, 1w)
Hoggard	13	0	49	2	(6nb)
Giles	26	4	93	0	
Vaughan	5	0	21	0	
Flintoff	25	6	71	4	(9nb)
SP Jones	17	3	57	1	

THE ASHES 2005
Fourth Test, Trent Bridge, 25–28 August

England won by 3 wickets

England won the toss
Umpires: Aleem Dar and SA Bucknor
Man of the Match: A Flintoff

Close of Play
Day 1: England 229/4 (Pietersen 33*, Flintoff 8*)
Day 2: England 477; Australia 99/5 (Katich 20*)
Day 3: England 477; Australia 218 & 222/4 (Clarke 39*, Katich 24*)

England 1st innings			Runs	Mins	Balls	4s	6s
ME Trescothick		b Tait	65	138	111	8	1
AJ Strauss	c Hayden	b Warne	35	99	64	4	0
*MP Vaughan	c Gilchrist	b Ponting	58	138	99	9	0
IR Bell	c Gilchrist	b Tait	3	12	5	0	0
KP Pietersen	c Gilchrist	b Lee	45	131	108	6	0
A Flintoff	lbw	b Tait	102	201	132	14	1
+GO Jones	c &	b Kasprowicz	85	205	149	8	0
AF Giles	lbw	b Warne	15	45	35	3	0
MJ Hoggard	c Gilchrist	b Warne	10	46	28	1	0
SJ Harmison	st Gilchrist	b Warne	2	9	6	0	0
SP Jones	not out		15	32	27	3	0
Extras	(b 1, lb 15, w 1, nb 25)		42				
TOTAL	(all out, 123.1 overs)		477				

FoW: 1–105, 2–137, 3–146, 4–213, 5–241, 6–418, 7–450, 8–450, 9–454, 10–477

Bowling	O	M	R	W	
Lee	32	2	131	1	(8nb)
Kasprowicz	32	3	122	1	(13nb)
Tait	24	4	97	3	(4nb)
Warne	29.1	4	102	4	
Ponting	6	2	9	1	(1w)

Australia 1st innings			Runs	Mins	Balls	4s	6s
JL Langer	c Bell	b Hoggard	27	95	59	5	0
ML Hayden	lbw	b Hoggard	7	41	27	1	0
*RT Ponting	lbw	b SP Jones	1	6	6	0	0
DR Martyn	lbw	b Hoggard	1	4	3	0	0
MJ Clarke	lbw	b Harmison	36	93	53	5	0
SM Katich	c Strauss	b SP Jones	45	91	66	7	0
+AC Gilchrist	c Strauss	b Flintoff	27	58	36	3	1
SK Warne	c Bell	b SP Jones	0	2	1	0	0
B Lee	c Bell	b SP Jones	47	51	44	5	3
MS Kasprowicz		b SP Jones	5	8	7	1	0
SW Tait	not out		3	27	9	0	0
Extras	(lb 2, w 1, nb 16)		19				
TOTAL	(all out, 49.1 overs)		218				

FoW: 1–20, 2–21, 3–22, 4–58, 5–99, 6–157, 7–157, 8–163, 9–175, 10–218

Bowling	O	M	R	W	
Harmison	9	1	48	1	(3nb)
Hoggard	15	3	70	3	(4nb)
SP Jones	14.1	4	44	5	(1nb)
Flintoff	11	1	54	1	(8nb, 1w)

Australia 2nd innings

			Runs	Mins	Balls	4s	6s
JL Langer	c Bell	b Giles	61	149	112	8	0
ML Hayden	c Giles	b Flintoff	26	57	41	4	0
*RT Ponting	run out (sub GJ Pratt)		48	137	89	3	1
DR Martyn	c GO Jones	b Flintoff	13	56	30	1	0
MJ Clarke	c GO Jones	b Hoggard	56	209	170	6	0
SM Katich	lbw	b Harmison	59	262	183	4	0
+AC Gilchrist	lbw	b Hoggard	11	20	11	2	0
SK Warne	st GO Jones	b Giles	45	68	42	5	2
B Lee	not out		26	77	39	3	0
MS Kasprowicz	c GO Jones	b Harmison	19	30	26	1	0
SW Tait		b Harmison	4	20	16	1	0
Extras	(b 1, lb 4, nb 14)		19				
TOTAL	(all out, 124 overs)		387				

FoW: 1–50, 2–129, 3–155, 4–161, 5–261, 6–277, 7–314, 8–342, 9–373, 10–387

Bowling	O	M	R	W	
Hoggard	27	7	72	2	(1nb)
SP Jones	4	0	15	0	
Harmison	30	5	93	3	(1nb)
Flintoff	29	4	83	2	(9nb)
Giles	28	3	107	2	
Bell	6	2	12	0	(3nb)

England 2nd innings

			Runs	Mins	Balls	4s	6s
ME Trescothick	c Ponting	b Warne	27	24	22	4	0
AJ Strauss	c Clarke	b Warne	23	68	37	3	0
*MP Vaughan	c Hayden	b Warne	0	8	6	0	0
IR Bell	c Kasprowicz	b Lee	3	38	20	0	0
KP Pietersen	c Gilchrist	b Lee	23	51	34	3	0
A Flintoff		b Lee	26	63	34	3	0
+GO Jones	c Kasprowicz	b Warne	3	25	13	0	0
AF Giles	not out		7	30	17	0	0
MJ Hoggard	not out		8	20	13	1	0
Extras	(lb 4, nb 5)		9				
TOTAL	(7 wickets, 31.5 overs)		129				

DNB: SJ Harmison, SP Jones

FoW: 1–32, 2–36, 3–57, 4–57, 5–103, 6–111, 7–116

Bowling	O	M	R	W	
Lee	12	0	51	3	(5nb)
Kasprowicz	2	0	19	0	
Warne	13.5	2	31	4	
Tait	4	0	24	0	

THE ASHES 2005
Fifth Test, The Oval, 8–12 September

Match drawn

England won the toss
Umpires: B.F.Bowden and R.E.Koertzen
Man of the Match: KP Pietersen
Men of the Series: A Flintoff/SK Warne

Close of Play
Day 1: England 319/7 (Jones 21*, Giles 5*; 88 overs)
Day 2: England 373, Australia 112/0 (Langer 75*, Hayden 32*; 33 overs)
Day 3: Australia 277/2 (Hayden 110*, Martyn 9*; 78.4 overs)
Day 4: Australia 367, England 34/1 (Trescothick 14*, Vaughan 19*, 13.2 overs)

England 1st innings			Runs	Mins	Balls	4s	6s
ME Trescothick	c Hayden	b Warne	43	77	65	8	0
AJ Strauss	c Katich	b Warne	129	351	210	17	0
*MP Vaughan	c Clarke	b Warne	11	26	25	2	0
IR Bell	lbw	b Warne	0	9	7	0	0
KP Pietersen		b Warne	14	30	25	2	0
A Flintoff	c Warne	b McGrath	72	162	115	12	1
PD Collingwood	lbw	b Tait	7	26	26	1	0
+GO Jones		b Lee	25	60	41	5	0
AF Giles	lbw	b Warne	32	120	70	1	0
MJ Hoggard	c Martyn	b McGrath	2	47	36	0	0
SJ Harmison	not out		20	25	20	4	0
Extras	(b 4, lb 6, w 1, nb 7)		18				
TOTAL	(all out, 105.3 overs)		373				

FoW: 1–82, 2–102, 3–104, 4–131, 5–274, 6–289), 7–297, 8–325, 9–345, 10–373

Bowling	O	M	R	W	
McGrath	27	5	72	2	(1w)
Lee	23	3	94	1	(3nb)
Tait	15	1	61	1	(3nb)
Warne	37.3	5	122	6	
Katich	3	0	14	0	

Australia 1st innings			Runs	Mins	Balls	4s	6s
JL Langer		b Harmison	105	233	146	11	2
ML Hayden	lbw	b Flintoff	138	416	303	18	–
*RT Ponting	c Strauss	b Flintoff	35	81	56	3	–
DR Martyn	c Collingwood	b Flintoff	10	36	29	1	–
MJ Clarke	lbw	b Hoggard	25	119	59	2	–
SM Katich	lbw	b Flintoff	1	12	11	–	–
+AC Gilchrist	lbw	b Hoggard	23	32	20	4	–
SK Warne	c Vaughan	b Flintoff	0	18	10	–	–
B Lee	c Giles	b Hoggard	6	22	10	–	–
GD McGrath	c Strauss	b Hoggard	0	6	6	–	–
SW Tait	not out		1	7	2	–	–
Extras	(b 4, lb 8, w 2, nb 9)		23				
TOTAL	(all out, 107.1 overs)		367				

FoW: 1–185, 2–264, 3–281, 4–323, 5–329. 6–356, 7–359, 8–363, 9–363, 10–367

Bowling	O	M	R	W	
Harmison	22	2	87	1	(2nb, 2w)
Hoggard	24.1	2	97	4	(1nb)
Flintoff	34	10	78	5	(6nb)
Giles	23	1	76	0	
Collingwood	4	0	17	0	

England 2nd innings			Runs	Mins	Balls	4s	6s
ME Trescothick	lbw	b Warne	33	150	84	1	–
AJ Strauss	c Katich	b Warne	1	16	7	–	–
*MP Vaughan	c Gilchrist	b McGrath	45	80	65	6	–
IR Bell	c Warne	b McGrath	0	2	1	–	–
KP Pietersen		b Mc Grath	158	283	187	15	7
A Flintoff	c &	b Warne	8	20	13	1	–
PD Collingwood	c Ponting	b Warne	10	70	51	1	–
+GO Jones		b Tait	1	22	12	–	–
AF Giles		b Warne	59	158	97	7	–
MJ Hoggard	not out		4	44	35	–	–
SJ Harmison	c Hayden	b Warne	0	1	2	–	–
Extras	(b 4, w 7, nb 5)		16				
TOTAL	(all out, 91.3 overs)		335				

FoW: 1–2, 2–67, 3–67, 4–109, 5–126, 6–186, 7–199, 8–308, 9–335, 10–335

Bowling	O	M	R	W	
McGrath	26	3	85	3	(1nb)
Lee	20	4	88	0	(4nb, 1w)
Warne	38.3	3	124	6	(1w)
Clarke	2	0	6	0	
Tait	5	0	28	1	(1w)

Australia 2nd innings		Runs	Mins	Balls	4s	6s
JL Langer	not out	0	2	4	–	–
ML Hayden	not out	0	2	–	–	–
Extras		0				
TOTAL	(for 0 wickets, 0.4 overs)	0				

DNB: *RT Ponting, DR Martyn, MJ Clarke, SM Katich, +AC Gilchrist, SK Warne, B Lee, GD McGrath, SW Tait

Bowling	O	M	R	W
Harmison	0.4	0	0	0

INDEX